# Finance and Accounting for Nonfinancial Managers

# Finance and Accounting for Nonfinancial Managers

Eliot H. Sherman

**AMA** American Management Association®

Printed in the United States of America

# Contents

About This Course    xi
How to Take This Course    xiii

## 1   Introduction to Finance    1

Overview
The Vocabulary of Finance
The Elements of Finance
   Bookkeeping
   Accounting
   Planning
   Cash Management
The Basic Financial Statements
   The Balance Sheet
   The Income Statement
   Statement of Cash Flows
The Structure of Business and the Impact of Financial Statements
   Proprietorship
   Partnership
   Corporation
   Other Business Structures
Recap
Review Questions

## 2   Introduction to Accounting    21

Overview
The Purpose of Accounting
   The Accounting System
   Who Uses Accounting Information?
Basic Terminology
   Financial Statements
   The Chart of Accounts

The Accounting Cycle
  Using Journal Entries to Record Transactions
  Closing Procedures
More Financial Concepts
Preparing Financial Statements
  The Key Financial Statements
  Trial Balance
Recap
Review Questions

## 3  Financial Analysis: Using Ratios          43

Overview
Analysis of Financial Information
The Purpose of Business
Who Performs Financial Analysis?
The Power of Ratios
  Comparative Analysis
  Trend Analysis
Trend Ratio Analysis
  Liquidity Ratios
  Activity Ratios
  Profitability Ratios
  Debt Management Ratios
  A Different Perspective
  Creating Other Ratios
  Conflicting Information
Recap
Review Questions

## 4  Managing Operating Performance          65

Overview
Making Your Information Useful
The Key Financial Statements
  Ratios That Help Tell the Company's Story
  Effect Ratios
  Crossover Indicators and Causal Ratios
Recap
Review Questions

## 5  Managing Short-Term Assets          83

Overview
The Management of Cash
  Reasons for Holding Cash
  Techniques for Managing Cash
The Management of Other Short-Term Assets
  Managing Marketable Securities

Managing Accounts Receivable
Managing Inventory
Prepaid Expenses
Other Current Assets

Recap
Review Questions

6    **Relating Risk and Return, Valuation,
     and Time Value of Money**                97

Overview
Risk
Defining Risk
Risk Aversion
Possibility of Loss
Characteristics of Different Types of Risks
The Determination of Interest Rates

Types of Risk
Default Risk
Inflation Risk
Maturity Risk
Liquidity Risk

Estimating Interest Rates
Capital Asset Pricing Model
Relating Risk and Return
Extending the Theory

Time Value of Money
Valuation
An Illustrative Example
Assessing Investments
Valuing an Investment

Recap
Review Questions

7    **Capital Investment Decision Making**    115

Overview
Calculating the Cost of Capital
The WACC Model
Initial Exercise in Estimating Financing Requirements
Calculating the Cost of Capital

Capital Budgeting
Types of Capital Investment Projects
Applying Cost of Capital
Determining Investment Cost
Determining the Cash Flows of a Project
Determining the Terminal Cash Flows

Evaluating Capital Investment Projects
Payback Period

Net Present Value
Internal Rate of Return (IRR)
Recap
Review Questions

## 8  Managing Long-Term Assets   135

Overview
Considering Asset Classification
The Investment in Fixed Assets
Depreciation
Fixed Asset Accounting
Acquisition of Fixed Assets
Other Long-Term Assets
Recap
Review Questions

## 9  Managing Liabilities   145

Overview
The Liabilities of the Business
Short-Term or Current Liabilities
Accounts Payable
Notes Payable
Taxes Payable
Accruals
Long-Term Debt
Choosing a Bank Lending Officer
The "C's" of Credit
Character
Capacity
Capital
Cash Flow
Collateral
Conditions
Competition
Credibility
Competence
Communications
Banking Relationships
Defining Debt
Bank Structure Dictates Loan Interest Rates
The Cost of Bank Funds
Operating Expenses
Loan Losses
Profit Criteria
Comparison to Traditional Business Cost Structure
Bank Debt Pricing
Loan Pricing Example

Recap
Review Questions

## 10 The Equity in the Business    173

Overview
Equity and Business Structure
    Preferred Stock
    Common Stock
    Additional Paid-In Capital
    Retained Earnings
The Investment Marketplace
Accounting for Equity
Recap
Review Questions

## 11 Financial Planning    183

Overview
The Essence of Financial Planning
Business Planning—A Continuous Process
    Roles of the Key Players
    Overview of the Financial Planning Process
    Planning Sequence
Different Kinds of Plans
    Business Plan
    Strategic Plan
    The Operative Plan or Annual Budget
Projecting the Financial Future
    Estimating Financial Requirements
    Capital Budgets
    Cash Budgets
Recap
Review Questions

## 12 Relating Departmental Performance to the Big Picture    201

Overview
The Inverted Triangle: Finance from Broad to Specific
    The Company
    Subsidiary
    Division
    Department
    Group
    Individuals
The Relationship Between Budgets and Actuals
Recap
Review Questions

Appendix: Time Value of Money Tables            209

Glossary                                        215

The Final Exam                                  225

Index                                           235

# About This Course

As one course among many offered in the American Management Association's curriculum, *Finance and Accounting for Nonfinancial Managers* introduces the reader to financial terminology, relates financial measures to operating information, and enables the student to understand and apply financial measures to operating performance. Today's managers, whether supervisors or senior executives, are expected to understand and use financial and operational measures, prepare and utilize budgets, respond to inquiries about the financial consequences of actions taken by them or by their department or team, and understand and use financial and accounting terminology—the common language of business measurement. Written in a conversational, easy-to-understand tone, the course treats finance and accounting from the perspective of users of financial information—it enhances their ability to communicate effectively with subordinates, other managers, senior executives, and accounting and finance professionals. It offers managers the ability to use and analyze financial information to improve the performance of their operations and to identify—and avoid—potential problems.

**Eliot H. Sherman,** CPA, has more than twenty-five years of financial management experience. He is currently Chief Financial Officer, Treasurer, and Director of Gloucester Co. Inc., a manufacturer of adhesives, sealants, and caulking materials. He is also Partner and Chief Financial Officer of Venture Builders, established in 1999, an advisory firm dedicated to helping entrepreneurs build successful businesses. Prior to the establishment of Venture Builders, he was principal of his own consulting firm providing strategic and operational planning assistance and financial management guidance to smaller, growing businesses. During his career, he was worked for businesses from the very small to the *Fortune* 50, from private to publicly held, from domestic to multinational to foreign-owned. He currently serves as a director or advisor to several corporations and nonprofit organizations in the Boston area.

Mr. Sherman was educated at Harvard College and earned masters degrees from The Amos Tuck School and Bentley College. He is currently a Senior Lecturer at Northeastern University, teaching both undergraduate and graduate courses in the Finance Department. He is also a member of the finance faculty and in the Corporate Education Department at Suffolk University. He teaches regularly for several state societies of CPAs and for the American Institute of Certified Public Accountants, a major developer of professional education courses marketed to state CPA societies and other national organizations.

## ACKNOWLEDGMENTS

The publisher would like to thank the following people for their review of the manuscript of this course:

Henry H. Goldman, Associate Professor, Touro University International, Los Alamitos, California

Shahriar Khaksari, Associate Professor, Suffolk University, Boston, Massachusetts

David Filipek, CPA, Associate Professor, Rhode Island College, Providence, Rhode Island

# How to Take This Course

This course consists of text material for you to read and three types of activities (in-text exercises, the final exam, and end-of-chapter review questions) for you to complete. These activities are designed to reinforce the concepts brought out in the text portion of this course and to enable you to evaluate your progress.

## The Text

The most important component of this course is the text, for it is here that the concepts and methods are presented. Reading each chapter twice will increase the likelihood of your understanding the text fully.

We recommend that you work on this course in a systematic way. Only by reading the text and working through the exercises at a regular and steady pace will you get the most out of this course and retain what you have learned.

In your first reading, concentrate on getting an overview of the chapter's contents. Read the learning objectives at the beginning of the chapter first. They will act as guidelines to the major topics of the chapter and enumerate the skills you should master as you study the text. As you read the chapter, pay attention to the headings and subheadings. Find the general theme of each section and see how the theme relates to others. Don't let yourself get bogged down with details during the first reading; simply concentrate on remembering and understanding the major themes.

In your second reading, look for the details that underlie the theme. Read the entire chapter carefully and methodically, underlining key points, working out the details of the examples, and making marginal notations as you go. Complete the exercises.

## The Review Questions

After reading a chapter and before going on to the next, work through the review questions. Answering the questions and comparing your own answers to those given will help you to grasp the major ideas of that chapter. If you perform these self-check exercises conscientiously, you will develop a framework within which to place material presented in later chapters.

## The Final Exam

The final exam is made up of a series of straightforward questions on what you have studied in both the text and the review questions. Answer the questions using the enclosed scannable answer form and mail the form in one of the return envelopes to:

**American Management Association**
## Educational Services
**P.O. Box 359**
**Natick, MA 01760**

All tests are reviewed thoroughly by our instructors and will be returned to you promptly.

## Grading Policy

The American Management Association will continue to grade examinations and tests for one year after the course's out-of-print date.

If you have any questions regarding the tests, the grading, or the course itself, call Educational Services at 1-800-225-3215, ext. 600.

**1**

# Introduction to Finance

*focus*

## Learning Objectives

By the end of this chapter, you should be able to:

- Explain and use basic financial terms and concepts.
- Define the key financial statements and accounting equations and explain their purposes and contents.
- Describe the different forms of business structure and recognize similarities and differences among them.

## OVERVIEW

Change is a given in business today, and managers are expected to do more and understand more than they ever had to in the past. How often have you heard statements just like these—often from your own managers?

> Act like you own the business.
> Everyone is self-employed.
> If what you're doing isn't adding value to the business, then stop
> what you're doing.

In today's businesses, managers are expected to be active participants in and leaders of self-directed teams, they are supposed to be empowered, they are responsible for their own training and their own careers. You may be asked to come up with ways to help the company increase the **bottom line,** or to lead a team investigating new technologies. Functional expertise isn't enough any more. You've got to understand the relationship of the work you do to the overall financial success of your organization.

1

Finance and accounting give you tools that you can use to understand how the decisions you make and the jobs you perform affect the long-term success of the entire organization. Understanding the language of finance and accounting will allow you to present your ideas persuasively and precisely, to be more comfortable when discussing results or forecasts with your financial staff or outside investors. It will help you to understand the financial news and how financial markets can affect your own firm. And it will help you make better decisions about your personal finances and investments.

Accounting has been called "the language of business." This chapter introduces the basic terminology and concepts of financial management. You'll see how these terms and concepts relate to your everyday responsibilities, and you'll look at the basic financial statements, which will provide a starting point for everything that follows. This chapter will also describe the three major business structures and explain their similarities and differences.

### Are You a Financial Manager?

Bob had just been hired as the controller of a small, semiautonomous division of a publicly-held company that was experiencing severe growing pains. Rapid expansion strained the cash resources of the company as well as its human resources. Bob decided to introduce open-book management to the employees, but he knew he'd have to give people some basic tools before the company's financial information would make much sense to them.

He called the first group together and asked, "How many of you are financial managers?" Every hand stayed down. Then he asked, "How many of you have a checking account?" Most of the hands went up. "How many of you make mortgage or car payments?" Again, most of the group had loans they were paying off. When he asked, "How many of you have MasterCard or VISA cards?" nearly everyone raised their hand.

Bob pointed out that the managers in the group were managing cash, making investments and incurring loans, handling credit, and looking out for their own financial well-being. They all had plenty of experience that they could use as they analyzed the financial results of the company. When he asked the group, "How many of you really are financial managers?" nearly everyone responded affirmatively.

How would you have responded to these questions? Many managers, even those in senior positions, do not realize how much financial management they understand, and how much financial management they practice. In the next eleven chapters we will look at the whole range of basic financial management activities, relating them to the rest of business responsibilities. Nearly everything that goes on in a business has financial consequences. The understanding you gain as you take this course will help you relate your everyday activities, whether at work or within your family responsibilities, to the broader financial picture.

## THE VOCABULARY OF FINANCE

Finance is not a foreign language, understood only by those who have studied it for years. Everyone who functions in today's society has a basic understanding of the principles of finance. The daily transactions of comparing prices, writing checks to pay for purchases, using credit cards, and maintaining a bank account are all financial management activities. Understanding and managing the financial activities of a business is a logical extension of understanding and managing your personal financial activities.

Financial management comprises the tools and capabilities used to produce monetary resources and the management of those monetary resources. The language of finance allows different businesses to compare monetary results. Whether the business makes cars or sells hamburgers, people can describe their results in monetary terms. In order to take part in this discussion, it's important to understand the words and concepts that people use. Throughout this course we will employ the vocabulary of finance. New terms will be highlighted and defined. You'll find all of the definitions in the Glossary at the back of this text.

In its simplest definition, **finance** is managing money. What else can we say about the tasks and the focus of finance and financial management?

1. Finance, whether personal or business, is managing money on behalf of owners and creditors.
2. Managing money includes attracting it and spending it or investing it according to a plan of action.
3. Financial management is the management of that plan.

We can apply this description to **financial management** this way:

- Business finance is the managing of money for a business.
- Personal finance is the managing of money for oneself.

The rules and practices of managing money are essentially the same, regardless of whose money is being managed.

Exhibit 1–1 demonstrates just how close the business definitions and personal definitions of several important words and concepts are. It should be clear from these comparisons that the definitions of these terms are very similar whether viewed in a business or a personal context. You already know more than you may think, and you should feel confident that you will be able to understand and use the terms and concepts of financial management effectively.

**xhibit 1–1**

**Representative Terminology**

| Term | Business Finance | Personal Finance |
|---|---|---|
| Revenue | Sales | Salaries and wages |
| Expenses | Cost of sales | Expenses associated with work |
|  | Operating costs | Household and personal costs |
| Profit | The difference between sales and costs | Savings and amounts invested |
| Loss | When costs exceed revenues | When costs exceed revenues |
| Sources of financing | Banks, investors | Banks |
| Cash flow | The receipt of money, generally from sales | The receipt of money, generally from salaries and wages |
| Credit | The ability to borrow money or buy now, pay later | The ability to borrow money or to buy now, pay later |
| Sound investment strategies | Investments that return an acceptable profit | Investments that return an acceptable profit |
| Success | Increasing sales and profits | Increased income and improved lifestyle resulting from high enough salary and sound investments and accumulated savings |

## THE ELEMENTS OF FINANCE

This course describes four basic elements of finance:

1. **Bookkeeping**—the accurate and timely recording of transactions, providing the reader with clear financial information
2. **Accounting**—analysis and evaluation of past events and results, showing how we arrived at the current financial position
3. **Planning**—building on the past to direct the future, permitting the manager to manage proactively rather than simply reacting
4. **Cash Management**—concentrated attention on a scarce essential resource, assuring that the available resource can be managed effectively

As we describe these elements, the basic structure of financial information will become clearer.

### Bookkeeping

**Bookkeeping** is the accurate and timely recording of transactions. As we will see in the next chapter, this definition of bookkeeping is what most people mean when they talk about "accounting."

Without a sound bookkeeping system, all of finance is really only guesswork. No financial planning can take place if the books and records from which information is drawn are not reliable. If the systems and procedures that provide financial information are not dependable, the first step must be to correct the data and assure that future reporting is sound and timely. But the information gathered in the accounting process is too detailed in its raw form to be very useful for decision making. The data is used to generate financial statements, which follow set rules to provide consistent information to the people who use them—managers within the business, vendors and customers who do business with the business, and investors. Generating financial statements is really only the last step of the bookkeeping responsibility.

The production of these statements must follow a logical process, must conform to **generally accepted accounting principles** (GAAP), and must be timely. They must follow a logical process to ensure completeness. They must follow generally accepted accounting principles so that everyone who needs to understand them will be able to analyze and interpret them in a meaningful way. They must be timely so that management can take action effectively. When managers make good use of the information provided by the accounting system and the financial information it provides, they can achieve continuous improvement of financial performance by maintaining and enhancing positive results and correcting negative or unsatisfactory results.

## Accounting

**Accounting** is the analysis and evaluation of past events and results.

Accounting's primary focus is determining what really happened and why. The purpose of the accounting function is not to affix responsibility; nor to give credit for success or blame for shortfalls. Accounting has the absolute crucial responsibility of understanding what happened that caused the financial results reported through the financial statements.

Once financial statements have been prepared, the accounting staff and others evaluate them. This look at historical performance—whether for the most recent month, for the prior month, or for some prior year—establishes relationships that provide a starting point for forecasting financial performance.

The accounting analysis, as part of regular reporting, explains how or why the company achieved the financial results it did. In accounting analysis, managers and analysts examine the results reported in the financial statements and identify the actions or activities that caused or contributed significantly to the results reported. To be most valuable, they must perform this analysis while the operating circumstances are still fresh. Analysis of old results cannot contribute nearly as much to future success as can analysis performed while the situation is still clearly in focus. And since corrective action is not possible until managers have analyzed the results, failure to act quickly allows problems to continue longer than they should. We will examine techniques of **financial analysis,** the interpretation of financial results and positions to guide the future actions of the company, in more depth in Chapter 3.

In addition to helping management understand the recent past, this analysis, this accounting, provides the basis for judging forecasts of future performance. If the forecasts prepared as part of the planning process differ from the results that would be expected based on the past, the accounting function must be able to explain why the projected differences are valid. Otherwise, the forecasts are flawed and will yield unrealistic performance projections.

## Planning

**Planning** is building on the past to direct the future.

Planning starts from the understanding of what happened in the past and uses forecasts and estimates to project the future. If the results of the past were satisfactory, then managers develop a plan that will perpetuate past practices to reach the goals for the future. If, however, the results of the past were less than satisfactory, management must use its understanding of what happened to identify what must be changed in order to arrive at a more desirable future result.

Planning uses the analysis of what has happened in the past to guide the future. It answers the questions:

- Do we like the results of the past?
- What can we do to improve them?

In reality, the past is the starting point in developing a projection of future performance. If the manager and the organization feel that the past performance was satisfactory or exemplary, then they build on that to build for the future. If, on the other hand, the performance was not satisfactory, they must incorporate significant change into the projection. In a properly prepared plan, the projected results must identify those factors that will make the result differ from the past. We will consider planning in much more detail in Chapter 11.

## Cash Management

**Cash Management** is concentrated attention on a scarce, essential resource.

Cash is the focus of much of the public discussion of financial issues. Because cash is considered a scarce but essential resource, people believe it requires special treatment and attention. As you will see in Chapter 5, the essence of good cash management may be described as:

- collect it as quickly as you can
- hold it as long as you can
- release it as slowly as you can
- have little or none on hand

Often included in a discussion of cash management are a number of specific responsibilities that fit into the treasury responsibility. These functions include managing the relationship between the company and its bank so that necessary financing and bank services will be available, risk management so that the company is insured for casualty losses, and investment management to assure that the company earns a proper return on its excess cash.

The process of cash management is different from all other aspects of finance and requires a particular understanding. Specifically, the idea that we should have little or no cash requires an explanation.

A business holds cash (whether in currency or in a checking account) to facilitate transactions. However, cash held earns little or no interest. Therefore, the prudent manager would prefer to invest the cash where it will earn a greater return. The manager can't invest or use too much of the cash, however, or the business will not have enough on hand to make purchases, to pay bills, to pay salaries, or to pay taxes. The business must find just the right amount of cash to keep on hand. This is not as hard as it sounds, because most people and most businesses have predictable, and reasonably consistent, cash flows. It is not necessary to hold large amounts of cash because the account at the bank is being replenished continuously.

As you progress through this course, the effects on cash of the various aspects of financial management decision making will be clear. So, too, will opportunities to manage the cash resource.

## THE BASIC FINANCIAL STATEMENTS

All but the smallest businesses prepare financial statements. People inside the business use the statements to analyze their results. How is the business doing? Are there any warning flags that require changes? Is the business growing faster or slower than its competitors? What can it do better? Investors use financial statements to see whether their money is invested wisely. Are they getting the kind of return for the money they've invested? Would they do better to invest elsewhere? Should they work for a change in management? Is the company a likely target for acquisition? Vendors use the financial statements to determine whether the company is a good credit risk. Can the business pay its bills? Customers use financial statements to evaluate whether the company is likely to be around to provide services and support in the future?

How can one set of financial statements provide so much information about so many businesses to so many people?

Long ago, authors and theorists broke financial management information into two accounting equations, essential relationships that have been used to describe financial management. These two equations, which provide the basis for the first two financial statements, are:

1. ASSETS = LIABILITIES AND EQUITY—the basis for the Balance Sheet
2. REVENUES – EXPENSES = PROFIT—the basis for the Income Statement

The first of these accounting equations

ASSETS = LIABILITIES AND EQUITY

is also referred to by some as the "fundamental accounting equation." Using basic algebra, this equation may also be written as

$$ASSETS - LIABILITIES = NET WORTH$$

This equality may be described more simply as:

What you have = What you owe + What you own

or

What you have − What you owe = What you own

## The Balance Sheet

The accounting equation, whichever form it takes, establishes the essence of the Balance Sheet, a financial statement that describes for a reader the financial condition of a business (or an individual) at a point in time. You can think of it as a snapshot of an organization's financial position.

Clearly, then, your **net worth**—the **equity** you have in your personal assets or in your business—is a function of the resources you have and how you acquire and use them. If you can acquire those assets for less than they are worth or will generate, you will increase your net worth, or owner's equity. The objective of financial management is to increase what you own, your equity.

If that is the point of financial management, you might wonder why businesses use debt. If they didn't owe anything, they wouldn't have to subtract liabilities from assets. A quick look at the way people operate will show that this is an oversimplified view. The wise use of other people's money will, after providing an appropriate return for its use, enhance your ability to increase your own net worth. And we all understand that: if we can, we borrow funds to buy a house because we expect that, over time, that home will increase in value beyond what we paid for it and what we could have earned by investing the funds. Using borrowed funds to make the purchase will, therefore, increase our equity. The same is true for any productive or valuable asset that is properly chosen and managed.

The Balance Sheet is presented as of a specific date, most frequently the end of the financial year, and recognizes the effects of all of the financial activity that took place up through the Balance Sheet date. On the following pages we will present and describe the basic elements of the Balance Sheet. In the next chapter we will describe the activities that affect the Balance Sheet.

This presentation occurs when the Balance Sheet is presented for only one year. When multiple years are presented, the Balance Sheet is presented in vertical format to facilitate year-to-year comparisons.

## Exercise 1–1: Examining Your Company's Balance Sheet

*INSTRUCTIONS:* ☛ Get a copy of your company's Balance Sheet or the Balance Sheet of another company you are interested in. Compare the format of the Balance Sheet below with the one you are looking at. Identify the sim-

**E** **xhibit 1–2**

**The Balance Sheet—Annotated**

### Assets

| | |
|---|---|
| Cash | Liquid resources to be spent on goods and services or additional assets for the organization |
| + Accounts Receivable | Amounts due to the organization for goods or services or as the result of a contractual agreement |
| + Inventory | If the organization sells product, stocks of product to be sold |
| + <u>Prepaid Expenses</u> | Expenditures made in anticipation of future services or obligations, often interest, advertising, or insurance |
| = Current Assets | Those assets expected to be converted into cash or used within one year |
| + Fixed Assets | Those assets and resources owned by the organization expected to last more than one year, including such assets as land, buildings, furniture and fixtures, machinery and equipment, leasehold improvements, vehicles, and similar physical assets |
| + <u>Intangible Assets</u> | Valuable nonphysical assets owned by the organization, such as trademarks and patents |
| = <u>Total Assets</u> | The sum of all assets owned by the organization |

### Liabilities

| | |
|---|---|
| Accounts Payable | Amounts owed to others for goods or services previously purchased on credit |
| + Notes Payable | Amounts borrowed by the organization and due within one year |
| + <u>Accruals</u> | Amounts that will be owed to others based on the calendar date of the statement but not yet due as of the date of the statement, such as payroll or taxes |
| = Current Liabilities | The sum of all obligations expected to be converted to cash or paid within one year |
| + <u>Long-Term Debt</u> | Amounts borrowed by the organization and due beyond one year from the date of the statement |
| = +Total Liabilities | The sum of all amounts owed to creditors by the organization |
| + Preferred Stock | Investment in the company which generally does not represent ownership, but which gains the investor a right to preferences in distribution of dividends and in certain other situations |
| + Common Stock | Investment in the company in return for an ownership position, with the right to participate in the election of directors, in certain distributions, and in certain company decisions |
| + Retained Earnings | The cumulative earnings of the company less any dividends distributed to preferred and common stock holders |
| = +Equity | The difference between the total assets and the total liabilities, representing the net worth of the organization, the value of the owners' investment |
| = <u>Total Liabilities and Equity</u> | A total equal to the total assets that confirms that all obligations of the organization have been identified; also defined as the sum of all claims against the assets of the corporation |

**xhibit 1–3**

**The Balance Sheet—An Alternative Presentation**

| ASSETS | | LIABILITIES AND EQUITY |
|---|---|---|
| Cash | | Accounts Payable |
| Marketable Securities | | Notes Payable |
| Accounts Receivable | | Accruals |
| Inventory | | |
| Prepaid Expenses | | |
| Total Current Assets | | Total Current Liabilities |
| Fixed Assets | | Long-Term Debt |
| Intangible Assets | | |
| | | Preferred Stock |
| | | Common Stock |
| | | Retained Earnings |
| Total Assets | = | Total Liabilities and Equity |

ilarities and differences between this generalized Balance Sheet and that of a specific company. It is likely that your company's presentation of the Balance Sheet is similar to the one presented here. Different companies may alter the presentation of the Balance Sheet to reflect the specifics of the company more clearly. For example, you may see Fixed Assets described as Property, Plant and Equipment. Your company may break the classifications of assets and liabilities and equity into broader or narrower subcategories. To the extent that the examination of your company's financial statements raises questions, ask someone in the accounting or finance department to clarify what you have seen.

### The Income Statement

The second accounting equation relates to ongoing activity.

$$REVENUES - EXPENSES = PROFIT$$
$$Income - Outgo = Outcome$$

We measure our progress by comparing what we generate (revenues) with what it costs us (expenses) and keep track of the difference (profit). We compare that result against targets or objectives and get both absolute and relative measures of our success and achievement.

And we develop plans, programs, and actions that we expect will improve on our performance, our results. Over the remainder of this course we will examine some of these tools and techniques and consider how to strengthen our basic financial management skills.

This second accounting equation reflects the second major financial statement, the **Income Statement.** When the income statement, which is also known as the **Profit and Loss Statement,** is presented, it is expressed as covering a period of time, with the beginning and ending dates shown. Most frequently, this period is the accounting year, beginning on the first day (e.g., January 1, XXXX) and ending on the last day (e.g., December 31, XXXX). It summarizes all of the financial activity that took place during the period captioned. On the following pages we will present and describe the basic elements of the Income Statement. In the next chapter we will describe the activities that are incorporated into the Income Statement.

To understand the financial performance of a business, it is necessary to measure the revenues and expenses and to compute the **profit.** To be successful, all businesses, even those identified as "nonprofit," need to make a profit. That is, their revenues must exceed their expenses. Beginning with the Income Statement, we assess the performance of the business. The next chapter will present more detail, permitting you to following the Income Statement transactions, and see how they affect the Balance Sheet, enabling you to evaluate the financial condition of the enterprise.

In an annual report of a public company these last segments (Dividends and Change in Retained Earnings) may be presented as a separate reconciliation, called Statement of Stockholders' Equity or Statement of Retained Earnings. Conventions and regulations determine how information is

---

### xhibit 1–4
#### The Income Statement—Annotated

| | |
|---|---|
| Sales | Revenues received or to be received from the sale of the products or services offered by the business |
| – Cost of Sales | Those costs and expenses expended to generate revenues, including expenses specifically incurred in the production or acquisition of goods to be sold |
| = Gross Profit | |
| – Operating Expenses | Expenses incurred to support the general activities of the company, excluding investments in capitalized assets |
| = Earnings before Interest and Taxes, also known as Operating Profit | |
| – Interest | Expenses incurred in support of debt undertaken by the organization to finance its activities or the acquisition of assets and resources |
| = Earnings before Taxes | |
| – Taxes | Amounts required by the governmental authorities holding jurisdiction over the company, applied to profits earned by the company |
| = Earnings after Taxes | |
| – Dividends | Amounts paid out to shareholders, a distribution of after-tax earnings |
| = Change in Retained Earnings | Amounts retained in the company to help finance operations and growth |

---

presented to external users. This often differs from the way information is presented to internal managers for internal decision making.

## Exercise 1–2: Examining Your Company's Income Statement

INSTRUCTIONS: ☛ Compare this Income Statement format above with the one from your company or another company whose financial statements you have access to. Identify the similarities and differences between this generalized Income Statement and that of a specific company. As with the Balance Sheet, ask someone in the accounting or finance department to clarify anything that causes confusion.

For example, your company may show revenue from different sources separately or break down expenses in more detail. Individual industries, such as banking and insurance, may have some unique reporting practices that will cause their statements to differ somewhat from this format.

## Statement of Cash Flows

Because many people view cash as indicative of a business's financial well-being, a great deal of attention is directed toward cash, cash management, cash availability, and a range of other issues surrounding cash and cash equivalents. The third major financial statement, the Statement of Cash Flows, represents an effort to present the management of cash in a manner that can be understood by the various interested parties.

Over the years this interest in cash has gone through an evolution, from a relatively simple *Sources and Uses of Cash* statement to the *Cash Flow Statement* to today's *Statement of Cash Flows* in a form that addresses the interests of management, lenders, and investors in the same document.

The Statement of Cash Flows summarizes the changes in the Balance Sheet during the reporting period, separated into transactions reflecting operating activities, investing activities, and financing activities. It identifies where the company got the funds it used and what it did with them, and it facilitates assessment of management's effectiveness in directing the business.

The results of the Statement of Cash Flows reflect the change in the cash balances of the company. If an item, or a total, is negative, it represents cash outflow; if positive, it reflects inflows. On the following pages we will present and describe the basic elements of the Statement of Cash Flows. In the next chapter we will examine the way that financial activities are incorporated into the Statement of Cash Flows.

For internal management each contributor to cash flow may be computed separately as part of an effort to track amounts and causes and consequences. This detailed approach is known by some as the Direct Method Cash Flow Statement and the one presented in Exhibit 1–6 is known as the Indirect Method Cash Flow Statement.

The simple structuring of cash flows in Exhibits 1–5 and 1–6 helps you to recognize the double entry nature of bookkeeping entries and the effect that a transaction will have on cash resources. It demonstrates clearly the re-

## xhibit 1–5

**Statement of Changes in Financial Position (Cash Flow Statement)**

| | |
|---|---|
| | Net Profit after Taxes |
| + | Depreciation |
| + | Decreases in Current Asset Accounts (individually identified) |
| − | Increases in Current Asset Accounts (individually identified) |
| + | Increases in Current Liability Accounts except Notes Payable or Current Portion of Long Term Debt (individually identified) |
| − | Decreases in Current Liability Accounts except Notes Payable or Current Portion of Long Term Debt (individually identified) |

| | |
|---|---|
| = + | Cash Flow from Operations |
| +/− | Change in Gross Fixed Assets |
| +/− | Change in Any Business Investments |

| | |
|---|---|
| = + | Cash Flow from Investment Activities |
| − | Decrease in Notes Payable |
| + | Increase in Long Term Debt |
| +/− | Changes in Stockholders' Equity |
| − | Dividends Paid |

| | |
|---|---|
| = + | Cash Flow from Financing Activities |

| | |
|---|---|
| = | <u>Net Change in Cash and Cash Equivalents</u> |

lationship of cash to other accounts on the Balance Sheet and permits you to test the effect of a transaction before you undertake it.

If you include cash and cash equivalents in your generation of this table, the two columns will be equal. If you exclude cash and cash equivalents, the difference in the two columns is the change in liquid assets. If this table is produced as part of the planning process, the difference between the columns (and it will generally be negative) is the cash generated (+) or the cash needed (−) for the period being projected.

## xhibit 1–6

**Alternative View of Cash Flow Statement**

| Sources of Funds | = | Uses of Funds |
|---|---|---|
| Decreases in Assets<br>Increases in Liabilities | | Increases in Assets<br>Decreases in Liabilities |

# THE STRUCTURE OF BUSINESS AND THE IMPACT OF FINANCIAL STATEMENTS

The legal structure of a business may take many forms. All businesses, regardless of their legal structure, prepare and utilize financial statements the same way. While in some cases certain line labels differ, the meaning and interpretation of the financial statements and the essential elements of financial management are the same. In fact, the essence of financial management is the same for a business and for individuals and their families. Individuals practice many, if not most, of the same techniques with regard to their own financial condition as financial managers do for the businesses that employ them. A brief look at the most common business structures will help make this clear.

## Proprietorship

A **proprietorship** is the simplest form of business structure. It is a business that is owned by one person who runs the business actively and treats it as an extension of him or her. A proprietorship is the easiest form of a business to establish, requiring only that the proprietor meet local and state registration and licensing requirements. Because the business is treated as an extension of the owner, the owner retains liability for the business' obligations and recognizes all of the assets, liabilities, profits or losses as belonging to the owner. Income taxes, for example, are paid as part of the personal tax return of the owner, with no other reports or filing requirements. In summary, a proprietorship is easy to establish and easy to terminate; its assets and liabilities belong to the owner directly; its taxes and obligations are taxes and obligations of the owner.

A proprietorship faces some limitations as well. Because it is an extension of the owner, the business faces limits on the debt it can incur because lenders are lending to the entrepreneur and make their credit decisions based on the creditworthiness of the individual. The proprietorship encounters difficulties in attracting professional managers because the owner is often reluctant to grant authority to someone else to establish personal liabilities and obligations for the owner, and managers are reluctant to have their authority and responsibility so limited. Also of importance is the fact that a proprietorship does not survive the proprietor. That is, the business terminates with the death or withdrawal of the owner.

## Partnership

A **partnership** is an agreement between two or more people to work together and share in the ownership and operation of a business. Such an operation shares some of the benefits of a proprietorship, such as a single incidence of annual taxation, on the individual tax returns of the partners and based on the share of the profits or losses each has agreed to take. However, the establishment of a partnership often involves definition of rights and responsibilities for each partner as well as the documentation of share and other agreements. Such documentation costs much more than does the establishment of a proprietorship.

There are some significant disadvantages to a partnership as well. Perhaps the most important one is that each partner is liable for all the debts of the partnership, so, if one partner cannot pay his or her share, all the other partners, or even just one, will be responsible for the obligation. Under certain circumstances, a partner may agree to provide funds for the business, but otherwise to remain uninvolved in the operations. In such cases the partner may be a limited partner, with rights to share in the financial success, but not in the liabilities (beyond the investment). Such a partnership is known as a limited partnership. The normal structure, with all partners actively participating in the organization is known as a general partnership.

Partnerships have more access to debt financing because the credit of the partnership is based on the creditworthiness of the partners, rather than on only one individual. Similarly, a partnership may have access to more and better management talent because the manager might have the opportunity to be a partner at some time. Until recently, most professional organizations (accountants, lawyers, architects, etc.) were partnerships. Today, many are structured as Limited Liability Partnerships (LLP) or Limited Liability Companies (LLC), new forms of structure that provide more liability protection to the partners and owners.

Just as a proprietorship terminates with the death or departure of the owner, so, too, a partnership dissolves with the death or withdrawal of a partner. However, it is possible to establish a partnership arrangement that immediately reconstitutes the partnership after such a dissolution.

## Corporation

Establishing a **corporation** requires more formality and more legal involvement than a proprietorship or even a partnership. This is in part because a corporation is deemed to be independent of its individual shareholders and can, therefore, continue to exist even if a shareholder dies or transfers shares to someone else.

This ability to transfer ownership, or to change the number of shares to attract additional owners, makes a corporation facilitate the attraction of professional management, who can hope to receive ownership shares if they are successful. It also makes it easier to attract financing because the lender/investor knows that the corporation will continue to exist, even if part of management leaves. This makes their debt potentially more secure.

Among the advantages of financing a corporation is the limitation of liability that is associated with corporations. Because the corporation survives the owners, it is deemed to undertake its own responsibility. Therefore, the shareholders and managers of the corporation are protected from liability for the debts and obligations of the corporation.

A major disadvantage of a corporation is the tax treatment applied to corporate earnings. Again because of the independent identity of the corporation, it is taxed directly on its earnings. If the corporation distributes its earnings to the shareholders as dividends, these dividends are taxed at the recipient level even though the corporation was taxed when the profits were made.

While most businesses are proprietorships, these proprietorships only represent a small percentage of the business value in the United States. While the number of businesses that are corporations is the lowest among the three structures, corporations account for more than 90 percent of all business value in the country. It is for this reason that presentation of financial statements normally follows the corporate format.

Financial statements for proprietorships and partnerships differ from those of corporations only in the presentation of the equity portion of the Balance Sheet. For these other entities the owners' equity is often identified as "owner's capital" or "partners' capital" or some similar term, whereas, a corporation's equity section refers to common stock (or capital stock), additional paid-in capital, and retained earnings.

## Other Business Structures

In recent years a number of variations of these legal structures have been developed to accommodate the needs of owners and changes in legal interpretations. Among these are "S" Corporations, which are corporations legally, but which are taxed as partnerships; Limited Liability Companies and Limited Liability Partnerships, which provide protection for the owners from responsibility for debts incurred through the actions of others; Trusts, such as Real Estate Investment Trusts, established to protect investors from risk in real estate transactions in which they are only investors; and other types of entities created to satisfy particular needs. The financial reporting for these entities is essentially the same as for corporations, except in the equity section, and the statements they prepare are similar to those presented earlier in this chapter.

Finance is managing money on behalf of owners and creditors. In business finance, the tools of financial management are applied consistently to all types of business so that owners, creditors, and anyone else who is interested, can review and understand the financial performance and condition of the organization. The basic means of communication regarding the financial management of a business is through financial statements:

- The Balance Sheet, which describes the financial condition of a business at a point in time, reflecting the first accounting equation,
Assets = Liabilities + Equity
- The Income Statement, which describes the performance of the business entity over a period of time, reflecting the second accounting equation,
Revenues − Expenses = Profits
- The Statement of Cash Flows, which identifies the sources and uses of the funds that passed through the organization
- The Statement of Changes in Shareholders' Equity, which reconciles the Income Statement and the Equity section of the Balance Sheet

Financial information is presented in the same manner regardless of the legal structure of the business, and because this is so, financial statements are consistently understood across all industries and business structures. Businesses can take any one of several legal forms, depending on the desires and concerns of the owners.

- Proprietorships—owned and actively operated by one person who retains all the benefits and undertakes all the liabilities, easily formed and dissolved, incurring a single level of taxation, terminating with the withdrawal of the owner
- Partnerships—owned and operated by more than one person, sharing the benefits and the liabilities, more complex to establish and run, incurring a single level of taxation, dissolving with the withdrawal of a partner
- Corporations—owned by one or more stockholders, considered a legal entity separate from its owners, taxed at the operating level, existing beyond the transfer of stock ownership

## Review Questions

INSTRUCTIONS:   *Here is the first set of review questions in this course. Answering the questions following each chapter will give you a chance to check your comprehension of the concepts as they are presented and will reinforce your understanding of them.*

*As you can see below, the answer to each numbered question is printed to the side of the question. Before beginning, you should conceal the answer in some way, either by folding the page vertically or by placing a sheet of paper over the answers. Then read and answer each question. Compare your answers with those given. For any question you answer incorrectly, make an effort to understand why the answer given is the correct one. You may find it helpful to turn back to the appropriate section of the chapter and review the material of which you were unsure. At any rate, be sure you understand all the review questions before going on to the next chapter.*

1. Which of the following is not included in financial management?     1. (d)
   (a) Purchasing office supplies using a credit card
   (b) Making a deposit into a retirement account
   (c) Making a mortgage payment on time
   (d) Choosing the background for your checks

2. The Balance Sheet depicts:     2. (b)
   (a) revenues and expenses of a company for the past year.
   (b) the financial condition of a company at a point in time.
   (c) the current month's payment due on the building mortgage.
   (d) the profit before interest and taxes.

3. Holding large balances in cash:     3. (c)
   (a) is the smartest way to manage your money.
   (b) assures the maximum income a company can earn.
   (c) earns a company less that it could make with careful investments.
   (d) provides comfort for the senior management.

4. The Income Statement of a company tells the reader:     4. (c)
   (a) how much cash the company has.
   (b) whether the company is a corporation or a partnership.
   (c) revenues and expenses of a company for the past year.
   (d) the net worth owned by the shareholders.

Do you have questions? Comments? Need clarification?
Call Educational Services at 1-800-225-3215, ext. 600,
or email at ed_svcs@amanet.org.

**5.** The Statement of Cash Flows summarizes:                        5. (a)
   (a) the sources and uses of cash in a business for the past year.
   (b) whether or not the current cash balance is adequate for next
       year.
   (c) the level of sales achieved last year.
   (d) the changes in retained earnings from one year to the next.

$2$

# Introduction to Accounting

*focus*

## Learning Objectives

By the end of this chapter, you should be able to:

- Explain the difference between accounting and finance.
- Prepare a Balance Sheet and an Income Statement from financial data.
- Describe how transactions affect the financial statements of a company.

## OVERVIEW

Accounting is different from finance and this chapter will explain the differences. The definition and demonstration of basic accounting tools will provide you with the understanding you need to participate in discussions of financial matters with others. This chapter will cover such information as the definition and application of debits and credits to managerial understanding, the explanation of GAAP, and the application of double-entry bookkeeping.

### *Accounting Is Not Just Cash*

Bob welcomed the group and let them know that he appreciated how hectic it was around the plant these days. "I know a lot of you have been putting in a lot of extra hours, so I really appreciate the effort you're making to get together." Bob asked how many of the group had looked at the company financial statements on the intranet. Only a few hands went up.

"We've just started talking about accounting and finance, so those statements will still be hard to understand. Even so, the sooner you start looking at them, the sooner you'll start to see the story they can tell you. After you begin to get familiar with our financial statements, you might go to the Internet and look up some of the publicly traded companies we compete against to see what their financial statements look like. . . . Chris, I see you've got a question."

"Bob, I did take a look at our statements and I don't see why it has to be so complicated. At home, I pay all my bills, pay my mortgage, and put a little bit away. When I balance my checkbook at the end of the month, I can look at what's left and see how I did. Why can't we just check the company's cash balance? We're growing, right? And we have plenty of new orders. Why do we need all that other information?"

"Chris, the accounting system lets us record all transactions properly and on a timely basis and in the proper time period so that all kinds of people can make better decisions by looking at them.

"Because we're growing so fast right now, just looking at the cash we have in the bank at the end of the month could give a lot of people the wrong idea about the company. Our sales are increasing quite rapidly, but we don't get the cash for those sales at the same time we get the orders. We're buying larger quantities of raw materials every month lately, and we're running extra shifts—which means we're spending more on labor. We have to lay out that cash before we get the revenue for the new sales. The accounting system, by recording transactions in the proper period, lets me see how much cash we're going to need—and explain to the bank why we need to increase our credit line. It's not because we're managing badly, it's because we're growing fast.

"That's why I want every manager in this company to understand what's happening around here and what kind of impact it will have on the results we share with the board of directors, our creditors, and the bank. That kind of understanding will help you explain to your people why we have to be so careful about controlling costs."

## THE PURPOSE OF ACCOUNTING

The American Institute of Certified Public Accountants (AICPA) described in 1970 the purpose of accounting: "To provide quantitative information, primarily financial in nature, about economic entities that is intended to be useful in making economic decisions." The key word here is "useful." If the information is not useful, there is no sense in going through the effort. The following pages will look at the accounting information and identify its usefulness.

If we handle like transactions or activities in the same way all the time, it is easy for us to interpret the transactions and understand what is happening to our business. Accounting provides the structure that enables us to process business transactions in a way that permits consistent treatment, reporting, and interpretation. While this portion of financial management was labeled Bookkeeping in the first chapter, it is generally known as the accounting system.

### The Accounting System

The **accounting system** is the bookkeeping portion of financial management. It defines what goes in what category on the Income Statement or the

Balance Sheet. In addition, an accounting system accomplishes the following functions:

- **Identifies and records all transactions**—The accounting system needs to handle and control all transactional documentation quickly and correctly: incoming and outgoing invoices, incoming and outgoing payments, orders, payroll items, and all other business activities.
- **Describes accounting events on a timely basis**—As we noted earlier, immediately recording and recognizing financial effects allows organizations to respond effectively and quickly to challenges or opportunities.
- **Measures the value of transactions properly**—The accounting system must assign appropriate values to transactions, particularly those for which the value is not obvious, such as the inventory value and, therefore, cost of product produced or held for sale. The accurate valuation will help assure accuracy, which is necessary if an organization is to manage effectively.
- **Ensures recording in the proper time period(s)**—Financial reporting is most valuable when it provides an accurate assessment of the status of the business. By recording transactions in the appropriate time period, plans and forecasts as well as operations themselves can be properly evaluated.
- **Presents and discloses accounting events properly**—Proper treatment permits outsiders to evaluate the success of the business whether they are the board of directors, investors, lenders, vendors, customers, or anyone else. Timely reporting and disclosure increases the value of everything about the business.

## Who Uses Accounting Information?

Accounting information is valuable to everyone included in a list of **company stakeholders,** the various people and organizations that have an interest in the company. Among the stakeholders are

- the Board of Directors
- the management
- the employees
- the shareholders
- the bankers and other lenders
- the customers
- the vendors
- the competitors
- the various federal, state, and local governmental agencies that are interested in the company, its industry, taxes, and regulatory compliance
- the community as a whole
- anyone else with an interest in the company or its industry

These different parties use the information produced from the accounting records of the company, but obviously, all of them have different interests and perspectives to apply to this information. With all these different concerns, the quality of the accounting information becomes paramount. The accounting system and the processes followed require special attention.

In preparing the financial statements the bookkeepers and accountants must be aware of the needs and expectations of the various stakeholders. Consider the examples of the different stakeholders that follow.

The Board of Directors makes policy decisions and develops the future plan for the company based on the financial performance and condition of the company as reflected in the statements. They also take into account the financial performance of the company's competition. The importance of accuracy and timeliness is obvious.

Similarly, company management makes current and shorter-term decisions using the same information. Their decisions often respond to the signals found in the statements and in the changes in results from period to period. They also respond to the financial activities of customers, vendors, and competitors.

In turn, customers, vendors, and competitors analyze financial information for indications of financial strength or weakness, improved or deteriorated performance and prospects. They will make buying, selling, or market response decisions based on their interpretation of financial results. As we will see in Chapter 3, analysis of financial statements provides a real window into business operations.

Employees and prospective employees look at financial information as they make personal decisions as to employment and personal financial expectations. In today's competitive employment marketplace it is very common for a prospective employee, before committing to a job offer, to request copies of company financial statements to analyze.

The regulatory agencies of the federal, state, and local governments and the community as a whole are interested in the performance of the company and how it fits into the overall financial picture the viewer is concerned with.

Investors examine financial information of the company before making, retaining, or disposing of investments in the company. In some cases they rely on the analysis of financial analysts employed by securities brokers and dealers to provide guidance for their investment decisions.

Bankers and other lenders analyze financial information before deciding to make loans to the company. Then they examine the periodic financial statements to determine the appropriate actions with regard to the loans they have already made. If they see a weakening performance, they will be more apt to take protective actions to assure that their loans are secure. If they see strengthening of the financial performance of the company, they will be more likely to extend further credit and make more money available. As we will see, this improvement in performance that facilitates further borrowing is important to a company, because, in many cases, business growth creates the need for additional outside funding.

## BASIC TERMINOLOGY

To understand how accounting works, we need to understand the basic terminology of the discipline and to recognize how these terms and concepts are used.

## Financial Statements

This section of the chapter introduces the key financial statements from which analysts and managers identify the areas of success within the company, those that need improvement, and develop the understanding necessary to reach conclusions and make decisions that will guide the business going forward. The essence of financial management is gathering information, taking actions based on that information, and then reviewing and reassessing before progressing again.

Exhibits 2–1 and 2–2 lay out the first two of the basic financial statements. These two statements are the building blocks for all of the financial information managers need to fulfill their responsibilities.

These basic financial statements have already been introduced. Now we will consider how the information gets into these statements. To do so we must understand terms such as debits and credits, revenues and expenses, assets and liabilities. Back in the fifteenth century a Franciscan monk named Luca Pacioli, who first described the essentials of double-entry bookkeeping, identified the most basic elements of today's bookkeeping process.

He recognized that establishing a process of checks and balances enhanced information control. We follow that premise today, reflected in the Balance Sheet, where Assets = Liabilities + Equity. Using a basic principle of algebra, once established, the integrity of an equality must be preserved. Therefore, whenever we make an entry to affect one side of the equation, we must identify a companion transaction that either offsets that effect on the same side of the equal sign or reflects a complementary effect on the other side.

From this we have developed the essence of **debits** and **credits.** In double-entry bookkeeping, for every debit amount there must be an equal credit amount. Debits are used to increase the assets or decrease the liabilities and equity, and credits are used to decrease the assets or increase the liabilities and equity.

---

## xhibit 2–1

**The Balance Sheet**

| ASSETS | | LIABILITIES AND EQUITY |
|---|---|---|
| *Current Assets* | | *Current Liabilities* |
| Cash | | Accounts Payable |
| Marketable Securities | | Notes Payable |
| Accounts Receivable | | Accruals |
| Inventory | | *Long-Term Debt* |
| Prepaid Expenses | | *Equity* |
| *Fixed Assets* | | Common Stock |
| *Intangible Assets* | | Retained Earnings |
| TOTAL ASSETS | = | TOTAL LIABILITIES AND EQUITY |

---

**xhibit 2–2**

**The Income Statement**

|   |   |
|---|---|
| + | Sales or Revenues |
| − | Cost of Sales |
| = | Gross Profit |
| − | Operating Expenses |
| = | Earnings before Interest |
| − | Interest |
| = | Earnings before Taxes |
| − | Taxes |
| = | Earnings after Taxes |
| − | Stock Dividends |
| = | Change in Retained Earnings |

For example, if we purchase $100.00 worth of inventory for cash, we would make financial entries that would have the following effect:

Debit Inventory (an Asset) for $100.00 to reflect the value of the inventory acquired.
Credit Cash (an Asset) for $100.00 to reflect the reduction in cash used to pay for the inventory.

In the Balance Sheet it would be reflected as:

|   | **Dr (Debit)** | **Cr (Credit)** |
|---|---|---|
| Cash |   | $100.00 |
| Inventory | $100.00 |   |

The reason that the credit is reflected first in this example is that in our Balance Sheet cash comes before inventory.

If we had purchased the inventory on credit, promising to pay for it at a later date, it would appear as:

Debit Inventory (an Asset) for $100.00 to reflect the value of the inventory acquired.
Credit Accounts Payable (a Liability) for $100.00 to reflect the value of the inventory that we now owe to the vendor.

In the Balance Sheet it would be reflected as:

|   | **Dr (Debit)** | **Cr (Credit)** |
|---|---|---|
| Inventory | $100.00 |   |
| Accounts Payable |   | $100.00 |

To begin, bear in mind that the Income Statement reflects activities that are intended to reward the shareholder; that is, to increase the wealth of the shareholders through the generation of profit. As we saw in Chapter 1, the wealth of the shareholder is reflected in the Equity section of the Balance Sheet. Recording credits to the Equity accounts, therefore, increase them. Generally, except for the direct sale of stock, we only affect equity through transactions reflected in the Income Statement.

Therefore, to ultimately increase Equity, we must show Revenues in the Income Statement as credits, because, if revenues exceed expenses, the result is profit that must reflect on the Balance Sheet as an increase in—a credit to—Equity.

If we show Sales as credits, then we must show Expenses as debits in order to generate accurate accounting results. In its simplest terms then, we would show a sale of that inventory or credit as follows:

|  | Dr (Debit) | Cr (Credit) |
|---|---|---|
| Sales (Revenue) |  | $150.00 |
| Accounts Receivable (Asset) | $150.00 |  |
| Cost of Sales (Expense) | $100.00 |  |
| Inventory (Asset) |  | $100.00 |

These two transactions both balance, but the Balance Sheet no longer appears to be balanced because we increased Assets by $150.00, but then decreased them only by $100.00. However, the Income Statement now shows a profit of $50.00, the difference between sales and expenses. This profit, at the end of the accounting period, is recognized through a journal entry that closes out the period's income statement by removing the profit from the Income Statement through a debit and increasing the Equity on the Balance Sheet through a credit. Now the Income Statement result has been zeroed out, making it ready for the next accounting period, and the Balance Sheet has been balanced. Consider the following:

|  |  | Dr (Debit) | Cr (Credit) |
|---|---|---|---|
| BS | Accounts Receivable | $150.00 |  |
| BS | Inventory |  | $100.00 |
| IS | Sales |  | $150.00 |
| IS | Cost of Sales | $100.00 |  |
| IS | Profit | $50.00 |  |
| BS | Retained Earnings (Equity) |  | $50.00 |

Now, the Balance Sheet (BS) balances and the Income Statement (IS) reflects the activity of the period, closed out at the end of the period to the Balance Sheet.

## The Chart of Accounts

People develop accounting systems to make it easier to process accounting transactions and to generate financial statements and other financial information. To process the accounting transactions such as those in the preceding section, accountants have developed a systematic account numbering system that helps assure that transactions are properly reflected in the financial statements.

Such a systematic numbering system, called the **Chart of Accounts,** provides a shorthand entry control system for assuring that related transactions are accumulated together. Properly constructed, the chart of accounts should lead directly to the production of financial statements, making it easy to close the books each period, produce financial statements, and provide consistent information for analysis and interpretation. Thus, the accounting system and the processing of transactions contribute to the timely and effective management of the operations.

The numbering system in a well-constructed chart of accounts will reflect the same sequence as appears in the financial statements, beginning with cash, the first Balance Sheet asset account, and continuing through taxes, an expense reflected at the bottom of the Income Statement. The result of such a structure is that as the accountant closes the books for the period these basic financial statements will be automatically prepared.

A typical chart of accounts might be constructed like the one in Exhibit 2–3.

As you can see in Exhibit 2–3, the structure of the numbering system leads directly to the presentation of financial statements.

- 1000s are Assets
- 2000s are Liabilities
- 3000s are Equity Accounts
- 4000s are Revenues
- 5000s are Cost of Sales accounts
- 6000s are Operating Expenses
- 7000s are Other Income and Expense accounts
- 8000s are Taxes

This type of structure makes it very easy for the accountants and managers to review the results of the accounting period and report to management, and to other interested parties, the summarized results and the reasons behind them.

As a company becomes more complicated, with divisions or subsidiaries, with multiple departments, or with other specialized reporting interests, the accounts within each category may be expanded by inserting numbers or adding additional digits to permit reporting by smaller or more specific units. For example, Peachtree Accounting Software, an inexpensive PC-based accounting software package, permits a chart of accounts numbering system of up to 15 characters, both letters and numbers. Such a chart of accounts permits as much detail as any smaller business might want or need.

In fact, the availability of 15 characters would permit such detail as would be needed to track the costs of a specific project or activity within a department within a facility within a division within a subsidiary within a company. At the same time, by sorting on specific digits within the account code, management could determine how much was spent on a particular expense category, such as Telephone or Delivery.

As an example of a 15 digit account number consider the following:

AAA-BBBB-CCC-DDDDD

Where:

AAA     = Company, subsidiary, division or affiliate
BBBB   = Account number
CCC     = Department or responsibility
DDDDD = Project, territory, class of trade

With this type of structure a company can identify spending activity in almost any combination of ways to provide all managers with the information they need to manage their area and level of responsibility.

---

 **xhibit 2–3**

**Chart of Accounts**

| | | |
|---|---|---|
| 1010 | Cash | Asset |
| 1020 | Accounts Receivable | Asset |
| 1030 | Inventory | Asset |
| 1040 | Prepaid Expenses | Asset |
| 1510 | Fixed Assets | Asset |
| 1910 | Intangible Assets | Asset |
| 2010 | Accounts Payable | Liability |
| 2020 | Notes Payable | Liability |
| 2030 | Accrued Expenses | Liability |
| 2210 | Long Term Debt | Liability |
| 3010 | Preferred Stock | Equity |
| 3510 | Common Stock | Equity |
| 3710 | Retained Earnings | Equity |
| 4010 | Revenues | Revenues |
| 5010 | Raw Materials Expense | Cost of Sales |
| 5020 | Direct Labor | Cost of Sales |
| 5030 | Factory Overhead | Cost of Sales |
| 6010 | Salaries | Operating Expense |
| 6020 | Employee Benefits | Operating Expense |
| 6030 | Advertising | Operating Expense |
| 6040 | Bank Charges | Operating Expense |
| 6050 | Delivery, including Postage | Operating Expense |
| 6060 | Legal and Audit | Operating Expense |
| 6070 | Office Expense | Operating Expense |
| 6080 | Property Taxes | Operating Expense |
| 6090 | Rent | Operating Expense |
| 6110 | Repairs and Maintenance | Operating Expense |
| 6120 | Supplies | Operating Expense |
| 6130 | Telephone | Operating Expense |
| 6140 | Travel | Operating Expense |
| 6145 | Meals and Entertainment | Operating Expense |
| 6150 | Miscellaneous | Operating Expense |
| 7010 | Interest | Other Expense |
| 8010 | Federal Income Taxes | Taxes |
| 8020 | State Income Taxes | Taxes |

---

# THE ACCOUNTING CYCLE

Accountants collect financial information as it occurs but report it based on predetermined accounting time periods, generally months, quarters, and years. It could, however, be reported for any time period that management or some interested party decided was important.

## Using Journal Entries to Record Transactions

During the specified time period, the transactions that occur are tracked using the same journal entry structure discussed in the last section. All activity is recorded using debits and credits, preserving the balance that was established before, but changing totals to incorporate the current activity. In the actual accounting system these journal entries are often established with one side understood and calculated automatically, such as when a bill is paid, the debit is recorded as an expense or a charge to accounts payable. The credit side is automatically charged to Cash, to recognize the actual payment. Only when the credit is to go to some other account is it necessary to record the credit entry. Nevertheless, the journal entry balances and the basic accounting equality is preserved. A brief look at some of these transactions will clarify this discussion. Then a series of exercises will provide a little practice in making journal entries and following the transactions into the financial statements.

Consider a purchase of $1,000 of special widgets needed for a special project.

> The office manager would place an order with the local office of Specialty Widget Corporation for the supplies. This action would have no impact on the accounting system.

When the supplies are shipped, Specialty Widget issues an invoice for $1,000. On Specialty Widget's books this transaction is recorded as:

|  | Debit (Dr) | Credit (Cr) |
|---|---|---|
| Sales |  | $1,000.00 |
| Accounts Receivable | $1,000.00 |  |
| Cost of Sales | $700.00 |  |
| Inventory |  | $700.00 |

You will recognize that Specialty Widget has achieved a $300 contribution to profit on this transaction. The difference between sales and cost of sales is known as **gross profit.**

On the purchasing company's books, the same transaction appears as:

| | | |
|---|---|---|
| Supplies Expense | $1,000.00 | |
| Accounts Payable | | $1,000.00 |

The supplies are not generally treated as inventory because they are not for resale, are not held for longer than a year, and are not to be stored for use as part of the product to be sold.

When the purchasing company pays for the supplies, after 30 days or whatever credit period was determined in negotiation between the two companies, the respective entries are as follows:

On the books of the purchasing company:

| | | |
|---|---|---|
| Accounts Payable | $1,000.00 | |
| Cash | | $1,000.00 |

And on the books of the Specialty Widget Corporation:

| | | |
|---|---|---|
| Cash | $1,000.00 | |
| Accounts Receivable | | $1,000.00 |

You can see from this example that each entry is balanced. Following these entries to the financial statements will highlight some additional important considerations.

On the books of Specialty Widget, the Sales exceed the Cost of Sales by an amount which, were this the only transaction of the month, would result in a profit of $300. This profit, when closed to Retained Earnings during the closing process, would assure that the balance sheet balanced because the increase in assets of $300 (the absolute difference between the increase in Accounts Receivable [later transferred to Cash] and the decrease in Inventory) is equal to the increase in Retained Earnings

On the books of the purchasing company, the $1,000.00 in Supplies Expense, were it the only transaction of the month, would result in a reported loss of $1,000.00. This amount, when closed to Retained Earnings at the end of the month, would result in balancing the Balance Sheet, as the decrease in Cash of $1,000.00 would equal the decrease in Retained Earnings of $1,000.00.

In traditional accounting education, each of these transactions would be recorded in an appropriate **Journal,** a book of transactions that would be summarized as the first steps in the monthly closing process. In practice today, these journals are generally automatically recorded and summarized within the computerized accounting system. Let's see how this would look for an ordinary individual. If you pay all your bills by check and record all transactions in your checkbook, the checkbook is the journal, and you could prepare personal financial statements every month using the checkbook as the basis for all your closing entries.

If you analyze your business, you will recognize a series of journals that you can visualize as the accounting system:

- **Sales Journal**—Records all sales orders.
- **Cash Receipts Journal**—Records all cash receipts. The Cash Receipts Journal should confirm deposit information appearing in the bank statement.
- **Purchases Journal**—Records all purchase orders that have been fulfilled. It records obligations before they have been paid. Payments appear in the Cash Disbursements Journal.

- **Cash Disbursement Journal**—Records all payments made. The difference between the cash disbursements journal summary and the cash receipts journal summary will be the net entry to Cash on the Balance Sheet.
- **Payroll Journal**—Records all payroll transactions. The amounts entered into the payroll journal will also show up as transactions in the cash disbursements journal.
- **General Journal**—Records all adjusting entries, summary totals from the other journals, and all transactions that do not affect cash receipts or cash disbursements. The general journal provides the link to the financial statements for all accounting activities that do not pass through the other journals or other detailed records of the company.

Remembering that because each accounting period is suppose to provide a complete and accurate summary of financial transactions and financial conditions, it is sometimes necessary to recognize the financial effects of transactions that have not yet happened or are not yet complete. Consider the partial completion of some production. You would need to record the value of the work completed to date, even though it is not yet finished. The accounting for value added to work in process needs to be recorded, but for the next period, you need to undo, or reverse, this entry in order to record the final value of the now completed product. Such an entry, and there are many of them, will be handled in the accounting system as a **reversing journal entry,** that is, an entry that will be reversed in the next accounting period. Each period will then have the right amounts in it. The first entry, in the first period, will record the work completed to date. The second set of entries, in the following period, will record a negative amount for the work completed earlier and the full value of the completed product. The net of these two parts will equal the value added in the second period.

> Therefore, reversing journal entries will be part of the general journal and will normally be recorded separately, permitting their immediate (at the beginning of the next accounting period) reversal, setting the stage for the next accounting cycle.

There are also some transactions that occur every accounting period. These can be summarized in a series of **Standard Journal Entries** that simplify the accounting process. For example, the depreciation of Fixed Assets occurs every month, generally recognized as one-twelfth of the annual depreciation amount. (Sometimes a company will recognize depreciation based on the number of days in a month or as some other predictable amount.)

> Therefore, also in the General Journal, Standard Journal Entries will be recorded every month, providing a basis for the recognition of all relevant financial consequences in the appropriate accounting period.

## Closing Procedures

At the end of each accounting period, all of the transactions for that period are entered, even if the entry takes place after the last day of the accounting period. Accounting is more interested in accuracy than in getting everything done as quickly as possible. This sometimes creates conflicts between the accountants and the operating managers. Operating managers want to know as soon as possible what the results were and what happened. After all, it is easier to make corrections in practices if you know about the problems soon enough. Think about training a puppy. To change a behavior, you must educate the puppy while he still remembers what you are training him about.

To satisfy both the accountants and the managers, a closing schedule is established that brings most of the relevant accounting information to the accounting department quickly. The few transactions that are missed are generally not **material.** That is, they will not significantly affect the final results.

As soon as the last of the transactions are recorded, the accountants summarize the general journal, perhaps automatically as part of the computerized accounting system, making closing journal entries that bring the current period to a close. These entries bring the Income Statement balances for the period back to zero by transferring the net amount to the equity side of the Balance Sheet, creating a balance between the assets and the liabilities. At this time, the system is ready to start the next period's Income Statement.

## MORE FINANCIAL CONCEPTS

To complete this introduction to accounting, there are some additional terms and concepts that need explanation. The first of these is **GAAP, generally accepted accounting principles.**

From time to time you will hear people talk about GAAP (pronounced "gap"), perhaps asking if such and such has been handled according to GAAP. GAAP has been defined by the Accounting Principles Board as follows: "Generally accepted accounting principles encompass the conventions, rules, and procedures necessary to define accepted accounting practice at a particular time."

This definition is not particularly helpful, especially to the non-accountant. However, because all public companies and most others prepare their financial statements and accounting information according to GAAP, what it means, and what GAAP really does, is assure that financial information is prepared consistently and may be understood in the same way as other financial information similarly prepared. Therefore, GAAP assures that analysts and other readers of financial statements should understand the same structures and descriptions the same way and can compare financial statements and arrive at reasonable and supportable conclusions.

Other accounting terms such as accrual accounting, materiality, and auditor's opinion also create confusion. This is an appropriate place to define some of these terms as well.

**Accruals** and **accrual accounting** recognize that it is important to match revenues and expenses in the same time period. They also acknowledge that the recording of accounting transactions cannot always be completed quickly enough to produce timely, usable financial statements. Accruals, therefore, are accounting transactions that estimate revenues, or, more probably, expenses so that the period's financial reports will reflect that period's results appropriately. Accruals also reflect transactions that were not really complete at the end of the accounting period but that should be reported. An example of such is Accrued Wages, wages earned during the period, but not due or payable at the end of that period. For example, assume that December 31 falls on a Wednesday and that payday is Friday. The wages earned in December should be reported as December transactions, but the amount so earned is not due or payable on December 31, the end of the accounting period. The wages earned through December 31 will, therefore, be accrued, charged into the December accounting period.

**Materiality** is another attempt to make the accounting process reasonable. Some transactions are really very small relative to the operations of the entire business, but to be perfectly accurate, need to be recognized. The concept of materiality acknowledges that if we try to account for all the transactions at the end of a period, we may spend far more time or energy than will be worthwhile when compared to the value of the transactions involved. Therefore, GAAP recognizes that if not accounting for such a transaction properly will not change the quality or usefulness of the overall financial information, the transaction may be deemed not material. Accountants have agreed that if a transaction is not material, it does not have to be completed or reported if such reporting will delay the completion of the reporting. Therefore, you may hear people talk about some information as not being material.

The **auditor's opinion** is one place where GAAP and materiality come together. All public companies and many other companies employ outside auditors to review the accounting information to assess its accuracy and completeness. The auditor reviews the records and transactions of the company and provides an opinion as to whether or not they "present fairly, in all material respects, the financial position of the company as of December 31, XXXX." Analysts, investors, management, and others use this opinion as an assurance that a competent outsider has reviewed the accounting information and found it sound. These people then feel they can rely on the information to make managerial or investment decisions.

Sometimes, the auditors believe that there is a problem with the company or its records. They will, under those circumstances, issue a "qualified" opinion and will explain the qualification they have identified. The users of the financial statements, thus informed, can make appropriate decisions. The management, after receiving a qualified opinion, will be under great pressure to correct whatever deficiency has been identified.

## PREPARING FINANCIAL STATEMENTS

The final step in what is really the bookkeeping process (the accurate and timely recording of transactions) is the preparation of financial statements. This is the summarization of the recorded transactions into standard format for review and analysis. The next chapter will focus on the analysis and interpretation of these financial statements, which we referred to as accounting in the last chapter.

## The Key Financial Statements

Chapter 1 introduced the financial statements and this chapter has described their creation. The following exercises will provide an opportunity to try your hand at some financial statements and then to apply the journal entries described earlier to them to see their effect.

## Exercise 2–1: Prepare a Balance Sheet

*INSTRUCTIONS:* ☛ From the following account information, prepare the Specialty Widget Corporation's Balance Sheet as of December 31, XXXX.

| | |
|---|---:|
| Accounts Payable | $ 52,763.79 |
| Accounts Receivable | 83,895.76 |
| Accruals | 1,696.57 |
| Cash | 42,568.25 |
| Common Stock | 10,000.00 |
| Fixed Assets | 141,960.00 |
| Inventory | 65,361.59 |
| Long-Term Debt | 100,000.00 |
| Notes Payable | 65,985.00 |
| Retained Earnings | 103,340.24 |

Use the format in Exhibit 2–4 to prepare your answer.

 **xhibit 2–4**

**Specialty Widget Corporation**

Balance Sheet
(As of December 31, XXXX)

| Assets | | Liabilities and Equity | |
|---|---|---|---|
| Cash | _____ | Accounts Payable | _____ |
| Marketable Securities | _____ | Notes Payable | _____ |
| Accounts Receivable | _____ | Accruals | _____ |
| Inventory | _____ | | |
| Prepaid Expenses | _____ | | |
| **Total Current Assets** | _____ | **Total Current Liabilities** | _____ |
| Fixed Assets | _____ | Long-Term Debt | _____ |
| Intangible Assets | _____ | | |
| | | Common Stock | _____ |
| | | Retained Earnings | _____ |
| Total Assets | = | Total Liabilities and Equity | |

## Exercise 2–2: Prepare a Personal Balance Sheet

*INSTRUCTIONS:* ☛ Prepare a personal Balance Sheet (or one for your family) confidentially, using personal information. Structure it as if you were a business, with the equity section equal to the difference between the value of your assets and the amounts of money you owe to others.

Personal Balance Sheet

| ASSETS | | LIABILITIES AND EQUITY | |
|---|---|---|---|
| Cash | _____ | Accounts Payable | _____ |
| Marketable Securities | _____ | Notes Payable | _____ |
| Accounts Receivable | _____ | Accruals | _____ |
| Inventory | _____ | | |
| Prepaid Expenses | _____ | | |
| **Total Current Assets** | _____ | **Total Current Liabilities** | _____ |
| Fixed Assets | _____ | Long-Term Debt | _____ |
| Intangible Assets | _____ | | |
| | | Capital | _____ |
| | | Retained Earnings | _____ |
| Total Assets | = | Total Liabilities and Equity | |

## Exercise 2–3: Prepare an Income Statement

*INSTRUCTIONS:* ☛ From the following information, prepare an Income Statement for Specialty Widget Corporation for the year ended December 31, XXXX.

| | |
|---|---|
| Administrative Cost | $48,127.62 |
| Each Unit Cost | .73 |
| Interest Was | 15,278.80 |
| Selling Cost | 62,197.89 |
| Sold | 237,596 units at $1.45 per unit |
| Taxes | 30 percent of pre-tax profits |

Use the format in Exhibit 2–5 to prepare your answer.

## Exercise 2–4: Prepare a Personal Income Statement

*INSTRUCTIONS:* ☛ Prepare your own Income Statement confidentially (or one for your family), using personal information.

Structure this income statement as if you were a business, with:

- sales equal to your salary
- cost of sales equal to your work-based costs
- operating expenses equal to the remainder of your living expenses
- interest equal to the interest you pay on debt (including credit cards)
- taxes equal to the net income taxes (in this case including all payroll taxes withheld)

**xhibit 2-5**

Income Statement

Specialty Widget Corporation
(for the year ended December 31, XXXX)

+ Sales                               _____
− Cost of Sales                       _____
= Gross Profit                        _____
− Operating Expenses                  _____
= Earnings before Interest            _____
− Interest                            _____
= Earnings before Taxes               _____
− Taxes                               _____
= Earnings after Taxes                _____

The net income of your personal Income Statement from Exercise 2–4 should be the additions you have made to retirement, investment, and bank accounts. The effect of borrowing to purchase assets will not appear on your Income Statement, but it should have been shown on your personal Balance Sheet. Similarly, debt payments for mortgages, loans, and principal payments on credit card debt will not show on your Income Statement, but will show on your Balance Sheet (Exercise 2–2).

After some practice in preparing financial statements, the next step in putting accounting into perspective is to see the effect of transactions on these financial statements. For this exercise, assume that you are preparing the financial statements for the Specialty Widget Corporation. When we achieved the sale for $1,000, we prepared a journal entry.

To prepare this journal entry, apply the journal entries we created earlier for the sale of special widgets. In that transaction, we sold $1,000 worth of these widgets on credit.

 **xhibit 2-6**

Personal Income Statement

+ Sales                               _____
− Cost of Sales                       _____
= Gross Profit                        _____
− Operating Expenses                  _____
= Earnings before Interest            _____
− Interest                            _____
= Earnings before Taxes               _____
− Taxes                               _____
= Earnings after Taxes                _____

The entries we made were:

|  | **Dr (Debit)** | **Cr (Credit)** |
|---|---|---|
| Sales |  | $1,000.00 |
| Accounts Receivable | $1,000.00 |  |
| Cost of Sales | $700.00 |  |
| Inventory |  | $700.00 |

## Exercise 2–5: Revising the Financial Statements

*INSTRUCTIONS:* ☛ Reflect the impact of this transaction on the Balance Sheet and Income Statement of Specialty Widget Corporation.

When you complete the entries for Exercise 2–5, you see that sales and cost of sales have increased, but by different amounts, creating additional gross profit, operating profit, taxes, and net income. At the same time, in order to assure that the Balance Sheet remains balanced, accounts receivable increase, inventories decrease, and to make the statement balance, retained earnings must also increase.

If we continue to record the transactions, when the purchasing company pays our invoice, we will increase cash and reduce accounts receivable by the same amount, $1,000.00, maintaining the balance at all times.

## Trial Balance

During the course of an accounting period, a company will record many, many such transactions, tracking every activity of the company through the financial records. When the period ends, the accountants will summarize all of the transactions, determining the amounts to be recognized in each account. When all of the accounts in the chart of accounts are listed, with their respective balances, in a single, sequential statement, it is called a **Trial Balance.** A properly completed trial balance will reflect everything that has occurred during the period and when added together will total zero. That is, the debits will equal the credits and since they are all added together, they offset each other. Once this zero balance has been achieved, the accountants recognize that by separating the Balance Sheet accounts from the Income Statement accounts, they have prepared two financial statements which when added separately, reach the same net amount, but with opposite signs, one positive and the other negative. If the company has made a profit, the Income Statement has a total that reflects a net credit, and the Balance Sheet has more assets than liabilities, by the amount of the net credit. The final entry made, then, is to clear the net credit from the Income Statement and to add to the Retained Earnings account the profit for the period, bringing the Balance Sheet back into balance. From here the formal preparation and delivery of financial statements is only a function of printing the final results.

The Income Statement and Balance Sheet are the direct outcome of the accounting system recording and reporting process. The preparation of the Statement of Cash Flows follows easily from the completion of the Balance Sheet. The Statement of Cash Flows, as we noted in Chapter 1, summarizes information reflected on the Balance Sheet into a standardized structure, permitting analysts to understand and interpret how the company handled its cash during the period. Since cash and cash equivalents facilitate the completion of all business transactions, tracking the cash flows provides the analysts with a window into the company. We will consider this further in Chapter 3 when we discuss Financial Analysis.

Accounting is the process of recording and reporting financial information for the use of management and outsiders. The process of accounting recognizes the nature of financial transactions and provides a systematic and consistent method for communicating the essential information about the company, its financial strength, and its operating performance.

- Transactions are recorded using a system of debits and credits to relate different parts of the transactions to each other,
- The sum of the debits must equal the sum of the credits,
- The transactions must be recorded consistently, and
- All transactions for a period must be recognized in the financial statements for that period.

When this is done, financial reports will be accurate, timely, consistent, and prepared and presented in accordance with generally accepted accounting principles.

As a result, users of the financial statements will

- understand them
- be able to reach reasonable conclusions
- make logical decisions based on the information presented

## ANSWERS TO EXERCISES

### Exercise 2–1

**Specialty Widget Corporation**
Balance Sheet
(As of December 31, XXXX)

| ASSETS | | LIABILITIES AND EQUITY | |
|---|---|---|---|
| Cash | $42,568.25 | Accounts Payable | $52,763.79 |
| Marketable Securities | 0.00 | Notes Payable | 65,985.00 |
| Accounts Receivable | 83,895.76 | Accruals | 1,696.57 |
| Inventory | 65,361.59 | | |
| Prepaid Expenses | 0.00 | | |
| **Total Current Assets** | **$191,825.60** | **Total Current Liabilities** | **$120,445.36** |
| Fixed Assets | 141,960.00 | Long-Term Debt | 100,000.00 |
| Intangible Assets | 0.00 | | |
| | | Common Stock | 10,000.00 |
| | | Retained Earnings | 103,340.24 |

**Total Assets  $333,785.60  =  Total Liabilities and Equity  $333,785.60**

### Exercise 2–3

**Income Statement**
**Specialty Widget Corporation**
(for the year ended December 31, XXXX)

| | |
|---|---|
| + Sales | $344,514.20 |
| − Cost of Sales | 173,445.08 |
| = Gross Profit | 171,069.12 |
| − Operating Expenses | 110,325.51 |
| = Earnings before Interest | 60,743.61 |
| − Interest | 15,278.80 |
| = Earnings before Taxes | 45,464.81 |
| − Taxes | 13,639.44 |
| = Earnings after Taxes | $31,825.37 |

## Review Questions

**1.** Reversing journal entries are used to:
   (a) correct mistakes.
   (b) undo entries the accountant decides not to make.
   (c) record partially completed transactions into the correct accounting periods.
   (d) record activities that occur every period.

1. (c)

**2.** Debits reflect:
   (a) increases in assets, decreases in liabilities, and increases in expenses.
   (b) decreases in assets, increases in liabilities, and decreases in expenses.
   (c) increases in revenues, increases in profits, and increases in retained earnings.
   (d) increases in cash, increases in sales, and increases in increases in fees.

2. (a)

**3.** GAAP stands for:
   (a) Good and Appropriate Procedures.
   (b) Government Accounting and Auditing Practices.
   (c) Generally Accepted Accounting Principles.
   (d) General Accounting and Auditing Practices.

3. (c)

**4.** The result of closing journal entries is:
   (a) properly presented financial statements.
   (b) that the company no longer operates.
   (c) that the Income Statement balances.
   (d) that the company's bank account is reconciled.

4. (a)

**5.** The Chart of Accounts is:
   (a) structured into debits and credits.
   (b) a listing of all of the accounts into which entries may be made.
   (c) a graphical picture of the balances of the company's assets.
   (d) a comparison of financial results covering at least three years.

5. (b)

Do you have questions? Comments? Need clarification?
Call Educational Services at 1-800-225-3215, ext. 600,
or email at ed_svcs@amanet.org.

# Financial Analysis: Using Ratios

## Learning Objectives

By the end of this chapter, you should be able to:

- Compute analytical ratios from the data contained in a company's financial statements.
- Assess the financial condition of a business.
- Identify key areas for management focus to protect or improve business performance.

## OVERVIEW

Financial analysis refines the understanding of financial statements, taking on a scientific, structured focus that facilitates the interpretation of results. Using the tools of financial analysis, you will evaluate management by interpreting its financial results. The use of both traditional and nontraditional ratio analysis will show you what other analysts see. Your growing ability to analyze problems will lead to the development of management actions, and a discussion of alternative courses of action.

### Seeing Results

"Good morning. Please help yourself to some of the pastries and sodas on the table. Your efforts are really paying off. Our sales growth hasn't slowed down at all, and our numbers tell us that we're keeping our operations under control. Take a minute to congratulate yourselves for a job well done.

"You were going to analyze some of the ratios that weren't under the obvious control of your department before we got together today. What did you look at and why did you select that ratio? I'll be extremely interested to find out what you've learned from your investigation. And I really want to hear how our performance today compares with what we were doing before we started this program to teach everyone in the firm the basics of finance and accounting."

Pat was the first person to respond. "My department's been looking at a couple of these ratios and talking about how we can improve them during our weekly department meetings. We never really thought about how customer service could affect receivables before. But now that we understand how important it is to our overall results, some of our customer service reps have come up with really interesting techniques to resolve the problems some of our customers have been having with the A300 line and to encourage them to pay us faster. You can see that our average collection period was 65 days before the program started. It's down to 56 days today, and when I had lunch yesterday with Mary from accounts receivable, she said she'd noticed a real difference since we initiated this new effort."

## ANALYSIS OF FINANCIAL INFORMATION

Traditional ratio analysis, a process used for many years by many financial analysts and managers, looks at financial information in terms of liquidity, activity, profitability, and debt management, considering each measurement by itself. This analysis method helps the analyst develop an assessment of the company at the time of the statements analyzed. Nontraditional ratio analysis considers the relationships between financial data from an interpretive perspective, permitting the analyst or manager to make judgments or decisions related to operations. Nontraditional ratio analysis recognizes that some information is as indicative of future performance as it is of past performance.

Financial analysis incorporates some of the tools used by analysts and managers to assess the financial status and the financial condition of a company. Such analysis, utilizing financial ratios and analytical logic, provides information for assessment and is used by a wide range of interested parties. This chapter will explore these techniques, and provide experience in analyzing financial statements and seeing the story the numbers can tell.

Exercises and interactive examples will demonstrate how the techniques of financial analysis may be applied to functional responsibilities at the company level and at managerial levels throughout the organization. Sources of comparative information will be identified and use of the analytical tools will be explained in depth.

Everyone in business wishes they had a crystal ball and could anticipate future challenges and opportunities, allowing them to take appropriate and effective managerial action. Through the careful application of the tools of financial analysis, the manager can gain insight that is close to that crystal ball.

To begin this discussion and concentrate the process of financial analysis, consider this question: What is the purpose of business?

**Exercise 3–1: The Purpose of Business**

*INSTRUCTIONS:* ☛ Before continuing, write a brief response to the question: What is the purpose of business?

_____

_____

_____

# THE PURPOSE OF BUSINESS

To define the purpose of business, consider the relationships between business elements. Here are some alternatives:

1. Is it to maximize sales? If so, how would we do it?
2. Is it to maximize profits? If so, how would we do it?
3. Is it to maximize the wealth of the shareholders? If so, how would we do it?

As we develop our response to these questions, we will look at the techniques of financial analysis and the tools of financial management. First, however, we will develop answers to these questions in the context of a small company.

Consider a very small business—the company of you. You have an income and expenses, assets and liabilities. Therefore, an examination of your business may shed some light on this whole area. If we recast these questions, we can extrapolate easily from your personal business to a company of any size.

What is the purpose of your business? . . . Really?

Is it to maximize sales? You might then have to work extraordinary hours to maximize your revenue. If you worked that many hours, you would not have time to enjoy your wealth and you might burn yourself out without achieving your objective.

Is it to maximize your profits? You might choose to increase your profits by depriving yourself of everything but the barest of necessities, reducing your expenses to the minimum and increasing your savings. However, this option is also not very attractive, certainly over a long time period.

It should be obvious from this simple example that the superficial answers really do not yield the most attractive results. In reality, we work to achieve long-term goals. These long-term goals are not really described in a revenues context, yet they may appear to involve profits or accumulated profits. However, if the profits are accumulated at too great a sacrifice, that's not it either. The sacrifice detracts from our satisfaction, or wealth, which on a personal level is more than just financial. Our personal business objective is to maximize the wealth, from a satisfaction perspective, of the shareholder, our self.

We can easily extrapolate this analogy to a more general purpose of business, to maximize the wealth of the shareholders and to do so over the long run. To accomplish this, we must manage efficiently and effectively, making our resources, including people, productive. This, in turn, requires that we support and compensate the workers so that they can and want to be successful. Therefore, there is no conflict between the long-term objectives of the owners (shareholders) and the workers.

Financial analysis allows us to measure a business' success in achieving the wealth maximization goal. Wealth maximization is measured by the net worth of the company, and, more specifically, by the net worth of the company per share. There is a general belief that, for a public company, successful performance over time makes the company's stock attractive in the market. That is, strong operating performance is directly related to strong stock market performance, assuring that the market will reward shareholders, regardless of when they acquire their stock, appropriately.

At this point it is appropriate to consider the stock market and what it means. After all, shares of common stock represent ownership and the equity on the balance sheet, when divided by the number of shares, should equal the value of the shares. In fact, this calculation determines the **book value** of the shares.

However, the price of the stock in the market is generally different from the book value, frequently much higher. Chapter 6 discusses the time value of money and explains that the price of a financial asset, for example, a share of stock, is equal to the present value of future cash flows, the sum of dividends and sale price to be received in the future, discounted to current value. If a company is profitable, the profits belong to the shareholders, so the accumulated value of those profits, when discounted, will be valued in the stock market at a share price higher than the current book value of the stock.

## WHO PERFORMS FINANCIAL ANALYSIS?

Almost anyone can be a financial analyst. Different analysts look at financial information from different perspectives and make assessments based on the following criteria, criteria relevant to their individual focus. Exhibit 3–1 lists several different analysts and what they look for.

## THE POWER OF RATIOS

The analysis of financial information provides a window into the success of a business. While the analysis of financial statements starts with some straight-

## xhibit 3–1

### What Financial Analysts Look For

| Analyst | Objective of the Analysis |
|---|---|
| Current Investor | Safety, value, and possible opportunities for successful exit. |
| Prospective Investor | Profit opportunity based on predicted results. |
| Stock Analyst | Past performance and present condition as it relates to current and future value. |
| Banker | Security of existing or projected borrowing. |
| Older Owner | Prospects for profitable sale and exit. |
| Younger Owner | Prospects for future income and wealth. |
| Manager | Business condition and job preservation. |
| Customer | Business strength and reliability of supply. |
| Vendor | Prospect for payment and continuing sales. |
| Tax Authority | Value of ownership position and generation of tax revenue. |
| Current Employee | Security and continuity of employment. |
| Prospective Employee | Company stability and prospect of continued and expanded job. |
| Competitor | Competitive strength and opportunities for competition. |

forward calculations, it is really based on answering the same questions we were all taught to ask when we were in grade school:

**Who?**
**What?**
**Why?**
**When?**
**Where?**
**How?**
**How much?**

We will use some consistent and easily applied tools to provide a context and a framework for conducting the analysis. Keep these questions in mind throughout this chapter and whenever you are looking at financial information.

## Comparative Analysis

Financial analysis is generally cast as a comparative analysis, in a comparative analytical structure. The comparisons are based on the current company information and either industry or competitive information or historic company information. When the comparison is to other companies in the industry, whether identified as direct and specific competitors or averages drawn from industry summaries, the analysis is described as cross-sectional or competitive analysis. It serves to benchmark a company against other members of its industry and gives management an idea of the company's relative performance.

This kind of analysis, however, is often of limited managerial use because the companies in an industry are frequently not comparable, particularly if the company is relatively small. In addition, companies often define their data differently, making comparisons difficult. Also, management philosophies differ, resulting in different practices and choices of financing and operations, again making comparisons difficult.

If you choose to undertake an industry or competitive analysis, it is important to have reliable source data and to understand its limitations. There are a number of published sources for industry data and it is presented in a number of ways. Here are a few industry data sources:

### Dun & Bradstreet (D&B)

Drawn from corporate filings and company-provided information, D&B statistics provide information by Standard Industrial Classification (SIC) code. However, while company-provided data is summarized and presented by D&B, it is not independently validated or confirmed.

### Robert Morris Associates (RMA)

Drawn from information provided by the bank members of RMA, industry data is presented in quartile form. (Exhibit 3–2 illustrates a quartile presentation.) There is some belief that, because it comes from filings made with their banks, the company-provided data may be more reliable than data from some other sources. RMA also segregates its quartile data into company size quartiles as well.

### Trade Associations

Trade association data may be more specific than D&B or RMA data by general SIC code, but it may be of limited value because of reporting rules. For example, the trade association, mindful of the confidential nature of proprietary information, may restrict data that would identify a specific company. This renders the comparisons of limited value.

### Investment Analysts

Investment analysts publish industry data as part of the investment research function. Here, too, the particular opinions and biases of the analysts may influence the presentation of data.

**xhibit 3–2**

**Financial Ratios as Quartile Data**

| Industry Identification | Current Ratio | Quick Ratio | Average Collection Period | Inventory Turnover | Return on Equity | Return on Sales |
|---|---|---|---|---|---|---|
| 25% | 3:2 | 1.8 | 35.6 | 8.3 | 35.7 | 7.8 |
| 50% | 1:9 | 1.1 | 56.6 | 4.6 | 17.3 | 3.7 |
| 75% | 1:4 | 0.7 | 85.5 | 3.2 | 9.5 | 0.9 |

Financial ratios are frequently presented as quartile data. The quartiles represent the average ratios for companies falling into the respective quartiles, in terms of annual sales volume, within their industry, usually determined by Standard Industrial Classification (SIC), a classification system used by the United States Department of Commerce to categorize companies by the type of business they do.

Ratio analysis as illustrated in Exhibit 3–2 is quite informative. It may not tell the whole story. To be a good performer in a poor performing industry may merely mean that you aren't in quite as desperate a condition as others, but not that you are safe, secure, or a good investment. Another problem with general statistics is that they are just that, general. Consider the example in Exercise 3–2.

### Exercise 3–2: Comparative Performance

*INSTRUCTIONS:* ☞ Company A has, for the last five years, performed above the industry average on most performance measures, such as profitability or liquidity. Company B has, during the same time period, performed below the industry average in the same categories. Which of these two companies, A or B, would seem to be the more likely to be successful?

Now that you have made your choice, look at Exhibit 3–3. Is this consistent with your expectation? Are both companies equally likely to succeed? Explain your answer.

_____

_____

_____

### Trend Analysis

By contrast to industry comparison, comparing a company to itself over time, called **historic or trend analysis,** permits the analyst to track progress. In most cases, whether financial or not, an analysts looking at historic analysis knows whether the company is improving or not. If a company is improving year after year, that is good. Even if it trails the industry averages, continuous improvement is a predictor that it won't be behind for long.

The chart in Exhibit 3–3 highlights the limitations of an industry comparison and the clarity of historic analysis at the same time. For this reason, many analysts try to incorporate elements of both types of analysis into their assessments.

## TRADITIONAL RATIO ANALYSIS

Financial analysts, in conducting a financial analysis, generally compute and interpret several ratios, which are drawn from financial statements, followed

## xhibit 3–3

### Comparative Performance

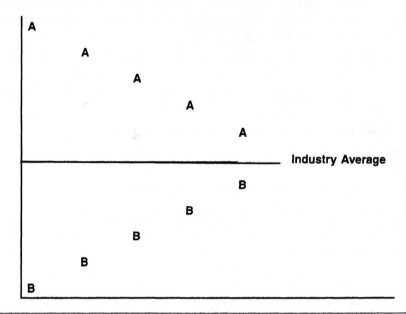

by a written interpretation of the results of the computations. Ratios can be represented in one of the following ways:

- Comparative analysis, often called cross-sectional analysis or industry analysis, may provide some meaningful benchmarks for performance.
- Trend analysis, also known as historical analysis, compares a company against itself over time.
- Ratios may be a combination of both of the above.

Ratios are grouped as follows:

- liquidity—assessing the ability to meet maturing obligations
- activity—assessing the effective utilization of assets
- profitability—assessing operating performance
- debt—assessing the management of borrowed funds, sometimes known as "coverage" ratios

## Liquidity Ratios

**Liquidity ratios** assess the ease with which a company can generate the cash to pay its bills, service its debt, and assure that it will satisfy the requirements of its current account creditors. Liquidity ratios recognize the relationships between the current assets and the current liabilities in the Balance Sheet.

*Current Ratio*

This ratio assesses the company's ability to pay its bills on time, to meet its maturing obligations.

$$\text{Current Ratio (CR)} = \frac{\text{Current Assets (CA)}}{\text{Current Liabilities (CL)}}$$

The Current Ratio provides a measure of the company's ability to meet its debts by comparing those assets the company expects to be converted to cash within one year to those obligations of similar time frame. Bearing in mind that the liabilities are often of shorter duration than, for example, the inventory, traditional analysis measures as acceptable a current ratio significantly greater than 1:1. However, a current ratio that is too large might indicate excessive liquidity, more liquidity than is required for normal operations. If liquid assets are too large, and too large relative to current liabilities, the assets in excess may not be earning as much return for the shareholders as they should.

*Quick Ratio*

$$\text{Quick Ratio (QR)} = \frac{\text{Current Assets} - \text{Inventory}}{\text{Current Liabilities}}$$

Similar to the Current Ratio, the Quick Ratio, also known as the Acid Test Ratio, removes Inventory, recognizing that it may be hard to turn Inventory into cash quickly. Analysts from creditors look for a company to have more quick assets than current liabilities. Comparison of the Current Ratio and the Quick Ratio quickly demonstrates the importance of inventory to the assets of the company. Because inventory is less liquid than the other current assets, this comparison helps assess the overall riskiness of the company.

*Net Working Capital (NWC)*

An alternative measure, not really a ratio, NWC indicates how much current asset value is in excess of current obligations. It is expressed in the following formula:

$$\text{Net Working Capital (NWC)} = \text{Current Assets} - \text{Current Liabilities}$$

## Exercise 3–3: Analyzing Ratios

*INSTRUCTIONS:* ☛ It would seem that the greater the liquidity ratios, the more cash-convertible assets a company has and therefore the better off they are. Is this necessarily true? Consider this question:

If a Current Ratio of 2 is considered good, and 2.5 is considered better, why might a Current Ratio of 5 be considered bad?

_____

_____

_____

_____

_____

_____

_____

## Activity Ratios

The **Activity Ratios,** also known as Asset Utilization Ratios, assess how well the management is managing the company's assets and using them to generate revenues for the company. Since assets cost money, the efficient management of assets is a highly desirable criterion for good management practice.

### Average Collection Period

Average Collection Period is also known as Days' Sales Outstanding (DSO). It is particularly useful in doing corporate cash planning.

$$\text{The Average Collection Period (ACP)} = \frac{\text{Accounts Receivable}}{\text{Sales}/360}$$

The denominator is described as average daily sales. ACP tells the analyst many things:

- It assesses the quality of accounts receivable.
- It provides a measure of credit management.
- It provides a measure of overall management.
- It indicates of how long it takes to turn a sale into cash.
- It may indicate future profits.

Note: The "360" in the denominator is important:

- It should reflect the relevant time period.
- There are really 365 days in the year, but the result is meant to be approximate, but analysts commonly use 360 because the computations are simpler.

A companion ratio, Receivables Turnover, indicates how many times a year the average accounts receivable balance is collected.

$$\text{Receivables Turnover} = \frac{\text{Sales}}{\text{Accounts Receivable}}$$

### Inventory Turnover

$$\text{Inventory Turnover} = \frac{\text{Sales}}{\text{Inventory}} \text{ or } \frac{\text{Cost of Sales}}{\text{Inventory}}$$

Inventory Turnover measures the movement of inventory, and potentially, inventory salability. Different analysts measure inventory turnover in different ways. With the first example shown, it may be easier to get the information to calculate. In trend analysis it is a reasonable formula because the company will generally account for inventory consistently from year to year. In industry analysis, there may be more difficulty with comparisons as different companies have different gross profit margins, and therefore will have noncomparable turnover ratios. This is why many analysts prefer the second formula; both cost of sales and inventory have the same valuation basis, computed without any profit.

Similar to the assessment of accounts receivable, inventory turnover can easily be converted to measure average days in inventory by using a ratio similar to the days sales outstanding:

$$\text{Average Days in Inventory} = \frac{\text{Inventory}}{\dfrac{\text{Cost of Goods Sold}}{360}}$$

### Fixed Asset Turnover

This ratio assesses how well the company utilizes its investment in capital assets (i.e., its productive capacity).

$$\text{Fixed Asset Turnover} = \frac{\text{Sales}}{\text{Fixed Assets}}$$

A high result is generally perceived to be positive, but it may result from high sales relative to fixed assets or low fixed assets relative to sales.

If the *high ratio results from high sales*, it may indicate active and favorable use of expensive and important investment assets, *but* if the high ratio results from low fixed assets, it may indicate:

- old, fully depreciated assets in need of replacement
- a small investment in just the right productive assets

If the ratio is low, it may be the result of low sales relative to fixed assets or of high fixed assets. If the *sales are low:*

- This is a problem in itself.

If the *fixed assets are high*, it may indicate:

- excessive investment in capital assets
- prudent investment in the latest, as yet undepreciated, equipment positioning the company for superior performance for many years to come

### Total Asset Turnover

This ratio evaluates the utilization of all resources to generate sales:

$$\text{Total Asset Turnover} = \frac{\text{Sales}}{\text{Total Assets}}$$

Many analysts use asset turnover to assess overall management performance as well as to measure the effective utilization of invested funds. Studies have shown that low asset turnover is a strong indication of severe financial risk.

## Profitability Ratios

**Profitability Ratios** are performance measures, assessing the company's ability to cover expenses and reward investors. They measure the quality of sales and point to profitability and sales success.

### Gross Profit Margin

$$\text{Gross Profit Margin} = \frac{\text{Sales} - \text{Cost of Goods Sold}}{\text{Sales}}$$

Calculating the Gross Profit Margin will tell the analyst if the company's products cover the cost of managing the company and bringing the product to market.

### Operating Profit Margin

This ratio may be a better measure of profitability than the ratio above. It measures the profitability of sales, without regard to source of financing. Operating Profit is Earnings before Interest and Taxes:

$$\text{Operating Profit Margin} = \frac{\text{Earnings before Interest and Taxes}}{\text{Sales}}$$

Operating Profit Margin is not affected by accounting policies or financing methods. It may be a better measure of business performance than either Gross Profit Margin or Net Profit Margin because it is calculated after accounting for all normal operating expenses, without regard for particular accounting or classification practices.

### Net Profit Margin

This ratio is also known as Return on Sales. It measures profit as a percentage of sales dollars.

$$\text{Return on Sales} = \frac{\text{Profit after Taxes}}{\text{Sales}}$$

This ratio is the most frequently used business performance measure, and is often used to compare one company's results against others or against an expectation. It provides a measure of the overall performance of the company.

### Return on Assets (ROA)

ROA measures profit earned as a percentage of the value of the assets:

$$\text{Return on Assets} = \frac{\text{Profit after Tax}}{\text{Total Assets}}$$

It assesses how well management uses the assets to produce profits. Because the assets require financing, the effective use of the assets leads to an acceptable return for the sources of the financing.

### Return on Equity (ROE)

ROE measures the reward to the shareholders:

$$\text{Return on Equity} = \frac{\text{Profit after Tax}}{\text{Shareholders' Equity}}$$

This ratio serves as the basis for investors' assessment of the business. They care most about the return provided to the shareholders. As far as they are concerned, the other evaluations are interesting, but are most important when considered from the specific perspective of the shareholder.

## Exercise 3–4: Calculating Ratios

*INSTRUCTIONS:* ☛ Calculate these ratios for five years using the financial statements in Exhibit 3–4 at the end of this chapter:

Return on Sales    _____

Return on Assets    _____

Return on Equity    _____

## Debt Management Ratios

Debt management ratios help the analyst to assess the risk level and the effective utilization of debt funds. Recognizing that debt is an important, but challenging source of financing, evaluating how well debt is managed is a critical part of financial analysis. The following three ratios are used towards accomplishing that end.

### Debt to Assets

This ratio measures the percentage of total assets paid for with other people's money.

$$\text{Debt to Assets} = \frac{\text{Total Liabilities}}{\text{Total Assets}}$$

The higher this ratio, the riskier the overall business is because the lenders, whether banks, vendors, or others, have a priority claim on company resources if the management fails to meet its obligations.

### Debt to Equity

This ratio compares the dollars of borrowed funds per dollar of invested funds. There are two different formulas that are used and they tell us different things.

The first assesses the overall riskiness of the business:

$$\text{Debt to Equity} = \frac{\text{Total Liabilities}}{\text{Equity}}$$

The second measures the sources of long-term, or capital, funds:

$$\text{Debt to Equity} = \frac{\text{Long-Term Debt}}{\text{Total Equity}}$$

### Times Interest Earned

This ratio assesses the ability of the company to service the company's debt. The higher the ratio, the easier it is for the company to service its debt.

$$\text{Times Interest Earned} = \frac{\text{Earnings before Interest and Taxes}}{\text{Interest}}$$

## A Different Perspective

Some of these ratios can predict what's going to happen, even as they tell what has already happened.

## Exercise 3–5: Interpreting Ratios

*INSTRUCTIONS:*   ☞ Answer the following questions in the space provided.

1. Consider inventory turnover. What do we know about a company if the inventory turnover is too low?

_____

_____

_____

_____

_____

2. What does that imply about the company's actions in the future?

_____

_____

_____

_____

_____

**3.** What might the consequences of those actions be? Think in terms of the Income Statement and the Balance Sheet.

_____

_____

_____

_____

### Exercise 3–6: Computing the Cost of Excess Accounts Receivable

_INSTRUCTIONS:_ ☞ Similar expanded analysis is possible with the Average Collection Period computation. Consider the following problem:

XYZ Co. has an average collection period of 50 days, and annual sales of $7,200,000. (Assume a 360-day year.)

**1.** What is the company's average accounts receivable balance?

_____

_____

_____

_____

**2.** If the industry Average Collection Period is 36, and the interest rate is currently 10 percent, how much do the excess receivables cost XYZ Co. annually?

_____

_____

_____

_____

### Creating Other Ratios

You can easily construct other ratios to tell you interesting information. Consider what you can learn by constructing a ratio such as Miscellaneous Assets to Net Worth, which may be very meaningful particularly in privately held companies.

Miscellaneous Assets are often those assets that make working for the company enjoyable but do not return any income to the corporation. They often include such things as loans to officers, loans to employees, recreation facilities for employees (such as a boat or a racquetball court), fine art for the company headquarters lobby, and investments (often in companies unrelated to the business).

These assets generally do not earn a return on their investment. In other words, sooner or later such nonprofitable investments can be expected to affect overall financial performance negatively. In addition, they have diverted funds, and possibly management attention, away from productive use by the company.

## Conflicting Information

Financial analysis requires that you examine alternative interpretations of the ratios.

### Exercise 3–7: Alternative Interpretations

*INSTRUCTIONS:* ☞ Consider Inventory Turnover again. What does it mean when the turnover number is high?

_____

_____

_____

Is it good?

_____

_____

_____

Could it be bad?

_____

_____

We need to ask more questions and examine other information to confirm our hypothesis.

## Exercise 3–8: Prepare a Trend Analysis

*INSTRUCTIONS:* ☞ Use the data in Exhibit 3–4 to compute the ratios below for all five years:

|  | Year 5 | Year 4 | Year 3 | Year 2 | Year 1 |
|---|---|---|---|---|---|
| Return on Sales (Net Profit Margin) | | | | | |
| Return on Equity | | | | | |
| Average Collection Period | | | | | |
| Inventory Turnover | | | | | |
| Current Ratio | | | | | |
| Quick Ratio | | | | | |
| Debt to Equity | | | | | |
| Times Interest Earned | | | | | |
| Fixed Asset Turnover | | | | | |

Prepare an analysis evaluating the trends in these and any other ratios you feel are appropriate. Identify the events or situations that have caused the changes in the ratios and the management actions and responses involved. Be as specific and explicit as you can. Assess overall management performance.

_____

_____

_____

_____

_____

_____

_____

_____

# **E** xhibit 3–4

**Financial Analysis Exercise**

Results from Continuing Operation (000)

| | 19X5 | 19X4 | 19X3 | 19X2 | 19X1 |
|---|---|---|---|---|---|
| Net Sales | 218623 | 179345 | 151803 | 154458 | 119840 |
| Cost of Sales | 171058 | 141508 | 122249 | 121233 | 98261 |
| Selling General and Admin Exp | 32619 | 24386 | 19803 | 19878 | 14903 |
| Operating Income | 14946 | 13451 | 9751 | 13347 | 6676 |
| Interest Expense | 2272 | 2285 | 1732 | 875 | 634 |
| Pretax Income | 12674 | 11166 | 8019 | 12472 | 6042 |
| Income Taxes | 5950 | 5370 | 3758 | 5835 | 3319 |
| Net Income from Contin. Oper. | 6724 | 5796 | 4261 | 6637 | 2723 |
| Avg. Shares (Adj. for Stk. Div.) | 2279 | 2257 | 2278 | 2314 | 2567 |
| Net Inc./Share from Cont. Ops. | 2.95 | 2.57 | 1.87 | 2.86 | 1.06 |
| Loss from Discon. Ops. | — | −2.7 | −0.99 | −2.7 | −0.52 |
| Reported Net per Share | 2.95 | −0.13 | 0.88 | 0.16 | 0.54 |

Year End Balance Sheets (000)

| | 19X5 | 19X4 | 19X3 | 19X2 | 19X1 |
|---|---|---|---|---|---|
| Cash and Short-Term Securities | 9082 | 12970 | 3563 | 4974 | 12770 |
| Receivables | 30542 | 25457 | 28104 | 28088 | 28249 |
| Inventories | 35173 | 31360 | 41993 | 35426 | 29248 |
| Other Current Assets | 526 | 1086 | 579 | 651 | 758 |
| Total Current Assets | 75323 | 70873 | 74239 | 69139 | 71025 |
| Net Plant and Equipment | 25530 | 16173 | 26126 | 25544 | 25074 |
| Other Assets (A) | 10143 | 5494 | 6388 | 7160 | 11318 |
| Total Assets | 110996 | 92540 | 106753 | 101843 | 107417 |
| Notes Payable | — | — | 6000 | 6000 | — |
| Accounts Payable | 14477 | 14962 | 14564 | 14186 | 22668 |
| Current Portion of LTD | 2452 | 2324 | 2454 | 2238 | 407 |
| Other Current Liabs. (B) | 13052 | 6725 | 7358 | 5011 | 6286 |
| Total Current Liabilities | 29981 | 24011 | 30376 | 27435 | 29361 |
| Other Liabilities | 1945 | 2114 | 2334 | 2687 | 2912 |
| Long-Term Debt | 37575 | 30544 | 36666 | 35525 | 36463 |
| Stockholders' Equity | 41495 | 35871 | 37377 | 36196 | 38681 |
| Total Liabilities and Equity | 110996 | 92540 | 106753 | 101843 | 107417 |
| Outstanding Shares (Adj.) | 2243 | 2220 | 2274 | 2274 | 2565 |
| Equity per Share | 18.5 | 16.16 | 16.44 | 15.92 | 15.08 |

(A) Other Assets at the end of 19X5 include $4,412 in escrow funds for construction projects.
(B) Other current liabilities at the end of 19X5 include a $6,452 income tax liability.

Financial analysis may be done by any of the stakeholders in a company. In each case the perspective will be different, but the assessment should be essentially the same. Financial analysis provides the analyst with a view into the company from the numbers in relation to one another and to a set of external numbers, industry averages.

Financial analysis usually takes the form of ratios, gathered into groups to provide confirmation of conclusions. The usual groupings include:

1. Liquidity Ratios
   • Current Ratio
   • Quick Ratio
   • Net Working Capital
2. Activity Ratios
   • Average Collection Period
   • Inventory Turnover
   • Fixed Asset Turnover
   • Total Asset Turnover
3. Profitability Ratios
   • Return on Sales
   • Return on Assets
   • Return on Equity
4. Debt Management Ratios
   • Debt to Assets
   • Debt to Equity
   • Times Interest Earned

## ANSWERS TO EXERCISES

### Exercise 3–6

1. $7,200,000/36 = $20,000, average receivables balance = $20,000 × 50 = $1,000,000
2. Industry average receivables from comparable sales would be $20,000 × 36 = $720,000. If the annual interest rate is 10 percent, $1,000,000 − $720,000 = $280,000. At 10 percent, the annual financing needed to pay for those assets would be $280,000 × .10 = $28,000.

In addition to the cost, the 50 days tells an analyst that a substantial amount of the money due is well over 60 days old. Because many customers pay on time or close to on time, in order to average 50 days, some receivables must be much older than that.

## Exercise 3–8

|  | Year 5 | Year 4 | Year 3 | Year 2 | Year 1 |
|---|---|---|---|---|---|
| Return on Sales |  |  |  |  |  |
| (Net Profit Margin) | 3.08% | 3.23% | 2.81% | 4.30% | 2.27% |
| Return on Equity | 16.20% | 16.16% | 11.40% | 18.34% | 7.04% |
| Average Collection Period | 50.29 | 51.10 | 66.65 | 65.47 | 84.86 |
| Inventory Turnover | 4.86 | 4.51 | 2.91 | 3.42 | 3.36 |
| Current Ratio | 2.51 | 2.95 | 2.44 | 2.52 | 2.42 |
| Quick Ratio | 1.34 | 1.65 | 1.06 | 1.23 | 1.42 |
| Debt to Equity | 1.67 | 1.58 | 1.86 | 1.81 | 1.78 |
| Times Interest Earned | 6.58 | 5.89 | 5.63 | 15.25 | 10.53 |
| Fixed Asset Turnover | 6.13 | 8.28 | 4.67 | 4.72 | 3.29 |

The volality of the profitability is the first indication of places to look—low in Year 1, up in Year 2, down sharply in Year 3, and up and leveling off in Years 4 and 5. A look at sales confirms that Year 2 was good and Year 3 was bad.

Perhaps the best way to start any analysis, however, is to look for the biggest change and ask questions from there. Times Interest Earned has the sharpest volatility, with a dramatic drop in Year 3. However, interest expense is the result of debt, and debt appears not to have changed significantly from Year 2 to Year 3, leading to the conclusion that the Note Payable must have been borrowed at the very end of Year 2. It was probably borrowed to pay for the expansion of inventory, particularly since accounts payable had been so high at the end of Year 1. And note that in Year 1, the company had substantial cash at the same time that payables were extremely high. This, it turns out, was because the cash was held to pay for a stock repurchase, identifiable by comparing average and year-end shares outstanding, and could not be used for Payables.

The next conclusion to be reached is that inventory was purchased to support the growth in sales, but sales slowed in the second half of Year 2, resulting in excess inventory, high payables, and the need to borrow. The Note Payable, due within one year, could not be paid off because Year 3 was a difficult year, and, therefore, had to be rolled over. The bank agreed reluctantly (as evidenced by the high interest expense in Year 4), requiring that the company take an action to repay the loan in Year 4.

The company, late in Year 4, sold a division (note the sharp drop in fixed assets and inventory) and used the cash received to pay back the bank, to pay off a long-term mortgage, and to hold in cash at year-end, confirming that the transaction took place late in the year. Also serving as confirmation of the timing is the level of interest expense remaining high with a significant reduction in debt.

In Year 5, the company purchased another company, adding substantial fixed assets, increasing debt and consuming some cash. The high level of cash at the end of Year 5 is needed to pay the tax obligation, due within 75 days of year-end.

While there are other identifiable actions and management decisions, these represent some of the most significant and they make up a coherent and defensible story.

**Review Questions**

1. The purpose of business is to:                                          1. (c)
   (a) make the most profit you can.
   (b) achieve your maximum sales potential.
   (c) maximize the shareholders' wealth.
   (d) survive into old age.

2. The average collection period measures the:                            2. (a)
   (a) time it takes to turn a sale into cash.
   (b) time spent in the collection effort.
   (c) average time it takes to collect a target amount.
   (d) time before you turn a receivable over to a professional.

3. The operating profit margin is considered the best measure of          3. (c)
   performance because it:
   (a) is calculated after the cost of manufacturing has been measured.
   (b) includes financing costs.
   (c) is not affected by the method of financing.
   (d) is also known as profit before interest, taxes, depreciation, and
       amortization (EBITDA).

4. Computing financial ratios:                                            4. (b)
   (a) is good practice for learning the keyboard.
   (b) tells the analyst much about the company.
   (c) is often a waste of time.
   (d) is best done by a Certified Public Accountant.

5. Liquidity ratios tell an analyst:                                      5. (a)
   (a) how well the company can pay its bills.
   (b) how well the company will pay its bills.
   (c) how well the company manages its assets.
   (d) whether the company is as profitable as its competitors.

# Managing Operating Performance

## Learning Objectives

By the end of this chapter, you should be able to:

- Describe how traditional ratios can be used to identify managerial issues.
- Interpret ratios to determine appropriate managerial actions.
- Explain how corrective actions affect financial performance.

## OVERVIEW

When we apply the tools of financial analysis described in Chapter 3 to financial statements and information of outside firms, we ask ourselves, "What did they do? What should they have done? What will the consequences of what they did be?" When we apply these same tools to the financial statements of our own company, the questions become more personal. "What did we do? What should we have done? What do we do now? What should I do?" This chapter will draw on the information and tools presented in the first three chapters to consider these questions from inside the company. Using some of the ratios introduced in Chapter 3, we will identify issues facing an organization, indicating where to concentrate management attention. This chapter will draw on financial analysis techniques to tell the manager where to respond as well as predict what will happen, or more specifically, to predict what will happen if something is not done.

The chapter will consider both the Income Statement and the Balance Sheet, with particular emphasis on where managers have impact. This discussion will also tie the Income Statement to the various parts of the Balance Sheet, facilitating the establishment of logical links between operating performance and financial condition. Inclusion of interactive examples will make this information transparent to the reader and enable each student to draw on personal experience to strengthen his or her understanding of the material. The information in this chapter will provide a context for the information in Chapter 11.

We can relate financial analysis to operating action in many ways. In Chapter 1, we described planning as "Building on the past to direct the future." Before we can move the company in the right direction, we must understand what has already happened. The interpretive analysis of financial information leads to the action decisions we will concentrate on in this chapter.

### Having an Impact

"Hi, Bob. Well, my group looked at some areas where we can exert some direct control. We compared inventory turnover for the past three years, and we were pretty surprised by some of what we learned. Even though sales are rising pretty dramatically, this ratio is getting worse. We asked two of the people in your group if they could help us identify what was causing this.

"It seems we've been buying more materials for the A600 product line to make certain that we won't run short when we get hit with big new orders. In addition, the inventory of A200s is rising. Those sales aren't keeping up with the other increases. A couple of us met with the plant manager and then got together with Jan and Les in purchasing. Two of our machinists can convert one of the machines from the A200 to the A600 products in half a day and we're going to try to negotiate a better delivery schedule with our main supplier for A600 parts."

"That's terrific. When we have everybody looking at the numbers to see how we can improve performance, we can come up with great solutions."

## MAKING YOUR INFORMATION USEFUL

When we think about analyzing financial statements, we start with the chart of accounts, the systematic listing of categories into which we separate all financial information. If we set up the chart of accounts so that it is easily grouped into the sequential lines of the financial statements—by tradition the Balance Sheet comes first, followed by the Income Statement—the routine recognition of activities and obligations will almost automatically produce appropriate financial statements. Furthermore, the user of the financial statements, generally an owner or manager, will know exactly where to get additional detail whenever a particular account or financial statement line item raises questions, either favorable or unfavorable.

The representative financial statements presented in this course are all in standard format, and it is easy to see how the ability to analyze a particular line would be beneficial.

## Exercise 4–1: Think About It . . .

*INSTRUCTIONS:* ☞ How would a properly organized chart of accounts help you analyze an unusually large variance in administrative expenses?

_____

_____

If the chart of accounts is consistent with the reports, there would be a separate group of numbers for the administrative expenses. These expenses will be included in Operating Expenses. By focusing your review on those accounts, you can quickly and specifically identify the particular expense items that you need to analyze further. The process is quick and to the point. If, on the other hand, the chart of accounts were listed in alphabetical order, or in some other order, the analysis would be much, much harder.

## THE KEY FINANCIAL STATEMENTS

We will begin this analysis by looking at the Income Statement, followed by the Balance Sheet. We will then consider a variety of financial ratios grouped in a different way, tied to the source of the information or to links to other measures. Unlike ratios grouped by liquidity, activity, profitability, and debt management, looking at these ratios in the context of their interrelationships will provide a different insight.

As you remember, the Income Statement summarizes all of the financial activity that took place during the period shown in the statement heading. Because it covers only one period, it relates expenses and profits to revenues

**E** **xhibit 4–1**

**The Income Statement**

Sales
<u>− Cost of Sales</u>
= Gross Profit
<u>− Operating Expenses</u>
= Earnings before Interest
<u>− Interest</u>
= Earnings before Taxes
<u>− Taxes</u>
= Earnings after Taxes
<u>− Preferred Stock Dividends</u>
<u>= Change in Retained Earnings</u>

achieved. By comparing the income statement from one period to that of another, whether previous or future, we can validate our conclusions or impressions by looking at other statistics or by analyzing detailed information that may be available to us.

When we are inside the company, whether as analysts or as managers, we have access to detailed data that helps to explain the results summarized in the Income Statement. The ratios that we will look at in this chapter will help us to focus our analysis on the aspects of our operations that cause particular ratios and relationships to come out as they do.

## Ratios That Help Tell the Company's Story

Specifically, we will look at Gross Profit Margin, Efficiency Ratio, Operating Profit Margin, Net Profit Margin, Times Interest Earned, and Percent Change Measurements. These ratios will highlight the application of financial analysis tools and the type of information that such an analysis will provide. As we will see, they also give the analyst or manager a good idea of where to look for additional information.

*Gross Profit Margin*

$$\text{Gross Profit Margin} = \frac{\text{Sales} - \text{Cost of Goods Sold}}{\text{Sales}}$$

Profitability ratios measure the quality of sales and point to profitability and sales success. Calculating the Gross Profit Margin will tell you if the company's products cover the cost of managing the company and bringing the product to market.

Measuring Gross Profit Margin tells managers inside the company if the sales in the period under study have been as successful and effective as planned or desired. If the answer is affirmative, you'll want to understand what went right and how to perpetuate those results. If the answer is negative, you can examine individual products or product groups more specifically to identify particular products that are dragging the margin down, or you can consider other actions to improve margins by either raising prices or reducing costs. If you decide that costs have to be reduced, analyzing particular product or group margins may help you focus on specific costs to be addressed. As you can see, the analysis continues to drill into the information until you have a very clear idea of what caused the results you want to change. The whole approach is one of identifying causes and consequences and then identifying appropriate management actions to respond to what is learned in the analysis. Doing analysis without committing to act on the information gained is a waste of time and effort.

To the extent that managers can start with more focused information, such as the margins for products or product groups under their responsibility, they can begin this analysis at a lower, more detailed level and determine the appropriate actions more quickly. Therefore, as managers you should request information specific to your area of responsibility.

### Efficiency Ratio

$$\text{Efficiency Ratio} = \frac{\text{Selling, General, and Administrative Expenses}}{\text{Sales}}$$

The Efficiency Ratio measures the costs associated with bringing products to market and supporting them. If this ratio is high or is rising, the expenditure of support funds may be too great for the revenues and margin provided. A rising efficiency ratio is an early signal that spending is outstripping revenues and jeopardizing success. In part this is because Selling, General, and Administrative (S, G, and A) expenses are usually considered fixed expenses, that is, they are not expected to rise in proportion to sales. If they do, it suggests that spending is not completely under control. If the ratio is increasing, spending is rising faster than sales, indicating that management needs to invest more attention to either increasing sales or controlling the spending. In many companies the determination of the Efficiency Ratio is the earliest warning that the company has management control problems.

### Operating Profit Margin

$$\text{Operating Profit Margin} = \frac{\text{Earnings before Interest and Taxes}}{\text{Sales}}$$

Accounting policies or financing methods do not affect Operating Profit Margin. For that reason, this ratio may be a better measure of business performance than either Gross Profit Margin or Net Profit Margin because it is calculated after accounting for all normal operating expenses, without regard for particular accounting or classification practices.

From an internal analysis perspective, the combination of the Gross Profit Margin and the Efficiency Ratio help to explain the Operating Profit Margin. All three help a manager focus attention on the activities that are contributing to success or are detracting from it.

### Net Profit Margin

This ratio is also known as Return on Sales. It measures profit as a percentage of sales dollars.

$$\text{Return on Sales} = \frac{\text{Profit after Taxes}}{\text{Sales}}$$

This ratio is the most frequently used measure of business performance, and is often used to compare one company's results against others or against expectations. We frequently hear about Net Profit Margin when analysts are explaining significant volatility in a company's stock price.

The internal assessment of the Net Profit Margin may be more stringent, even than that of the outside analysis. Understanding the components of the margin computation, the manager should be able to identify the places within the organization where costs need to be controlled or where additional selling effort will yield higher returns to the company and its operations.

### Times Interest Earned

This ratio assesses the ability of the company to service the company's debt. The higher the ratio the easier it is for the company to service its debt.

$$\text{Times Interest Earned} = \frac{\text{Earnings before Interest and Taxes}}{\text{Interest}}$$

While management is less interested in this measure than the bankers are, the Times Interest Earned calculation provides an early warning system for the manager. If earnings are, or become, low relative to interest expense, the Times Interest Earned ratio provides a focused warning. It alerts the manager to a banker's concern before the banker recognizes it, giving management time to correct the problem or prepare the response that will satisfy the banker.

This same ratio may provide a vendor with important information as well because a company will generally pay the bank (often because the bank automatically deducts payment) before it pays a vendor.

### Percent Change

The comparison of statistics to comparable statistics from other time periods, sometimes referred to as "horizontal" analysis, helps the manager identify areas of concern. Using a relationship in which the growth (or decline) in sales provides a benchmark against which to compare, calculating percent change will focus attention on those statement lines, those account groupings, or even those specific accounts that are not performing as expected. Comparing one time period to another helps management concentrate its attention on those areas of company performance that are achieving or exceeding expectations and those that are falling short.

An extension of the percentage change analysis recognizes that many accounts included in the Income Statement should not keep pace with revenues. The analysis of period-to-period change should enable a manager to examine the reasons for increases in such ratios. Another way to recognize this is to compare the Income Statements of two or more years, not by dollars, but by percentage that the Income Statement lines are to sales. Consider the example in Exhibit 4–2, drawn from the company example at the end of Chapter 3.

Notice that when you examine Exhibits 4–2 and 4–3 the percentages that the Income Statement and Balance Sheet accounts represent to Sales (for the Income Statement) and Total Assets (for the Balance Sheet), year-to-year changes stand out. Look at cash, which fluctuates from a low of 3.34 percent of assets in 19X3 to a high of 14.02 percent in 19X4; or look at Selling, General, and Administrative Expenses, which were 12.44 percent of sales in 19X1 and were 14.92 percent of a much higher sales number in 19X5. When you recognize that Selling, General, and Administrative expenses are frequently made up of expense categories whose amounts that should not vary absolutely by very much from year-to-year, an increase of 2.5 percentage points may indicate spending that is out of control, even though the company did very well in 19X5.

Like the Income Statement, the Balance Sheet provides extensive information to an analyst.

## xhibit 4–2
### Common Size Statements

*A Financial Analysis*

### Results from Continuing Operations (000)

| | 19X1 | % of Sales | 19X2 | % of Sales | 19X3 | % of Sales | 19X4 | % of Sales | 19X5 | % of Sales |
|---|---|---|---|---|---|---|---|---|---|---|
| Net Sales | 119840 | 100.00% | 154458 | 100.00% | 151803 | 100.00% | 179345 | 100.00% | 218623 | 100.00% |
| Cost of Sales | 98261 | 81.99% | 121233 | 78.49% | 122249 | 80.53% | 141508 | 78.90% | 171058 | 78.24% |
| Selling General and Admin Exp. | 14903 | 12.44% | 19878 | 12.87% | 19803 | 13.05% | 24386 | 13.60% | 32619 | 14.92% |
| Operating Income | 6676 | 5.57% | 13347 | 8.64% | 9751 | 6.42% | 13451 | 7.50% | 14946 | 6.84% |
| Interest Expense | 634 | 0.53% | 875 | 0.57% | 1732 | 1.14% | 2285 | 1.27% | 2272 | 1.04% |
| Pretax Income | 6042 | 5.04% | 12472 | 8.07% | 8019 | 5.28% | 11166 | 6.23% | 12674 | 5.80% |
| Income Taxes | 3319 | 2.77% | 5835 | 3.78% | 3758 | 2.48% | 5370 | 2.99% | 5950 | 2.72% |
| Net Income from Contin. Oper. | 2723 | 2.27% | 6637 | 4.30% | 4261 | 2.81% | 5796 | 3.23% | 6724 | 3.08% |
| Avg. Shares (Adj. for Stk. Div.) | 2567 | | 2314 | | 2278 | | 2257 | | 2279 | |
| Net Inc./Share from Cont Ops | 1.06 | | 2.86 | | 1.87 | | 2.57 | | 2.95 | |
| Loss from Discon. Opers. | –0.52 | | –2.7 | | –0.99 | | –2.7 | | — | |
| Reported Net per Share | 0.54 | | 0.16 | | 0.88 | | –0.13 | | 2.95 | |

### Year End Balance Sheets (000)

| | 19X1 | % of Sales | 19X2 | % of Sales | 19X3 | % of Sales | 19X4 | % of Sales | 19X5 | % of Sales |
|---|---|---|---|---|---|---|---|---|---|---|
| Cash and Short-Term Securities | 12770 | 11.89% | 4974 | 4.88% | 3563 | 3.34% | 12970 | 14.02% | 9082 | 8.18% |
| Receivables | 28249 | 26.30% | 28088 | 27.58% | 28104 | 26.33% | 25457 | 27.51% | 30542 | 27.52% |
| Inventories | 29248 | 27.23% | 35426 | 34.78% | 41993 | 39.34% | 31360 | 33.89% | 35173 | 31.69% |
| Other Current Assets | 758 | 0.71% | 651 | 0.64% | 579 | 0.54% | 1086 | 1.17% | 526 | 0.47% |
| Total Current Assets | 71025 | 66.12% | 69139 | 67.89% | 74239 | 69.54% | 70873 | 76.59% | 75323 | 67.86% |
| Net Plant and Equipment | 25074 | 23.34% | 25544 | 25.08% | 26126 | 24.47% | 16173 | 17.48% | 25530 | 23.00% |
| Other Assets (A) | 11318 | 10.54% | 7160 | 7.03% | 6388 | 5.98% | 5494 | 5.94% | 10143 | 9.14% |
| Total Assets | 107417 | 100.00% | 101843 | 100.00% | 106753 | 100.00% | 92540 | 100.00% | 110996 | 100.00% |
| Notes Payable | 0 | 0.00% | 6000 | 5.89% | 6000 | 5.62% | 0 | 0.00% | 0 | 0.00% |
| Accounts Payable | 22668 | 21.10% | 14186 | 13.93% | 14564 | 13.64% | 14962 | 16.17% | 14477 | 13.04% |
| Current Portion of LTD | 407 | 0.38% | 2238 | 2.20% | 2454 | 2.30% | 2324 | 2.51% | 2452 | 2.21% |
| Other Current Liabs. (B) | 6286 | 5.85% | 5011 | 4.92% | 7358 | 6.89% | 6725 | 7.27% | 13052 | 11.76% |
| Total Current Liabilities | 29361 | 27.33% | 27435 | 26.94% | 30376 | 28.45% | 24011 | 25.95% | 29981 | 27.01% |
| Other Liabilities | 2912 | 2.71% | 2687 | 2.64% | 2334 | 2.19% | 2114 | 2.28% | 1945 | 1.75% |
| Long-Term Debt | 36463 | 33.95% | 35525 | 34.88% | 36666 | 34.35% | 30544 | 33.01% | 37575 | 33.85% |
| Stockholders' Equity | 38681 | 36.01% | 36196 | 35.54% | 37377 | 35.01% | 35871 | 38.76% | 41495 | 37.38% |
| Total Liabilities and Equity | 107417 | 100.00% | 101843 | 100.00% | 106753 | 100.00% | 92540 | 100.00% | 110996 | 100.00% |
| Outstanding Shares (Adj) | 2565 | | 2274 | | 2274 | | 2220 | | 2243 | |
| Equity per Share | 15.08 | | 15.92 | | 16.44 | | 16.16 | | 18.5 | |

(A) Other Assets at the end of 19X5 include $4,412 in escrow funds for construction projects.
(B) Other current Liabilities at the end of 19X5 include a $6,452 income tax liability.

**xhibit 4-3**

**The Balance Sheet**

*Assets*

|   |   |
|---|---|
|   | Cash |
| + | Accounts Receivable |
| + | Inventory |
| + | Prepaid Expenses |
| = | Current Assets |
| + | Fixed Assets |
| + | Intangible Assets |
| = | Total Assets |

*Liabilities*

|   |   |
|---|---|
|   | Accounts Payable |
| + | Notes Payable |
| + | Accruals |
| = | Current Liabilities |
| + | Long-Term Debt |
| = | Total Liabilities |

*Owners' Equity*

|   |   |
|---|---|
|   | Preferred Stock |
| + | Common Equity |
| = + | Total Equity |
| = | Total Liabilities and Equity |

As with the Income Statement, when we are inside the company, we have access to detailed data that helps to explain the balances reflected in the Balance Sheet. The ratios that we will look at here will help us to focus our analysis on the aspects of our operations that cause particular ratios and relationships to come out as they do.

## Effect Ratios

Specifically, we will look at a group of ratios that have been described as Effect Ratios:[1] the Current Ratio, the Quick Ratio, Net Working Capital, Accounts Receivable to Working Capital, Inventory to Working Capital, Debt to Assets, Debt to Equity, Short-Term Debt to Equity, and Short-Term Debt to Total Liabilities. We will also look at period-to-period change in these measurements. These ratios will highlight the application of financial analy-

---

[1] James MacDonald and Wallace Davidson have identified these ratios as Effect Ratios in *Financial Statement Analysis: Basis for Management Advice,* published as a Continuing Professional Education Seminar by the AICPA in 2000.

sis tools and the types of information that such an analysis will provide. As we will see, they also give the analyst or manager a good idea of where to look for additional information.

### Current Ratio

This ratio assesses the company's ability to pay its bills on time, to meet its maturing obligations.

$$\text{Current Ratio (CR)} = \frac{\text{Current Assets (CA)}}{\text{Current Liabilities (CL)}}$$

The Current Ratio provides a measure of the company's ability to meet its debts by comparing those assets we expect to convert to cash within one year to those obligations of similar time frame. Bearing in mind that the liabilities are often of shorter duration than, for example, the inventory, traditional analysis generally measures as acceptable a current ratio significantly greater than 1:1. However, a current ratio that is too large might indicate excessive liquidity, more liquidity than is required for normal operations. If liquid assets are too large, and too large relative to current liabilities, the excess assets may not be earning as much return for the shareholders as they should.

The internal analyst, considering the current ratio, would be concerned first with any covenant requirements imposed by a lender and then with how well the company is using its current assets. For example, if the company holds substantial amounts of cash and marketable securities, its current ratio may be well above 2:1, but the company may be sacrificing earnings for liquidity. This will result in less profit and less return to the shareholders, the real measure of success for a business. Cash provides a comfort to managers, so there is a tendency for companies to hold cash "just in case." Cash held as insurance may limit managers' flexibility to take full advantage of business opportunities. Therefore, the manager analyzing the Current Ratio and cash balances needs to consider managerial philosophy.

### Quick Ratio

$$\text{Quick Ratio (QR)} = \frac{\text{Current Assets} - \text{Inventory}}{\text{Current Liabilities}}$$

Similar to the Current Ratio, the Quick Ratio also measures liquidity. However, the Quick Ratio removes Inventory, recognizing that Inventory may be hard to turn into cash quickly. Analysts from creditors look for a company to have more quick assets than current liabilities.

Because inventory is harder to turn into cash, the quick ratio may be very important. If there is a significant disparity between the current ratio and the quick ratio, the level of inventory may be too high. In many companies the sales department likes to have finished goods inventory; it helps assure that orders can be filled promptly, satisfying customers. However, carrying substantial amounts of inventory costs a lot of money, making the operations less profitable. We'll discuss this more deeply in Chapter 5.

A real example of this relates to a company that had always paid its obligations precisely on time, up until the day it and its parent company filed for bankruptcy. Analysis of this surprise showed that while the parent had a Current Ratio of 1.42, it had a Quick Ratio of 0.23. This particular company had inventory equal to 1.19 times the value of its Current Liabilities. Although the Current Ratio indicated adequate liquidity, the company could not pay its bills.

### Net Working Capital (NWC)

An alternative measure, not really a ratio, NWC indicates how much current asset value is in excess of current obligations. It is expressed in the following formula:

$$\text{Net Working Capital (NWC)} = \text{Current Assets} - \text{Current Liabilities}$$

While it is difficult to assess Net Working Capital, the amount of net working capital that a company has will affect its ability to withstand a sales downturn. The level of net working capital is a measure of the financial strength and operational comfort of a company. The number also serves as the denominator of a number of ratios that help managers assess the riskiness of the business.

### Accounts Receivable to Net Working Capital

$$\text{Accounts Receivable to Net Working Capital} = \frac{\text{Accounts Receivable}}{\text{Net Working Capital}}$$

Extending the discussion of net working capital further, accounts receivable to net working capital provides a measure of risk or risk avoidance for a company. If this ratio is high, it suggests that if any accounts receivable are uncollectible or even delinquent, the company may have difficulty paying its bills on time.

### Inventory to Net Working Capital

$$\text{Inventory to Net Working Capital} = \frac{\text{Inventory}}{\text{Net Working Capital}}$$

Similar to the previous ratio, Inventory to Net Working Capital is a risk measurement. It is even more important than Accounts Receivable to Net Working Capital simply because inventory is harder to turn into cash. The higher this ratio is the greater the risk that some of the inventory is obsolete or otherwise unsalable. This will result in difficulty for the company to meet its obligations. While this ratio measures an already established condition, it also provides a window into the near future.

### Debt to Assets

This ratio measures the percentage of total assets paid for with other people's money.

$$\text{Debt to Assets} = \frac{\text{Total Liabilities}}{\text{Total Assets}}$$

It, too, is a measurement of risk. The higher this ratio, the riskier the overall business is because the lenders have a priority claim on company resources if the management fails to meet its obligations. Therefore, if this ratio is high, the lender may consider the loan at risk and may apply pressure to collect outstanding amounts, even if they are technically not due.

### Debt to Equity

This ratio compares the dollars of borrowed funds per dollar of invested funds. There are two different formulas that are used and they tell us different things.

The first assesses the overall riskiness of the business:

$$\text{Debt to Equity} = \frac{\text{Total Liabilities}}{\text{Equity}}$$

The second measures the sources of long-term, or capital, funds:

$$\text{Debt to Equity} = \frac{\text{Long Term Debt}}{\text{Total Equity}}$$

As with the previous ratios in this grouping, Debt to Equity, computed either way, is a measurement of risk. In this case, however, it may also be used to assess the managerial philosophy of the company. The greater this ratio, the more risk management is willing to take and the greater should be the return to the shareholders as a result.

As with Debt to Assets, if this ratio is high, the lender may perceive an uncomfortable level of risk, requiring personal guarantees by company principals or other measures to protect the lenders' interests.

### Short-Term Debt to Equity

$$\text{Short-Term Debt to Equity} = \frac{\text{Current Liabilities}}{\text{Total Equity}}$$

As with the previous ratios, this ratio, too, measures riskiness. In this case, however, the concern is with management's choices. The higher this ratio, the greater the risk because short-term debt requires cash for repayment sooner, leaving less time for other management concentration. However, it is also true that short-term debt is easier to obtain than other forms of financing, and it is also less expensive, either directly, in terms of interest payments required for other forms of debt, or in expected return, for equity. Therefore, the higher this ratio, the greater profits should be and the greater the percentage return on equity should be as well.

One significant issue that arises when this ratio is increasing is whether the increase is intentional or the result of lack of attention by management to the support requirements related to sales growth.

### Short-Term Debt to Total Liabilities

$$\text{Short-Term Debt to Total Liabilities} = \frac{\text{Current Liabilities}}{\text{Total Liabilities}}$$

As with the previous ratio, this can be used to measure riskiness and to assess managerial philosophy. The choice of financing indicates management's comfort with risk. Short-term debt is easier and less expensive to attract than long-term debt because it carries lower risk to the investor (as we'll discuss in Chapter 6). However, it is riskier for management because it must be repaid sooner. Therefore, the attractiveness of the lower cost must outweigh the importance of the repayment obligation for it to be attractive to management. If management is really conservative, the decision to fund with short-term debt will raise concerns in the mind of the analyst who would expect a less risky Balance Sheet structure.

## Crossover Indicators and Causal Ratios

In addition to ratios and relationships within the two key financial statements, there are many ratios that relate an element of the Income Statement to an element of the Balance Sheet. These ratios are also very valuable tools for assessing management and for identifying actions or situations that will affect future results.

Among these ratios are Return on Assets, Return on Equity, Average Collection Period, Inventory Turnover, Fixed Asset Turnover, Total Asset Turnover, and Sales to Net Worth.

### *Return on Assets (ROA)*
ROA measures profit earned as a percentage of the value of the assets:

$$\text{Return on Assets} = \frac{\text{Profit after Tax}}{\text{Total Assets}}$$

It assesses how well management uses the assets to produce profits. It is related to the Return on Sales (Net Profit Margin) and Asset Turnover ratios considered earlier. It is affected by the level of sales the organization achieves and by the amount of investment made to achieve those sales. If the company underutilizes its assets, this ratio will be low and the reward to the shareholders will probably also be low.

### *Return on Equity*
ROE measures the reward to the shareholders:

$$\text{Return on Equity} = \frac{\text{Profit after Tax}}{\text{Shareholders' Equity}}$$

Even though in public companies, and even in some private ones, the dollars in equity do not reflect the amount actually invested in stock of the company, Return on Equity is a useful measure of how effectively management is generating a reward for the shareholders. Recognizing that the profits of a company belong to the shareholders, the ability of a company to earn profits and reward shareholders is generally reflected in the market price of the stock. Profitable companies have higher stock prices relative to poor performers.

*Average Collection Period*

Average Collection Period is also known as Days' Sales Outstanding. The Average Collection Period divided into 360 (or 365) is known as Receivables Turnover. It is particularly useful for corporate cash planning, but it also provides many other insights for management.

$$\text{Average Collection Period (ACP)} = \frac{\text{Accounts Receivable}}{\text{Sales}/360}$$

The denominator is described as average daily sales. ACP tells the analyst many things:

- It assesses the quality of accounts receivable.
  Because most companies pay their bills on time, if the average collection period is high, it may indicate a problem with the collectibility of the accounts that are due.
- It provides a measure of credit management.
  If accounts are overdue, it may indicate that the credit managers are not doing an adequate job of evaluating the creditworthiness of customers or are not doing an adequate job of collecting accounts.
- It provides a measure of overall management.
  To the extent that receivables are an important asset to keep current as collection provides the cash needed to run the business, a high average collection period may suggest that overall management is not paying enough attention to this area of responsibility.
- It indicates how long it takes to turn a sale into cash.
  To the extent that the average collection period reflects the average time it takes to receive payment for sales made on credit, the Average Collection Period provides useful information for the company's annual budget and its cash budget.
- It may hold an indication of future profits.
  To the extent that a high average collection period indicates overly delinquent accounts, it may be masking truly uncollectible receivables. When management decides to recognize these uncollectible accounts, the accounting transaction to recognize them is:

Dr. Bad Debt Expense
Cr. Allowance for Doubtful Accounts

The consequence will be a reduction in profits by the bad debt, equal to the entire sale, as reflected in the uncollectible account. This will adversely affect profits in the period when the bad debt is recognized. At some time later, probably during the year-end closing, the accountant will create an adjusting journal entry to reduce both Accounts Receivable and the offsetting Allowance for Doubtful Accounts to remove the uncollectible account from the books.

If the Average Collection Period is higher than desired, management must analyze accounts receivable to identify the delinquent accounts and then develop an action plan to collect the overdue amounts and bring the Average Collection Period into line.

*Inventory Turnover*

$$\text{Inventory Turnover} = \frac{\text{Sales}}{\text{Inventory}} \text{ or } \frac{\text{Cost of Sales}}{\text{Inventory}}$$

Inventory Turnover measures the movement of inventory, and potentially, inventory salability. Different analysts measure inventory turnover in different ways. The first example shown may be easier to get information to calculate. In historical analysis it is a reasonable formula because the company will generally account for inventory consistently from year-to-year. In industry analysis, there may be more difficulty with comparisons as different companies have different gross profit margins, and therefore will have non-comparable turnover ratios. This is why many analysts prefer the second formula; both cost of sales and inventory have the same valuation basis, computed without any profit.

Inventory turnover is as important an indicator as the average collection period. If the number is low, it indicates that there may be excess inventory in the company. This, in turn, may indicate an obsolescence problem that will result in a write-off at some time in the future. Such an action will be reflected in Cost of Goods Sold and will reduce profits. The decision to write-off excess inventory also requires its disposal. To write the inventory off and then keep it means that management feels it still has, or might have, value which conflicts with the write-off decision.

If the inventory is salable, but there is just too much of it, alternative actions have similarly unfavorable consequences. A decision to stop or slow production will result in layoffs or unabsorbed costs, which will result in lower profits. A decision to stop or reduce purchases will distress vendors, particularly those to whom you owe money. They will seek to collect their receivables, your accounts payable, adding to the pressure on management just when it is concentrating on making the business better. Regardless of management action, the consequences of having excess inventory, reflected in a low inventory turnover rate, will be pressure on management and on profits.

*Fixed Asset Turnover*
This ratio assesses how well the company utilizes its investment in capital assets (i.e., its productive capacity).

$$\text{Fixed Asset Turnover} = \frac{\text{Sales}}{\text{Fixed Assets}}$$

A high result is generally perceived to be positive, but may result from high sales relative to fixed assets or low fixed assets relative to sales.

If the *high ratio results from high sales*, it may indicate active and favorable use of expensive and important investment assets, *but* if the high ratio results from low fixed assets, it may indicate:

- old, fully depreciated assets in need of replacement
- a small investment in just the right productive assets

If the ratio is low, it may be the result of low sales relative to fixed assets or of high fixed assets.

If the *sales are low:*

• this is a problem in itself.

If the *fixed assets are high*, it may indicate:

• excessive investment in capital assets
• prudent investment in the latest, as yet undepreciated, equipment poising the company for superior performance for many years to come

Clearly, as with so many ratios, the computation of fixed asset turnover leads to as many questions as it does answers, but generating the answers to these questions makes management smarter about the situation facing the business.

### Total Asset Turnover

This ratio evaluates the utilization of all resources to generate sales:

$$\text{Total Asset Turnover} = \frac{\text{Sales}}{\text{Total Assets}}$$

Many analysts use asset turnover to assess overall management performance as well as to measure the effective utilization of invested funds. Studies have shown that low asset turnover is a strong indication of severe financial risk.

Analysts also use total asset turnover to assess the overall health of the business. There is a very high correlation among businesses that have hard assets, that a low total asset turnover indicates a fundamental weakness in the business. Total Asset Turnover is the most important component of Edward Altman's "Z-score,"[1] which is used as an indicator of potential business bankruptcy.

The higher the Total Asset Turnover number, the more effective the company is in managing its assets and using them to generate sales. With sufficient sales, managing costs will lead to success. Without sales, without asset turnover, all the cost management effort will not be enough to make the company successful.

### Sales to Net Worth

$$\text{Sales to Net Worth} = \frac{\text{Sales}}{\text{Equity}}$$

Sales to Net Worth is also known as the **Trading Ratio.** The higher it is, the more difficult it will be to assure business success. The Trading Ratio

---

[1] Edward I. Altman, a professor at Stanford University, in 1968 identified through scenario analysis, a ratio based formula that provides a prediction of business distress and failure.

## xhibit 4–4

### Sales to Net Worth: Early Warning System

|  | 19X1 | 19X2 | 19X3 | 19X4 |
|---|---|---|---|---|
| Cash | 10,000 | 10,000 | 10,000 | 10,000 |
| Receivables | 100,000 | 200,000 | 400,000 | 800,000 |
| Inventory | 200,000 | 400,000 | 800,000 | 1,600,000 |
| Total Current Assets | 310,000 | 610,000 | 1,210,000 | 2,410,000 |
| Fixed Assets | 250,000 | 250,000 | 500,000 | 1,000,000 |
| Miscellaneous Assets | 5,000 | 5,000 | 5,000 | 5,000 |
| Total Assets | 565,000 | 865,000 | 1,715,000 | 3,415,000 |
| Notes Payable | 0 | 0 | 200,000 | 200,000 |
| Accounts Payable | 165,000 | 345,000 | 505,000 | 1,350,000 |
| Total Current Liabilities | 165,000 | 345,000 | 705,000 | 1,550,000 |
| Long Term Debt | 0 | 0 | 250,000 | 625,000 |
| Total Liabilities | 165,000 | 345,000 | 955,000 | 2,175,000 |
| Net Worth | 400,000 | 520,000 | 760,000 | 1,240,000 |
| Total Liabilities and Equity | 565,000 | 865,000 | 1,715,000 | 3,415,000 |
| Net Sales | 1,200,000 | 2,400,000 | 4,800,000 | 9,600,000 |
| Net Profit | 60,000 | 120,000 | 240,000 | 480,000 |
| Net Working Capital | 145,000 | 245,000 | 505,000 | 860,000 |

is an early indicator that a company is growing faster or has grown larger than its resources can support without creating excessive risk. With a high Trading Ratio, equity is low, implying that the company is utilizing substantial debt to pay for its assets. The consequences are high return on equity, satisfying the shareholders, and high risk, distressing the lenders. While high Sales to Net Worth by itself will not hurt the company, it makes the company very vulnerable to any downturn in sales. Consider the example in Exhibit 4–4.

As you examine these numbers, you will see a company that is growing very rapidly, is profitable, is retaining all of its profits, and is increasingly risky. The liabilities are increasing faster than the assets and much faster than the equity. The accounts payable, which reflect the means by which the company pays for much of its increase in accounts receivable and its inventory, are rising very quickly, making the company much riskier. While the company is successful by most measures, management, through its actions, is creating a situation where any slowdown in sales growth will jeopardize the company. An actual decline in sales and the company would be unable to pay its bills—possibly causing the vendors to force it into bankruptcy.

Each of these ratios, and others that you can create from your own knowledge and experience as being of particular significance to you or your organization, offer a range of interpretations. It is extremely important to remember that no one ratio, by itself, should be used as a basis for decisions or actions. Additionally, it is rare that one year, or a single other period, is sufficiently significant to warrant dramatic action in the absence of corroborating evidence. Nevertheless, we can look at these specific measurements and reach hypotheses that we can then substantiate and, if appropriate, respond to.

Effect ratios tell you something about what happened to bring the company to its present condition. These ratios include:

- Current Ratio
- Quick Ratio
- Net Working Capital
- Accounts Receivable to Net Working Capital
- Inventory to Net Working Capital
- Debt to Assets
- Debt to Equity
- Short-Term Debt to Equity
- Short-Term Debt to Total Liabilities

Crossover ratios and causal ratios not only tell you about past experience, they indicate future results as well. By focusing on causes as well as consequences, you, as a manager, can have a dramatic impact on future financial performance. These ratios include:

- Return on Sales
- Return on Assets
- Average Collection Period
- Inventory Turnover
- Efficiency Ratio
- Net Sales to Net Worth

## Review Questions

1. The efficiency ratio measures:                                          1. (a)
   (a) selling, general, and administration expenses as a percentage of
       sales.
   (b) manufacturing efficiency of production.
   (c) cost of goods sold as a percentage of sales.
   (d) cost of sales as a percentage of sales.

2. The current ratio and the quick ratio both measure liquidity. The       2. (b)
   difference between the two is:
   (a) quick ratio is quicker.
   (b) quick ratio excludes inventory.
   (c) current ratio excludes inventory.
   (d) current ratio includes all assets.

3. Short-term debt:                                                        3. (c)
   (a) has a higher interest rate than long term debt.
   (b) is subordinated to equity.
   (c) is less expensive than long-term debt or equity.
   (d) is riskier than long-term debt or equity.

4. Average collection period is important because it:                      4. (a)
   (a) provides a measure of the quality of accounts receivable.
   (b) measures sales manager success.
   (c) measures quality of prior period earnings.
   (d) measures the time it takes to collect from every customer.

5. A high fixed asset turnover:                                            5. (d)
   (a) can have only one meaning.
   (b) assesses the capital spending budget.
   (c) may mean that sales are very poor this month.
   (d) may indicate that fixed assets are old.

Do you have questions? Comments? Need clarification?
Call Educational Services at 1-800-225-3215, ext. 600,
or email at ed_svcs@amanet.org.

# Managing
# Short-Term Assets

*focus*

## Learning Objectives

By the end of this chapter, you should be able to:

- Describe the characteristics of the key short-term assets.
- Distinguish the effects of alternative management policies on working capital.
- Explain the cash conversion cycle.

## OVERVIEW

Starting with this chapter, you will take a step-by-step tour of the Balance Sheet. You will learn how the operating manager affects these accounts and how the financial information reflected in these accounts affects the operating manager. This particular chapter concentrates on short-term assets, those that make up the working capital assets. These short-term assets are often the most critical assets of a business, requiring a high degree of management attention and careful understanding to assure that these resources are properly utilized. This chapter will talk about proper management as well as the consequences of improper management of these important financial resources.

The management of short-term assets, also known as working capital assets, is a very, very important management function. As we will see, mismanagement of these assets, particularly inventories and accounts receivable, can consume resources that would otherwise be used to support and strengthen the business. It is important to recognize that management of these assets is a comprehensive function. One cannot focus on only one of these asset categories at a time.

We will also see that there is a direct relationship between the management of short-term assets and the management of short-term liabilities, part of the subject matter of Chapter 9. As we noted earlier, financial transactions that affect one part of the Balance Sheet will ultimately affect another part, because the Balance Sheet will always balance. Understanding the other side of the Balance Sheet effect will help us to understand the impact of management actions.

In this chapter we will concentrate on cash, accounts receivable, and inventories. The other current assets are generally relatively small and have little impact on the operations or the financial strength of the business. In those companies where these assets are important or significant, the manager whose function required the expenditure often holds specific responsibility for the prepaid expense or deposit.

### Attention and Improvement

"It's been awhile since we've gotten together. I thought we could revisit some of the initiatives you put in place already. Pat, has the customer service group continued to follow the ACP ratio?"

"We have, Bob. And Accounts Receivable began some initiatives of their own. Mary said that by collecting sooner, we've got cash coming in faster and we've been able to invest it in more raw materials for our fastest growing lines. This means we've had enough stock on hand to fill orders promptly—and my group is noticing a difference in the phone calls we're getting. Almost no complaints about late deliveries. That's helped the morale in customer service—as has knowing that our ideas for improving the ACP had a measurable effect on other departments and overall performance."

## THE MANAGEMENT OF CASH

Everyone knows what cash is. We also know, from our personal experience, what it is used for. Here we are less concerned with its uses than with the consequences of the choice of use we select. Cash is the most liquid asset, immediately available for use. As such it carries the least risk to its owner. However, if cash is not managed properly, several measurements used to assess the business may be adversely affected.

In Chapter 3 we looked at several ratios and other measurements that analysts use to evaluate the business and its management. Large cash balances will affect these measurements and lead to conclusions about the company. For example, if cash balances are high, the current ratio may be high, suggesting that the company has not used its cash to generate income for the company and return for the shareholders. If the cash balance is high and the current ratio is not, then it may be that the company has more interest-bearing debt than it should, reducing the income of the company and penalizing the return that the shareholders receive.

If we have a large cash balance, we must consider the alternative uses for cash that management has chosen not to employ. Suppose management decides to hold cash instead of paying down a note payable. Management may have recognized that if the company had paid the balance, it might not have been able to borrow that same amount at a later date. Therefore, management may have made the choice to retain the cash and incur the interest expense in order to retain the flexibility that the cash provides for a future time. As we study the financial statements, we may see this as an indication that the management must renegotiate the arrangement with the lender to permit a **revolving loan** rather than a **term loan.** And if we have extended credit to this company in the past, we may want to take a hard look at the situation before we extend any more. We will explore this further in Chapter 9.

Another possibility is that the retention of cash in a liquid form, generally in a checking account, provides management with a sense of security. After all, having cash makes a manager comfortable that, whatever may occur, there is a resource to take care of it. This is a very conservative approach. However, the very existence of that cash, if substantial, may make the company attractive for a takeover. An aggressive manager may recognize that same cash as an underutilized resource, capable of earning a significant return and may attempt to gain control of the company in order to take advantage of that resource. This belies the security that the earlier manager felt.

## Reasons for Holding Cash

College finance textbooks describe three purposes for holding cash: transactions, emergencies, or opportunities. Most of the cash we have is used to pay bills in the normal course of business. However, with a prior arrangement, the bank will provide "overdraft" protection for our checks, assuring that our check when presented will be honored, whether we have available cash or not. Therefore, if we have arranged for overdraft protection, or a revolving line of credit, we do not need to hold cash for transactions unless we are certain that the cash flow that normally occurs will not be sufficient, even with the overdraft credit, to meet our payment needs.

In the case of emergencies, unless we have extraordinary amounts on deposit, the cash balance may not be sufficient. Additionally, if our business is well managed, such emergencies should not be manageable only with cash. Here, too, a prior arrangement with the bank will enable us to deal with the emergency without having to hold cash.

In the third instance, opportunities, we cannot know in advance how much cash we will need. Therefore, it may be much more effective to establish the type of banking relationship, that, when appropriate, will give us access to the appropriate resource.

In all three of these situations, we have turned to the bank to cover our cash needs. Some managers do not like to use debt, but we all know that used properly, debt can enhance wealth. The most obvious example is in the purchase of a home. There are very few of us who can pay cash for a house. We borrow money, the mortgage, in order to be able to buy an asset that we believe will improve our lifestyle, help control our costs, and ultimately increase our wealth through the equity we build up as house prices rise and we pay down the mortgage. Clearly, the use of other people's money, in this case through the bank, is a means of increasing our own wealth as well as providing a return for the lender and the suppliers to the lender. It is the same way in business. The judicious use of other people's money increases our own ability to make money. Holding cash for comfort, or, "just in case," may not really be to our advantage.

## Techniques for Managing Cash

A manager of cash in a company recognizes that earning interest on cash on hand increases the overall profits of a company. Therefore, many managers take advantage of banks' need for cash to maintain their levels of reserves. Managers contract with the bank for the bank to use the cash the company has on deposit to increase the bank's overnight balances in return for interest. These **repurchase certificates** or securities (Repos) provide a modest income for the company on funds it otherwise would not earn anything at all on. If the funds are not needed for longer than just overnight, longer agreements will be established, and they will carry higher interest rates, to compensate for the longer time. The differences in interest rates are very slight, but if the balances involved are substantial, this may still result in some real income. If the funds will be available for longer, weeks or months, there are other investment instruments that may offer higher rates of return.

As part of this cash management process, companies with multiple locations will arrange to bring the cash from all the locations into a central account where it can be managed and invested more effectively. A manager can earn more money if there are larger amounts to invest as well as if the money can be invested for longer periods of time. The **sweeping** of these funds in a **concentration** account gives the manager more opportunities to manage the funds effectively.

However, when a company gets too caught up in the management and manipulation of such funds, bad things can happen as well. Several years ago, E.F. Hutton and Company, a major brokerage house, carried the management of funds to an extreme, using the record keeping associated with the transfer of funds to create fictitious balances on which they were paid interest amounting to millions of dollars. Ultimately, the scheme was discovered, several people were convicted of fraud, and E.F. Hutton and Company was sold and eventually combined into another brokerage house.

Nevertheless, used properly, the techniques of cash management, getting money into a central account and investing the funds intelligently, offers an opportunity to contribute significantly to the financial success of a company. These funds are often invested in short-term securities, known as Marketable Securities.

## THE MANAGEMENT OF OTHER SHORT-TERM ASSETS

Other short term assets, including marketable securities, accounts receivable, inventory, and prepaid expenses, are part of the company's working capital. The rest of this chapter will describe the management issues for each of these assets.

## Managing Marketable Securities

There are numerous instruments available to the company treasurer to help generate income while holding liquid assets. The list of such investments grows daily and includes instruments called "derivatives," whose value is "derived" from underlying assets or arrangements. One of the most interesting aspects of the derivatives market is the flexibility of the instruments that are being developed. Derivatives, which have received a lot of negative publicity in recent years but which offer the ability to tailor investments to particular needs or situations, may carry a level of risk inappropriate for liquid resources that a company will need in the near future.

A variety of short-term investment choices are listed in Exhibit 5–1.

Clearly, the array of choices offers great flexibility at a broad range of risk levels. Common stock is far riskier than savings accounts, but for the right situation it may offer the prospect of sufficiently high return to make the risk worthwhile. It should also be apparent from the breadth of the list in Exhibit 5–1 that a short-term investment instrument can be constructed to meet almost any need.

## Managing Accounts Receivable

One of principal ways that many companies generate sales is by offering to sell their products on credit. This is particularly true when the company is selling to other businesses. The sale on credit enables the purchasing company to use the product for a period of time before paying for it. They may convert the purchased product into some other product for ultimate sale, or they may resell the purchased product to downstream customers or they may consume the product themselves. In any event, the payment for the purchase is delayed, enabling the buyer to retain its funds and use them to generate income for the company.

---

 **xhibit 5–1**
**Short-Term Investment Choices**

| *Certificates of Deposit* | *U.S. Treasury Bills* |
|---|---|
| Commercial Paper | EuroDollar Deposits |
| Dollar Deposits in London Market (LIBOR) | Mutual Funds |
| U.S. Treasury Bonds | Corporate Bonds |
| Common Stock | Short-Term Notes |
| Repurchase Agreements (Repos) | Savings Accounts |
| Money Market Funds | Interest Bearing Checking Accounts |
| Stripped Securities | Bankers' Acceptances |
| Ready Asset/Managed Cash Accounts | Municipal Notes |
| Preferred Stock | Call Loans |
| Government Agency Issues | Zero CDs—Zero Coupon Discount Certificates of Deposit |

---

The delay in receiving payment for your sale increases the risk to your company, risk that you might not get paid at all, and risk because you need to borrow funds for the time you wait, lowering the return that you can earn because you do not have the money. Therefore, if you choose to sell on credit, it is important to manage your receivables to assure that you do receive the funds when you want and expect them.

Managing accounts receivable involves the assessment of credit risk, discussed in Chapter 9, as well as following up with customers to assure that they are satisfied with their purchase and will, therefore, pay for it when payment is due. The management of accounts receivable includes the maintenance of accurate and complete records of all sales and payments, monitoring the status of all accounts, and undertaking the collection effort necessary to keeping your investment in accounts receivable at the lowest level consistent with your other management policies.

Most managers do not like to call asking for money. Therefore, in many companies, accounts receivable are not well managed and customers are allowed to set their own schedule for payment. Because most companies, just as most people, pay their bills on time, that is, within the terms set by the seller, the longer a receivable remains unpaid, the riskier it is. Some companies borrow money, using accounts receivable as security for the loan. The bank, in assessing the accounts receivable, will limit the amounts that will be considered to those amounts that are current or only a little past due. The lender knows that receivables unpaid more than 30 days past due fall into the problem category, because the customer either can't pay (doesn't have the money) or won't pay (has a problem with the product or service). In either event the security for the loan is gone and the lender will not consider such an account as valuable.

As part of managing accounts receivable, management assesses the probability of collecting the amounts due. If there is some question as to whether the customer will pay the amount due, a reserve may be established. It might even be reasonable to create such a reserve based on the percentage of receivables, and therefore of sales, that has historically been uncollectible. This reserve, created by recording a "Bad Debt Expense" in the Income Statement and a "Reserve for Bad Debts" or an "Allowance for Doubtful Accounts" on the Balance Sheet, reduces the profits for the period and lowers the net balance of accounts receivable on the Balance Sheet. If a company chooses not to recognize this probability, no adjustment to income or assets occurs. As you can see, the evaluation of accounts receivable can change the financial performance.

In the past some companies adjusted their reported profits by manipulating this and other reserves, raising and lowering profits according to management choice or investor expectations. The Internal Revenue Service (IRS), Securities and Exchange Commission (SEC), and the Financial Accounting Standards Board (FASB) all felt this practice was sufficiently misleading so they established rules to limit the use of reserves. Today, reserves for bad debts must be specific, that is, based on specific accounts considered potentially uncollectible rather than on a percentage of receivables. Other reserves, such as a reserve for inventory obsolescence, may no longer be recorded on the Balance Sheet, but must be specifically identified and written off through the Income Statement, reducing the Balance Sheet balance. Any inventory thus written off must be disposed of. It cannot be held, to be sold at a later date, permitting the company to transfer the profits to the future.

In Chapter 3 we considered the calculation of the Average Collection Period, a measure of the effectiveness of the management of accounts receivable. This ratio tells us a lot about the credit management and the overall management of the company, the quality of the accounts receivable, and something about the future profitability of the business. As such this ratio is one of the first computed when a company is being analyzed, whether by an investor, a customer, or a competitor of the company.

## Managing Inventory

For many companies, inventory is as, or more, important as accounts receivable. The money spent on inventory takes longer to convert to cash, because it must be sold and the revenue collected, and is therefore more risky than accounts receivable. Because in many cases inventory goes through stages, it is more complicated to manage as well.

In a manufacturing company, inventory goes through three stages, raw material, work-in-process, and finished goods. In these companies the management function is more complex, requiring forecasts of requirements, an understanding of the production process, and an estimate of end customer demand. In other companies, ones that only handle the product after it is finished, the stages of inventory are not important, but the forecasting is more critical because, while raw materials may be used for several end products, and even work-in-process may be finished into a number of different items, finished goods are not easily changed into something else.

Because managing inventory is so critical, companies have developed complex systems to control the inventory and keep track of it. In recent years some of these systems, drawing on the capabilities of computers and systems, have been expanded to control all aspects of the manufacturing process. In the early years of computerization, companies developed inventory control systems that would track the quantities, cost, and physical location of stocks held. Later these systems were expanded to recognize ordered but not received materials as well as work in process by stage of processing. These systems evolved into planning and forecasting tools that took on the projection of materials requirements and the first Materials Requirements Planning (MRP) systems were developed. Rapidly, MRP systems evolved into Manufacturing Resource Planning (MRPII) tools, and from there to Enterprise Resource Planning (ERP) systems. These have in recent years been further expanded to recognize that the requirements for resources extend beyond the company to the suppliers and their suppliers and to the customers and their customers. Today companies are developing comprehensive computerized planning systems to tie the needs of all the parts of the supply chain into an integrated planning system that will provide status information about any stage of the entire processing chain from the very beginning to the very end to anyone with a need to know.

## xhibit 5-2

**Manufacturing Cash Cycle**

| | |
|---|---|
| Day 1 | Place a purchase order to a vendor. |
| | • Initiate a purchasing transaction to acquire raw material to be used in future production. |
| | • Vendor ships and bill merchandise ordered (payment due on Day 30). |
| Day 5 | Receive material ordered and place it in inventory. |
| | This transaction has no effect on the cash cycle. |
| Day 30 | Pay vendor for material. |
| Day 35 | Check is presented to company's bank and is honored. Payment amount is withdrawn from the company's account. |
| Day 45 | Inventory is transferred from raw material to work-in-process and production is started. |
| Day 66 | Production is completed and finished product is transferred to finished goods to be held awaiting sales order. |
| Day 94 | Sales order is received and goods are shipped and billed, receivable due in 30 days. |
| Day 124 | Customer pays the bill. |
| Day 129 | Customer's payment is received and deposited. |
| Day 131 | Bank recognizes the deposit as usable funds to the company. |

The model in Exhibit 5–2 will help to clarify the importance of the planning as well as the interrelationship of the different disciplines within a company. Consider this processing cycle for a manufacturing company shown in Exhibit 5–2.

### Exercise 5–1: Analysis of the Manufacturing Cash Cycle

*INSTRUCTIONS:* ☛ What disturbing pattern do you see in this manufacturing cash cycle?

_____

_____

_____

_____

_____

What is obvious from the example in Exhibit 5–2 is that there is a lot of time, 96 days, from the time the funds leave your account until the time when they are returned. This gap between cash out and cash in, known as the **cash conversion cycle**, requires the company to borrow funds to continue to operate during this time period. In this example we have assumed that our company and our customers pay their bills on time. If we delayed our payments, the amount of time from cash out to cash in would be reduced. If our customers were at all delinquent (and on the average companies' collection periods are longer than the credit terms), the period from cash out to cash in would be longer.

In this case the length of the conversion cycle is caused primarily by the need to hold inventory, a need that is based on the difficulty in forecasting demand. It highlights the importance of developing good forecasts and emphasizes the interrelationship between forecasting, management of assets, and the cost of managing the company. Consider the costs associated with carrying inventory in a company. The list of such expenses is shown in Exhibit 5-3.

It is estimated that when all these costs are added together, they equal approximately 30 percent of the value of the average annual inventory balance. This amounts to a substantial percentage of company profits and, excess inventory held "just-in-case" severely impacts potential profitability. This is one reason for the "just-in-time" emphasis on inventory management today.

The cost of carrying inventory, particularly when interest rates were very high in the early 1980s, raised management attentiveness to inventory issues. One concept that gained broad interest is that of **"Just-in-Time" (JIT) inventory management.** JIT requires a very strong knowledge of your customers and your suppliers to be successful. The essence of JIT is that inventory is only made available when it is actually needed. Consider the amount of time that inventory is held waiting for something to happen in the Cash Control Cycle exhibit. JIT reduces the investment in inventory as well as reducing the carrying costs incurred. However, it requires a great deal of work by many different people in different parts of the company and much cross-discipline communication to be successful.

Because inventory is such an important and complex asset, inventory control is a major issue in many companies. The computer system keeps track of the inventory balances and, perhaps, even tells us where the stock is. However, it is possible to make errors and it may be necessary to move inventory around. Therefore, in addition to the perpetual inventory system, companies are also expected to confirm the physical presence of the inventory reported. In part, regulators and the market require this because of large fraud cases

### Exhibit 5–3

**Inventory Carrying Costs**

- Warehouse Space Costs
- Shrinkage
- Property Taxes
- Utilities
- Inventory Handling Costs
- Interest/Opportunity Cost

- Insurance
- Obsolescence
- Damage
- Control Systems Costs
- Security

in the past, where companies reported inventories that did not exist, inflating their assets, overstating their profit, and therefore the company value. As a result of these cases and also just because of the importance of the investment on the Balance Sheet, companies take physical counts of their inventory at least once a year. These counts, taken under controlled conditions, confirm the computerized records or identify adjustments that affect the inventory balances and the profits or losses reported in the Income Statement. These counts are generally taken at or near the end of the year and are observed by the independent accountants who are asked to express an opinion on the financial statements of the company. The inventory is considered an important representation of the quality of financial controls, and these outside auditors use the comparison of actual inventories to the computerized records as a test of the accuracy of the entire financial control and reporting system for the company.

We can carry this concept of inventory management a bit further. Obviously, manufacturing, distribution, and retailing companies have inventory and are, therefore, affected by the type of analysis we just saw. But many other companies that do not have inventory in the traditional sense have similar managerial issues. Consider, for example, a professional services firm, such as a lawyer, doctor, CPA, architect, engineer, or consultant. While each of these professional organizations does not have traditional inventory, they sell time-based services. Therefore, they have to have time available to sell—professional and staff time. If there is no time available, they cannot generate additional revenue. If there is time available and they do not sell it, they still have to pay for it (staff wages). It is similar to grocery inventory that is no longer fresh; they pay for it and get no revenue. Therefore, many of these professional firms will agree to lower fees during slack periods. For example, a CPA firm charges full rates during "busy season," that time after the end of the year and before taxes are due. During the summer, however, they may have more staff than they need and will offer a lower rate to clients whose requirements occur during this slack time. Many not-for-profit organizations have fiscal year-ends that fit this time period and rates to these firms are often considerably lower. There are other industries that have similar seasonal patterns where a customer buying during a slow period can negotiate a better price for the product.

## Prepaid Expenses

Some industries require their customers to pay for an entire year's costs at the time they make a purchase. One such example is the insurance industry, where the customer generally purchases insurance for an entire year, and pays for it in advance. At the end of the accounting period, which is generally not the end of the policy year, a portion of that insurance policy remains unused. It still has value that should be recognized on the Balance Sheet as an asset. In fact, if the company were to cancel the policy at almost any time during the policy year, it would be eligible for a refund of a portion of the premium paid.

Other similar expenditures include advertising where purchasing a year's contract may qualify for a discount when compared to the individual insertion rate, certain borrowing arrangements where the interest is paid in advance, dues and subscriptions where a year's membership is paid up front, and professional fees where a retainer is paid in advance of the services rendered. In some cases there may be taxes, such as estimated income taxes, paid in advance that also need to be recognized. In all of these and similar cases, the unused portion of the prepayment represents value to the company, a value that should be included in the assets of the company. Therefore, Prepaid Expenses is another category of the Current Assets on the Balance Sheet. While these amounts are often relatively small, they may add up to a significant amount. In the effort to make the financial statements accurately reflect the financial condition of the company, these amounts need to be recognized and accounted for.

## Other Current Assets

There are several other types of assets that should be acknowledged. They are often insignificant, but in some cases may represent important managerial policies. For example, accounts receivable from employees, shareholders, or officers may be included as a subaccount in the accounts receivable section of the current assets. These receivables represent expenditures made by the company on behalf of these people and may or may not really be collectible. If the balances here are substantial, it is important that they be visible on the Balance Sheet. Another such category is deposits. Deposits may be down payments on rental space, capital assets, show space, or some other future expenditure. By recording them on the Balance Sheet the company can keep track of the expenditure and be sure that the money spent is utilized effectively. Sometimes, companies will account for deposits, especially for rental space or capital assets in the long-term assets section of the Balance Sheet because the deposit will not be returned or consumed until some years later.

The short-term assets on the Balance Sheet are also known as the working capital assets. These assets:

- cash
- marketable securities
- accounts receivable
- inventories
- prepaid expenses

represent significant investment for the company. These assets, particularly accounts receivable and inventory often grow as, or more, quickly than the company's sales, resulting in considerable demand for additional financial resources. Predicting this demand for cash helps management assure the ability to meet demand.

- The management of cash and short-term investments can have a significant impact on the earnings of the company and the risk with which the management is comfortable.
- The management of accounts receivable includes collecting funds from customers and making sure the funds are usable as quickly as possible.
- Inventory is a very expensive resource. It takes a relatively long time to turn the investment back into cash, and while it is being held, it costs up to 30 percent per year or more to hold it.
- The cash conversion cycle describes how long it takes the company to replenish the money it spends, an important measurement of management effectiveness.

## Review Questions

1. Working capital assets are:
   (a) the short-term assets.
   (b) the productive assets, machinery and equipment.
   (c) only inventory and machinery.
   (d) accounts receivable and accounts payable.

2. Sweeping cash is the practice of:
   (a) spending all cash from all sources.
   (b) cleaning out the wallets of the senior executives.
   (c) bringing all cash to a concentration account.
   (d) closing all cash accounts in a particular bank.

3. Accounts receivable on your Balance Sheet represent:
   (a) purchases your company has made on credit.
   (b) purchases your company has made for cash.
   (c) sales your company has made on credit.
   (d) sales your company has made for cash.

4. The investment in inventory is considered:
   (a) the least risky of all assets.
   (b) less risky than cash but more risky than accounts receivable.
   (c) more risky than cash but less risky than accounts receivable.
   (d) more risky than cash or accounts receivable.

5. The cash conversion cycle refers to the period between:
   (a) cash in and cash out.
   (b) the decision to purchase and the payment of cash.
   (c) sale and receipt of payment.
   (d) receipt of payment and availability from the bank.

1. (a)

2. (c)

3. (c)

4. (d)

5. (a)

Do you have questions? Comments? Need clarification?
Call Educational Services at 1-800-225-3215, ext. 600,
or email at ed_svcs@amanet.org.

# 6

# Relating Risk and Return, Valuation, and Time Value of Money

*focus*

### Learning Objectives

By the end of this chapter, you should be able to:

- Explain what risk is in a financial management context.
- Relate risk and return in financial decision making.
- Describe how risk affects return and therefore the risk tolerance of managers.
- Apply risk-return decision making in your daily activities.
- Evaluate financial options applying the time value of money principles.

## OVERVIEW

The discussion of these related topics provides a basis and a setting for much of the material in the next several chapters. Managerial decisions, whether they be investment or financing choices, are often made by applying the principles of the risk-return relationship. This discussion will demonstrate that most people, regardless of their responsibility, understand and apply these principles in their daily activities. However, it is also important to understand how these principles apply and how to measure the risk-return trade-off to permit sound decision making. Therefore, this chapter focuses on application and measurement. This material will lead directly into the capital investment decision-making discussion of the next chapter. It will also carry over into the discussion of financing choices for the business discussed in Chapters 9, "Managing Liabilities," and Chapter 10, "The Equity in the Business."

### Assessing Investment Choices

"Bob, we've been looking at some new office space in town. The mortgage rates the bank offered were 8.625 percent for 15 years, 8.75 percent for 30 years, and a quarter of a point less if we put up more than 20 percent. I feel I can make excellent contributions in the area of space and functionality, but I don't understand why we're being offered different rates or which deal is the best one for us."

"That's a good question. Let's see if anyone else in the group has any ideas."

"I think the difference in rates relates to risk and return. We're growing rapidly and we expect that to continue, but my parents still talk about the economic downturn in the late 1980s. Plenty of firms downsized and the residential real estate market collapsed. It's hard to predict the business cycle, and if we had a severe recession, our market demand might dry up overnight.

"The farther out you go in the future, the harder it is to predict, so the more return you have to demand."

"I agree with Les, Bob, but I think there's more to it than that. I think risk and return are also related to the amount we'd have to put up as a down payment. Bankers want buyers to have some of their own money at risk—they figure people will be more careful with their own money than with the bank's. But the difference in rates for different terms reflects the time value of money. We can calculate net present value to see which rates are better for us."

"Those are both good answers. This kind of thinking helps you make better decisions about company finances and about your own finances. You shouldn't finance any purchases without considering risk and return and the time value of money."

# RISK

When asked if they understand what risk is, most people will answer, "Yes," but when asked to define it, they hesitate. Go further and ask if they can tell which of two or more alternatives is riskier than the others, they again will answer affirmatively. But, when asked how much riskier, they will again have difficulty responding. This helps us understand the challenges that often face financial managers when making investment or managerial decisions.

Consider these choices: crossing the street in a rural town, crossing the street in a small city, and crossing the street in a major city. Clearly, they are not all equally risky. You have a sense of relative risk. But, can you quantify it? Is crossing the street in the small city two or three times as risky as crossing the street in the rural town or only a little riskier? Would you cross the street in the major city the same way you would in the small city or the rural town? The answer to this last question is obviously, "No," unless the reward for doing so was very high.

Thus, it is with all risk decisions for most people, and that applies to financial managers making financial decisions as well.

## Defining Risk

The dictionary defines risk as "possibility of loss." However, such a definition is not particularly helpful in financial decision making. Consider these three examples of possible investments: A, B, and C. You have carefully analyzed these three investment choices and have decided that you will invest, and will invest in one of these three.

Investment A has a 25 percent probability that things will not go as well as is expected that, as a result, Investment A will yield a return of 9 percent. You have also determined that there is a 50 percent likelihood that things will turn out exactly as anticipated, and as a result, Investment A will yield a return of 10 percent. And, you have determined that there is a 25 percent probability that things will turn out better than expected, and as a result, Investment A will yield an 11 percent return.

Investment B has a 25 percent probability that things will not go as well as is expected, that, as a result, Investment B will yield a return of 5 percent. You have also determined that there is a 50 percent likelihood that things will turn out exactly as anticipated and, as a result, Investment B will yield a return of 10 percent. And, you have determined that there is a 25 percent probability that things will turn out better than expected, and as a result, Investment B will yield a 15 percent return.

Investment C has a 25 percent probability that things will not go as well as is expected, that, as a result, Investment C will yield a return of −10 percent. You have also determined that there is a 50 percent likelihood that things will turn out exactly as anticipated, and as a result, Investment C will yield a return of −10 percent. And, you have determined that there is a 25 percent probability that things will turn out better than expected, and as a result, Investment C will yield a −10 percent return.

## Exercise 6–1: Comparison of Investment Options

*INSTRUCTIONS:* ☞ In tabular form this situation looks like this:

| Probability/Yield | Investment A | Investment B | Investment C |
|---|---|---|---|
| 25 Percent | 9% | 5% | −10% |
| 50 Percent | 10% | 10% | −10% |
| 25 Percent | 11% | 15% | −10% |

Which of these choices is least risky? _____

Why did you respond as you did? _____

_____

_____

_____

Many people respond that "A" is least risky, but the correct response is "C" because, in fact, C has *no* risk at all. You know exactly what the result of an investment in C will be. In financial decision-making terms, risk may be better defined as the *uncertainty of result* rather than the possibility of loss. In principle, the amount of that uncertainty can be measured. The chapter on risk and return in any finance textbook will provide a detailed discussion of the process of measurement and the statistical validity of such a measurement.

In this course, we will recognize that risk is determined by the range of possible outcomes. The wider that range and the greater the probabilities of high or low results, the greater the risk. To demonstrate how this all works in finance, identify which of the investments we just described you would invest in.

I would choose: _____

## Risk Aversion

Realizing that a loss of 10 percent is not at all attractive, it is easy to assume that you will not choose C, but between A and B, the decision is harder. You will note that the expected return on both A and B is equal to 10 percent. You can determine this by multiplying the probability by the related expected return and then adding up the results. If you chose A, you are like most people, averse to risk. Because both investment choices have the same expected result, you chose the one of lower risk. To consider choosing a higher risk option, you would have to be offered a higher return, and that higher return would have to reward you adequately for taking the higher risk. Crossing the street in the middle of the block in a major city is obviously more dangerous than crossing at the corner with the light. To take the additional risk, the reward for crossing there must be very attractive. Financial decisions are similar. For a risk-averse person to take a high risk alternative, the reward must be enough higher to overcome the aversion to risk.

If you chose B, you may be classified as a risk taker. This is because B is the higher risk choice, and, given that the expected result, 10 percent, is the same for both options, more attractive only to those who have a relatively higher risk tolerance. The risk taker gets some additional reward from the challenge; perhaps it is the excitement of the prospect of a high return, 15 percent, if everything goes better than expected. Perhaps it is a high level of optimism. Whatever it is, there must be an additional reward, not necessarily financial, beyond the expected return.

If you originally chose A, consider your response if the return resulting from better than expected performance were 20 percent. This would change the expected return (determined by the multiplication and addition process described above) to 11.25 percent, 12.5 percent higher than before. Would this be enough to persuade you to change to B?

This expands the definition of risk aversion: If two investments have equal return, the risk-averse investor will choose the investment with the lower risk. If two investments have equal risk, the risk-averse investor will choose the one with the higher return. And, further, the risk-averse investor will demand a higher return if asked to take a higher risk.

We can state this as an investment, and general, rule:

The greater the risk, the greater the return must be.

This is the essence of risk and return and serves as the basis for all financial decision making. It can be generalized to all investments, whether of time or money, whether personal or business.

## Possibility of Loss

Having demonstrated this financial principle, let's return for a moment to the dictionary definition. It is not altogether wrong.

In our example the choice of B, the riskier of the two reasonable instruments, A and B, entails the possibility that the yield will be 5 percent. If that comes to pass, then the investor will have incurred an opportunity loss since, had he or she chosen A and received the lowest yield, it would have been 9 percent. By choosing B, the investor incurred an opportunity loss of 4 percent.

## Characteristics of Different Types of Risks

In considering financial investment decisions, and financial investments obviously include the extension of business credit, there are a number of general risk types to evaluate. In particular, the investor must consider default, inflation, maturity, and liquidity issues. In addition, when dealing internationally, an investor must include currency risk, the possibility that due to changes in exchange rates, the value of a transaction will change between the time of its initiation and its completion.

## The Determination of Interest Rates

A logical next step is to examine the development of interest rates as a basis for determining how investment decisions are made. Interest will serve as a starting point for the examination of all rates of return.

If you had a cabin in the woods and someone wanted to use it for several months while writing a book, you might, assuming everything else checked out, be willing to allow this writer to use the cabin. You would expect to be paid some rent for its use, to compensate you for your costs and to reward you for not being able to use it yourself.

The same is true with money. If you lend money to someone else, you expect to be paid rent for its use and to compensate you for not being able to use it yourself. In addition to the charge for "rent" and for our lost opportunity, several other risks we can identify also require compensation.

# TYPES OF RISK

As a general rule we can define the return you should receive for the use of your money as rent plus compensation for the risks you incur, a premium determined by the types and severity of the risks. The types of risk may be gathered into four basic types, each of which has a different consequence and concept. These four types are:

- default
- inflation
- maturity
- liquidity

**Default risk** is the risk that you will not get your money, your principal, back on time or, perhaps, at all.

**Inflation risk** is the risk that when you do get your money back it will have lost some buying power.

**Maturity risk** is the recognition that if you have loaned your money to someone else you cannot use it yourself, even if a better opportunity arises. Therefore, maturity premium may also be considered an opportunity premium.

**Liquidity risk** is the risk incurred if you have to liquidate the loan before it matures. It is a measure of the potential penalty that would be imposed by the market.

Following are more detailed descriptions of these different types of risks and a discussion of the effect that they have on interest rates and, because interest rates are the starting point, on all rates of return.

## Default Risk

Whether an investment is a loan or a purchase of equity, when we make the investment, we want to protect our investment and assure ourselves that its value remains sound. In the case of a loan, we eventually, at maturity, want the money back. When we determine what interest rate to charge, we try to assess the probability that we might have difficulty getting repaid. We'll charge more if we think that probability is significant. What if we are sure we will get the money back, but we are not sure that it will be paid on time? We'll charge a higher premium for the uncertainty. Default risk is the risk type that immediately comes to mind in any discussion of interest charges.

If our investment is a purchase of equity, presumably we do not expect to receive our money back directly. However, we still want the money we invest to be safe and profitable. Therefore, we determine an expected rate of return on our equity, defined as the **cost of equity capital,** and expect the investment to generate enough increased value to provide us such a return.

Almost all borrowers are subject to some default risk, however small. Only the government of the United States (or of another sovereign nation) is not subject to default. If there were ever any possibility of default, the government would merely print more money and the risk of default would vanish. Such an action would adversely affect the inflation risk, but the default risk would be eliminated. Therefore, we consider government obligations to be free of default risk.

If we are concerned that an equity investment is abnormally risky, we require an abnormally high rate of return to compensate us for taking that risk. In the investment marketplace, equity investments in start-up and early stage companies are very risky and the risk perceived is a form of default risk. As a result, the investors (venture capital firms, for example) require extremely high expected returns to make the investments.

## Inflation Risk

Inflation has nothing to do with the specific investment. Nevertheless, it is a risk to the investor in that there is, in the United States, no provision for an inflation-based increase in the amount to be returned at the end of the investment term. (In some countries with continuously high inflation, there may be an indexing process that takes the inflation rate into account in determining the amount to be repaid.)

All borrowers are subject to inflation risk because there is nothing borrower-related in the determination of inflation. Even the borrowings of the United States government are subject to inflation risk. Therefore, inflation is described by some as a "nondiversifiable" risk and must be included in any return requirement regardless of borrower.

## Maturity Risk

Like inflation risk, maturity risk is not borrower-specific. Since it relates to time, the time your money is committed for, it is not diversifiable. Interest rates in the United States are expressed in annual terms, and maturity risk is a function of time. It applies to loans with a term longer than one year. The maturity premium increases the longer the term of the loan.

Consider this example. Suppose you agreed to lend your associate $10,000 for five years. You would agree on a rate and complete the transaction. Now suppose, two years into the term of the first loan, another associate offers you a better deal. Because the first loan used up the available money, you cannot take advantage of the new deal. The maturity premium provides the lender with at least some reward for the risk of missed opportunities. For this reason, the longer the loan contract, the higher the maturity premium. This is the principal reason that long-term interest rates are generally higher than short-term interest rates. If short term interest rates are higher, a circumstance that results in an **"inverted" yield curve,** it is an indication that rates are changing and an investor should reexamine his or her investment portfolio.

## Liquidity Risk

Sometimes you just have to get your money back sooner than you planned. The person to whom you loaned the funds was not planning to repay the loan this soon and simply cannot do so. What do you do? One choice is to sell the note you hold to someone else. How easily this is done, and how much of a discount you have to allow, is the essence of liquidity risk.

At the extreme, you could not sell the note to anyone. If you knew these circumstances in advance you would require a significant liquidity premium. At the other end of the spectrum is a loan to the United States government. A loan to the Treasury, in the form of a **Treasury bill**, note, or bond, has no liquidity risk for several reasons. First, there is a large and ready public market for Treasury securities. Second, the government has guaranteed a market for its securities, and, third, if pressed, just as with default, the government could print money to repay its debts, even early.

## ESTIMATING INTEREST RATES

Using the preceding section as a guide, the formula for interest rates would be:

$$I = BR + DP + IP + MP + LP$$

Where:

$I$ = the Interest Rate
$BR$ = Basic Rental cost of money, approximately 2 percent
$DP$ = Default Premium
$IP$ = Inflation Premium, currently running about 3 percent, increased because the Federal Reserve is concerned that the strength of the economy in 2000 would cause prices to rise
$MP$ = Maturity Premium
$LP$ = Liquidity Premium

Recognizing the premiums described we can easily arrive at an approximation for the "risk-free" rate, the interest rate paid by the U.S. Treasury. The risk-free rate, designated $R_F$, includes the basic rental cost of money, plus the premiums for inflation and maturity, the nondiversifiable risk elements.

As an example, U.S. Treasury Bonds, the long-term bonds the U.S. government issues, are currently offering an interest rate of approximately 6.0 percent. If we consider the basic rent plus the inflation premium plus the maturity premium, the risk premiums discussed above that apply to the U.S. government's obligations, we find that:

| | |
|---|---|
| Basic Rent | 2.0 percent |
| Inflation Premium | 3.0 percent |
| Maturity Premium | 1.0 percent |
| Interest rate | 6.0 percent |

Therefore, the interest rate on a loan to the U.S. government, described as "risk-free," is really free of the risks that the borrower can manage. In a similar vein, any corporate borrower can reduce the interest rate they have to pay, particularly on unsecured loans, by reducing their default risk and by improving their market presence, assuring that there is a ready market for their obligations.

## Capital Asset Pricing Model

This interest discussion establishes a basis for looking at other securities. After all, equity investors want a return that recognizes these same risk premiums and rewards the investor for giving up the right to a defined maturity, for taking a subordinated, lower priority role to other financing, and for giving up the right to a regular payment of income. Scholars have analyzed this relationship and identified a relationship that describes these needs. Finance theoreticians have described the Capital Asset Pricing Model (CAPM) as an equation that determines the return required of an investment having a particular risk relationship to the general market. This equation is:

$$k_j = R_F + \beta_j(k_m - R_F)$$

where:

$k_j$ = the Require Rate of Return on an investment j
$R_F$ = the risk-free rate
$\beta_j$ = "beta sub j" the risk coefficient that relates investment j to the market
$k_m$ = the rate of return available on a known portfolio in the relevant market, the basis for the comparison to j

The measure of beta has been the subject of much academic debate, but generally it relates the volatility or riskiness of a particular security to the general market for similar securities. That is, it relates a particular stock, j, to the performance of the Standard & Poor's 500 average, the Dow Jones Industrial Average, or some similar well-known market measure.

## Relating Risk and Return

While the CAPM equation, in current markets, does not really present a definitive market value relationship for an investment, by relating risk and required return for a prospective investment to the risk-free rate ($R_F$—the U.S. government bond rate) and the market ($k_m$) through an assessment of riskiness ($\beta_j$) and investor is able to apply a rational assessment of validity to a projected, estimated, or definitively required rate of return. The investor is then in a position to decide if the investment is attractive or not.

This defined relationship between risk and return leads to the old adage, "If it sounds too good to be true, it probably is." This saying applies to investments as well as, if not better than, to other situations. If someone offers an extraordinarily high rate of return, it must mean that there is an extraordinarily high risk associated with the opportunity. Despite any objections that might be raised, the relationship of risk and return is clearly valid and as such should be heeded.

## Extending the Theory

Over the years many sources of investment guidance have estimated the beta coefficients for different stock issues. Drawing on the difficulty of establishing just how much riskier one situation or investment is than another, we find that in these estimates of beta, very few company stocks are evaluated at a beta higher than 2. The consequence of this leads to an important result in the financial marketplace. Taking the CAPM equation and using 2 as beta, in the current market where $R_F$ is 6.0 percent and $k_m$ is estimated long-term to be approximately 10 percent, the consequence is a required rate of return of:

$$k_j = R_F + \beta_j(k_m - R_F)$$
$$k_j = 6 + 2(10 - 6)$$
$$k_j = 14$$

If beta is 2, frequently the highest beta coefficient because it is so hard to say that one opportunity is more than twice as risky, twice as volatile, as the market, then, to be attractive, a risky investment must offer the investor a rate of return greater than 14 percent. It is this recognition that has established a market for high risk, non-investment-grade securities. If a company that does not qualify as an investment-grade borrower offers a bond at a rate of, say, 15 or 16 percent interest, there will be some investors—risk takers—who, seeing a rate of return higher than their required rate of return, will invest, establishing the junk bond market and making it possible for riskier companies to attract the funding they need to move their businesses forward. To further explain how this works, remember that interest expense is deductible before computing taxes. Therefore, on an after-tax basis, which will be important when we consider capital investment decision making in Chapter 7, the cost of this high interest debt to the company is approximately 10 percent, well below the cost of equity.

## TIME VALUE OF MONEY

The importance of determining the risk-based required rate of return, k, cannot be overstated. All financial decisions should incorporate an assessment of this risk and the return required as a basis for action.

In essence, we use "k" to assess the real value of whatever we are considering. An essential element of understanding our business system is the recognition that we can always earn a return—an income—however modest, by investing our money in a low- or no-risk investment offering a basic interest rate—a basic rental cost for the use of our money.

We further recognize that if we leave our money invested for periods longer than the stated interest period the investment will continue to earn interest and will also earn interest on the interest. This lesson goes back to childhood when a parent took you to the savings bank and explained that if you deposit your money, the bank will pay you interest and that interest will compound, enabling your deposit to grow and grow. This understanding is our starting point. It can be described as "A dollar today is worth more than a dollar tomorrow."

Taking risk into account results in changing expectations of that return. The greater the risk, the greater the return *must* be to make taking that risk attractive to us. This premise makes it possible for us to evaluate alternative opportunities by judging the risk and then applying our requirements for return based on that risk. If after taking risk into account, the return is satisfactory, we will make the investment; if it is not, we will not.

The way we assess the investment is to relate the value of the money we pay out to the amount that money we will receive would be worth if it were computed in today's terms. Or, we relate the value that something will be worth in the future to what an acceptable investment would be worth, using the required rate of return, k, as the basis for the assessment.

To make this concept simple, assume you required a rate of return of 10 percent and you had $100 to invest for one year. To be attractive to you under these circumstances, you would need to receive at least your $100 back plus a 10 percent additional amount, or $10 ($100 × .10). Therefore, we can say that the **future value,** in one year, of the investment for which we will pay $100, must be $110.

Similarly, we can say that an investment that will pay us $110 in one year has a **present value** of $100 today if our required rate of return is 10 percent. It is important to recognize that such analysis goes both ways. We need to be able to compute the future value from the present and to compute the present value from the future. In fact, we can go either way. If we know any three of the four variables—Present Value, Future Value, Term, and Rate of Return—we can compute the missing variable and then assess the investment.

**Present Value**—The cost of an investment or the value today of monies to be received in the future.

**Future Value**—The dollar yield of an investment or the value of monies to be received at some time in the future from an investment made today.

**Term**—The life of the investment.

**Rate of Return**—The rate of return offered by an investment or required by the investor.

At the Appendix at the end of the course you'll find some tables that will help relate present value to future value, both for individual sums of money and for annuities, which are regular periodic payments of the same amount of money over a period of time extending beyond one period. As we will see in the next chapter, we can compute the present value of capital investments by applying the principles of Time Value of Money to the facts that we determine.

## VALUATION

We can use our understanding of Time Value of Money, along with the application of risk assessment, to evaluate investment opportunities. Therefore, we can determine that the value of an investment is a function of what we

**xhibit 6–1**

**Valuation Computations**

*Part 1*

Present Value = $85,000
Rate = 6 percent
Term = 20 years
Future Value Interest Factor (from Exhibit 6–2) = 3.207
Future Value = 85000 × 3.207 = $272,595

*Part 2*

Future Value = $272,595
Term = 20 years
Interest Rate = 10 percent
Future Value Interest Factor of an Annuity (from Exhibit 6–2) = 57.274
Annuity Required to accumulate necessary funds = 272595/57.274 = $4,759.49

will receive in the future, discounted to the date of the investment. Therefore, if we want an investment of $100 to yield 10 percent over 5 years, we can compute $100 × 1.10 × 1.10 × 1.10 × 1.10 × 1.10, which equals $161.05. Therefore, the future value of an investment of $100 at 10 percent for five years is $161.05. A look at the future value table shown in Exhibit 6–1, confirms that the future value of $1, at 10 percent interest, compounded annually, for five years is $1.6105. Therefore, the future value of $100 computed the same way will be $100 × 1.6105, or $161.05.

All investments can be assessed the same way. Therefore, the determination of the value of an investment depends on the present value (PV), future value (FV), interest rate (I) and term (N, for number of periods). We can also determine how much we will need at some time in the future, to buy something or to reach a desired milestone. Let's look at an example.

### An Illustrative Example

Suppose you want to purchase a retirement home when you retire in 20 years. You have a specific home in mind that is currently available for $85,000. You expect market prices to increase an average of 6 percent per year for the next 20 years. What will the house be worth when you are ready to buy it? Looking at the table for future values in the Appendix, under the 6 percent column across the 20 period line, we find the factor of 3.207, which tells us that the value of the house will be $85,000 × 3.207 or $272,595.

As a second part to this problem, let us determine how much we need to save each year if we can invest our savings at 10 percent for the entire time. Since we want to save the same amount each year for the twenty years, we are talking about an annuity. We need the annuity to be worth $272,595 in 20 years using a 10 percent interest factor. Looking at the future value of an annuity table (see Appendix), we see the factor for an annuity for 20 periods at 10 percent is equal to 57.274. Therefore, if we divide the $272,595 by the factor, 57.274, we find that if we save $4,759.49 each year for the twenty years, we will have accumulated enough money to pay for the house.

### Assessing Investments

We can use these tools to assess any investment, recognizing that the value of the investment is whatever we receive, related to what we paid in, and related to our expectation of return, which, in turn, depends on our assessment of risk.

To determine the attractiveness of an investment in a bond, therefore, we evaluate the interest payments we will receive and the return of the face amount of the bond at maturity and compare that result to our investment amount. Therefore, a bond which will pay us $100 per year for five years and will then pay us $1,000, the face amount of the bond, is worth $1,000.00 to us now if our required rate of return is 10 percent, but is worth $1,080.30 to us if our required rate of return is 8 percent, or $894.70 if our required rate of return is 12 percent. We can use the factors in Exhibit 6–2, taken from the Present Value Table, to see how we reach this conclusion.

These computations tell us many things. Not only do they tell us what such a bond is worth at different discount rates, but they also demonstrate the relationship between nominal interest rates, the 10 percent that the bond pays based on its face amount, and market rates. If the bond's interest rate exceeds the current market, the bond will sell at a premium, and, conversely, if the bond's interest rate is lower than the current market rate, the bond will

**xhibit 6–2**

**Assessing Investments**

| Payment | 10% | | 8% | | 12% | |
|---|---|---|---|---|---|---|
| | PV Factor | Extension | PV Factor | Extension | PV Factor | Extension |
| Year 1 $100 | .909 | $90.90 | .926 | $92.60 | .885 | $88.50 |
| Year 2 $100 | .826 | $82.60 | .857 | $85.70 | .783 | $78.30 |
| Year 3 $100 | .751 | $75.10 | .794 | $79.40 | .693 | $69.30 |
| Year 4 $100 | .683 | $68.30 | .735 | $73.50 | .613 | $61.30 |
| Year 5 $100 | .621 | $62.10 | .681 | $68.10 | .543 | $54.30 |
| Year 5 $1000 | .621 | $621.00 | .681 | $681.00 | .543 | $543.00 |
| Total Value | | $1,000.00 | | $1,080.30 | | $894.70 |

sell at a discount. This enables an investor to receive a return competitive with the market rate. If that were not possible, there would be no market for securities that offered returns different from the current market.

Equity investments can be evaluated in a similar manner. The investor, in considering an equity investment, has a desired rate of return in mind. This return is invariably higher than would be required for a risk-free or a low-risk investment as equity investments are clearly riskier. Additionally, an equity investment does not promise a regular cash income. Therefore, the expectation is that when the return is actually received, it will be significantly more rewarding.

The reward for an equity investment is a function, not of dividends, but of earnings. The earnings of a company belong to the shareholders so that a dividend, which is a distribution of the company's earnings to the shareholders, is actually a distribution by the company of money that already belongs to the shareholders. However, it is deemed to have a separate value. More important, however, than the dividends, is the market value of the stock. When someone purchases shares in a company, they do so in a market and with the expectation that, someday, they will resell those shares into the market. Therefore, the market price that a person pays for shares must be a reflection of the perceived present value of the money that the shareholders expects to receive in the future, when he or she sells the shares back into the market.

Unlike a bond, there is no certainty of timing for redemption or sale of the stock. The shareholder will hold the stock until the current market value of the shares is higher than the perceived present value of the future market performance, as determined using the investor's required rate of return. This all makes sense, but is probably not a picture of reality. Most investors make investment decisions largely on the basis of past performance and intuitive perception. However, underlying this perception is an assessment that the future market price will be higher, and will be enough higher to make it worthwhile to buy and hold this stock.

## Valuing an Investment

Valuing an investment involves applying the tools of time value of money to the expectation of return, recognizing the riskiness of the investment in determining the required rate that will be applied. That is, the value today of an investment is the present value of the future cash flows (whether periodic payments, maturity payment, or price received when sold) of the investment in question, discounted at the rate of return required by the investor and determined by applying a risk assessment to the investment.

The required rate of return that the investor establishes for a particular investment is used as the "k," the discount rate used to convert future cash flows into present value for comparison to the price of the investment.

## Exercise 6–2: Evaluating Investments

*INSTRUCTIONS:* ☛ The following problem highlights the flexibility of this tool.

Using the table below and the Time Value of Money tables, answer the questions which follow.

| Investment | Value at Maturity | Maturity |
|---|---|---|
| A | $30,000 | 15 years |
| B | 13,000 | 7 years |
| C | 20,000 | 10 years |
| D | 15,000 | 20 years |

1. At what price will each of these investments yield 10 percent?
2. What is the approximate yield (return on investment) percentage of each if the investment required today is $8,000?

The solution to this exercise appears at the end of this chapter.

Finally, let's consider a more comprehensive example related to personal financial planning. For this analysis, assume that you are a 25-year-old who wishes to retire in 40 years with $1,000,000 in the bank. While a million dollars won't be as attractive then as it is now, having it will be far better than not having it.

You want to consider how much you need to invest today, at a 10 percent rate of return, to have one million dollars as a retirement fund. What do we know?

- we know the future value: $1,000,000
- we know the term: 40 years
- we know the interest rate: 10 percent

Using the future value tables, we find the factor related to 40 years at 10 percent: 45.258. Dividing $1,000,000 by 45.258 equals $22,095.54, which tells us that if we were to invest $22,095.54 today in an investment that promised a 10 percent interest rate compounded annually, at the end of 40 years, we would have $1,000,000.

We can use the present value tables equally effectively. The present value interest factor for 40 years at 10 percent is .022. Multiplying $1,000,000, the future value, by .022, the present value interest factor, equals $22,000. This is essentially equivalent to the $22,095.54 determined using the future value interest factor. The difference is a result of rounding. In fact, if we had a table of four decimal places, the factor would be .0221 and the answer would be $22,100.00, very close to the $22,095.54.

Perhaps, however, as a 25-year-old, you do not have $22,000 available to invest for 40 years. You are able to save some money from your weekly salary. How much would you need to save each year from your compensation to accumulate a $1,000,000 fund when you retire (all tax considerations are ignored for this exercise).

Using the future value of an annuity table, we find the factor for the future value of an annuity for 40 years at 10 percent is 442.58. Dividing $1,000,000 by the factor 442.58 equals $2,259.48. Saving $2,259.48 over the course of each year for 40 years and investing that money at 10 percent will yield a retirement fund of $1,000,000.

Using the present value of an annuity table is slightly more complicated because we must cover two steps.

The present value of a $1,000,000 fund to be available in 40 years is, as we saw before, $22,100. The present value of an annuity factor for 40 years at 10 percent is 9.779. We need to work with the present value of the retirement fund to equate to the present value of the annuity that will equal that fund. Dividing the $22,100 by 9.779 equals $2,259.94, equal to the annuity computed using future value amounts.

As is obvious from all this, the use of time value of money techniques, coupled with an understanding of risk and return, enables an investor to decide whether an investment opportunity is appropriate for him or her or not. These tools are extremely powerful and are used for both personal and business investment decision making. As we will see in the next chapter, businesses use these same tools to judge capital investment opportunities.

Managing the time value of money has been part of our responsibility since we were very young. In business it takes on even more importance as we manage money on behalf of others, lenders, shareholders, and others in our company. The essence of time value of money is that "A dollar today is worth more than a dollar tomorrow." However, the things that affect this value are volatile and must be taken into account:

- Risk—the higher the risk, the higher the return must be.
- Specific Risks—default, inflation, maturity, liquidity.
- Required Return—the rate we must earn to satisfy the funding sources, a function not only of financial risk, but also of alternative opportunities, managerial philosophy, and general economic conditions.

The manager must take into account all of these factors when looking at investment alternatives.

## ANSWERS TO EXERCISES

### Exercise 6–2

Part 1:

|   | Future Value | Term | Interest Rate | Present Value Factor | Present Value |
|---|---|---|---|---|---|
| A | $30,000 | 15 yrs. | 10% | .239 | $7,170 |
| B | $13,000 | 7 yrs. | 10% | .513 | $6,669 |
| C | $20,000 | 10 yrs. | 10% | .386 | $7,720 |
| D | $15,000 | 20 yrs. | 10% | .149 | $2,235 |

To solve this problem, you could also use the future value interest factor by dividing the future value by the future value interest factor.

Part 2:

| Investment | Present Value Factor | Future Value | Term | Interest Rate | Interest Rate |
|---|---|---|---|---|---|
| A | $8,000 | $30,000 | 15 yrs. | 3.750 | Between 9% and 10% |
| B | $8,000 | $13,000 | 7 yrs. | 1.625 | Between 7% and  8% |
| C | $8,000 | $20,000 | 10 yrs. | 2.500 | Between 9% and 10% |
| D | $8,000 | $15,000 | 20 yrs. | 1.875 | Between 3% and  4% |

To arrive at the correct answers, you need to divide the future value by the present value to determine the interest factor.

To solve this problem you could also use the present value interest factor by dividing the present value by the future value.

## Review Questions

1. To undertake a greater risk, the risk-averse investor requires:
   (a) a return equal to all the other choices.
   (b) a greater return.
   (c) a lesser return because the thrill is its own reward.
   (d) no significant consideration one way or the other.

   1. (b)

2. Inflation risk affects all investments because:
   (a) inflation is an economic factor independent of the type of investment.
   (b) it increases the value of money.
   (c) some companies cannot pay their debts.
   (d) cash is important to have at all times.

   2. (a)

3. The Capital Asset Pricing Model tells you:
   (a) how much to pay for an investment.
   (b) that the required rate of return on an investment decreases in proportion to risk.
   (c) that risk and return are inversely related.
   (d) the return required of an investment having a particular risk relationship to the general market.

   3. (d)

4. The essence of the time value of money is:
   (a) the more money you have, the more money you need.
   (b) that a dollar today is worth more than a dollar tomorrow.
   (c) that it is better to wait for your money.
   (d) that if you have money, you can always get more time.

   4. (b)

5. If the market rate of interest is higher than the coupon rate on a bond, the price of the bond will be:
   (a) higher than the face amount of the bond.
   (b) lower than the face amount of the bond.
   (c) the same as the face amount of the bond
   (d) indeterminate from the information presented.

   5. (b)

Do you have questions? Comments? Need clarification?
Call Educational Services at 1-800-225-3215, ext. 600,
or email at ed_svcs@amanet.org.

# 7

# Capital Investment Decision Making

*focus*

### Learning Objectives

By the end of this chapter, you should be able to:

- Apply Time Value of Money tools to capital investment projects.
- Calculate the Weighted Average Cost of Capital.
- Explain why it is necessary to justify an investment.

## OVERVIEW

This chapter provides a bridge between the discussion of Risk and Return (Chapter 6) and Managing Long-Term Assets (Chapter 8). Operating managers who want their company to invest in a long-term asset that will help them achieve operating performance objectives are generally asked to "justify" the investment. In other words, the managers must demonstrate the financial return made possible by the investment. This chapter explains how capital investment decision making is done and why it is important and presents the concepts of time value of money.

### Addressing Capital Needs

"Morning, Bob. I was wondering if the group could focus on a problem I'm having today. Sales for the A600s are still going crazy and the sales forecast estimates another 18 percent increase next year and the year after that. With this kind of growth, we won't be able to get enough product through the plant to keep up with demand.

"I've requested that we purchase one of two machines—the Schroeder, which will cost $300,000 over 7 years, or the Worrener, which will cost $450,000 over 10 years. Either machine will eliminate the bottleneck in this department. Lee Cronin, the plant manager, said the request sounded reasonable but I'd have to submit a proposal with all the figures documented before he could take it to senior management. I've never prepared this kind of proposal before, so if anyone has any advice, I'd sure appreciate it."

"I think that's definitely worth the group's time. Does anyone have any ideas?"

"You know, I had to write up a similar proposal last year when we needed some new loading equipment in the warehouse. I started with an Introduction that described the current situation, described the anticipated growth, and listed the options. The next section included relevant tables from the sales forecast and business plan and described the effects of a bottleneck in production. Following that, I think you should provide calculations for the cost of capital and rate of return for both alternatives and then state your recommended course of action and the penalties for failing to act now. You might include some appendixes with machine specs and vendor qualifications."

"That sounds like a good plan to me. Would you all break up into smaller groups and help prepare the calculations today? The sooner the proposal is submitted, the sooner Hang Tan can move ahead."

## CALCULATING THE COST OF CAPITAL

In Chapter 6 you learned how to use the Capital Asset Pricing Model to incorporate the relationship between risk and return as you calculated the required rate of return on an investment. You saw the problems that can occur when you try to assess the relative riskiness of different investments. This same problem exists when you look at business investments, whether they be acquisitions of fixed assets or acquisitions of whole companies. This problem is compounded by the need to acknowledge and accommodate the requirements of different providers of funding to the company. One way to address this issue is through a computation known as the Cost of Capital.

The **cost of capital** is the return required to satisfy the provider of a particular type of capital to be used in the business. For providers of debt financing this cost is interest. For the provider of preferred stock financing the cost is the dividend that the stock receives. (We will discuss the specifics of preferred stock and common stock in Chapter 10.) The provider of common stock financing measures his or her return in terms of earnings per share and evaluates that return as a percentage of the price paid for the stock.

In finance textbooks, the return to the shareholder is described as the dividend on the common stock (known as the Gordon Model or the Dividend Capitalization Model) or more recently as the Free Cash Flow (the amount of money that can be withdrawn from a business) model. However, these descriptions become problematic for those companies that pay no dividends or that are growing and consuming all the funds generated, leaving no money that could reasonably be withdrawn. For these reasons, we will look at the return to the common shareholder as the earnings of the business, whether paid out or retained. After all, the earnings really do belong to the shareholders.

Cost of capital recognizes that each source of funds has its own cost. By calculating each element's cost and weighting the costs according to the weighting of the funding sources, you can easily compute the **weighted average cost of capital (WACC).**

## The WACC Model

The following model will demonstrate the cost of capital calculation. We will then develop a generic model before applying the computation to a more comprehensive example. We will draw on this latter example later to demonstrate the problems with assuming that a profitable company must have "free cash flow." Many lenders assess the ability of a company to support debt as a function of the free cash flow concept.

The capital of a business is all of the money invested in the business, whether debt, preferred stock, or common stock. These funds, which will be discussed in depth in Chapters 9 and 10, are the moneys that pay for the assets, particularly the long-term assets, that enable the company to function.

*Assumptions for the model:* If we assume that the interest rate on long term debt is 10 percent, then, the rate of the dividend paid on preferred stock must be higher, say, 12 percent. It must be higher because an investment in preferred stock is riskier to the investor than an investment in long-term debt. If the rate on preferred stock is 12 percent, then, the earnings per share, expressed as a percentage of the value of the common stock, must be higher, say 14 percent, because an investment in common stock is riskier to the investor than an investment in preferred stock.

Let's take a closer look at the interest cost to the company. The company will be able to deduct its business interest expense from its income before computing its taxes. From the viewpoint of shareholders, they receive all rewards on an after-corporate-tax basis. Therefore, the cost to the company of the interest it pays to the investor is really based on its after-tax cost. This is known as the *tax effect*.

The effect, in cost of capital calculations, of the deductibility of interest is to lower the cost of interest by the amount of the tax rate. If we assume that the tax rate is 40 percent, then the effective cost of interest is only 60 percent of the interest rate. We express this tax effect in computing cost of capital as $(1 - T)$, where T equals the tax rate. For this example, assume the tax rate is 40 percent. Since preferred stock and common stock are not subject to tax deductibility, there is no adjustment for taxes in computing the cost of these types of capital.

To adjust the computation for the mix of financing, we must take into account the relative weight that each investment source type is of the whole amount of long-term capital. For this example, assume that the company is funded 40 percent by long-term debt, 10 percent by preferred stock, and 50 percent by common stock and retained earnings. Note that we have now accounted for 100 percent of the long-term funding.

To compute the cost of each type of capital for a particular company, simply multiply the rate associated with each type times the tax effect times the weight.

**xhibit 7–1**

**Computing the Weighted Average Cost of Capital**

| Funding Type | Cost | Rate | Tax Effect | Weight | Cost of Capital |
|---|---|---|---|---|---|
| Long Term Debt | Interest | 10% | (1 − .4) | 40% | .10 × .6 × .40 = .024 |
| Preferred Stock | Dividends | 12% | 1 | 10% | .12 × 1 × .10 = .012 |
| Common Stock and Retained Earnings | Earnings | 14% | 1 | 50% | .14 × 1 × .50 = .070 |
| Weighted Average Cost of Capital | | | | 100% | .106 |

The weighted average cost of capital, WACC, that rate which will satisfy all of the investors, is the sum of the weighted costs of the different types of capital employed in the business. If an investment does not meet this required rate of return, it is not an acceptable opportunity for the company. As we will see a bit later, this rate needs to be adjusted before it can really be used to evaluate capital investment projects. Exhibit 7–1 illustrates how to compute WACC.

The weighted average cost of capital in Exhibit 7–1 is 10.6 percent. This means that, in order to satisfy all the providers of long-term funds to this business, an investment must earn at least a 10.6 percent rate of return.

Exercise 7–1 is an opportunity for you to try the computation for WACC yourself. The exercise only adjusts the assumptions slightly, but will emphasize the process as well as the importance of weighting and choice of financing source.

### Exercise 7–1: Try It Yourself: Compute the WACC

INSTRUCTIONS: ☞ Compute the Weighted Average Cost of Capital following the model in Exhibit 7–1, except use for the weighting: 50 percent for long-term debt, 10 percent for preferred stock, and 40 percent for common stock and retained earnings.

### Computing the Cost of Capital

| Funding Type | Cost | Rate | Tax Effect | Weight | Cost of Capital |
|---|---|---|---|---|---|
| Long Term Debt | Interest | ___% | _____ | ___% | _____ = ___ |
| Preferred Stock | Dividends | ___% | _____ | ___% | _____ = ___ |
| Common Stock and Retained Earnings | Earnings | ___% | _____ | ___% | _____ = ___ |
| Weighted Average Cost of Capital | | | | ___% | ___ |

What are the implications of the result you have just determined?

---

The solution to this exercise appears at the end of this chapter.

From this small example it should be obvious that the choice of financing will have implications for cost of capital and the number of investment opportunities that will be satisfactory. It also helps us to recognize how our funding choices effect the riskiness of our business. The more debt relative to equity, the lower is the cost of capital—due in part to the subsidy provided by the deductibility of the interest. However, the more debt relative to the equity, the riskier the business is to the shareholder because there are more funders ahead of the shareholder in the event the business runs into financial distress. However, to compensate for the higher risk to the shareholder, the lower cost of capital yields a higher profit opportunity because all investments that offer a rate of return in excess of the cost of capital will increase the reward to the shareholder. This is because the debt and preferred stock have fixed rates while the common stock and retained earnings get the benefit of everything that is left over.

## Initial Exercise in Estimating Financing Requirements

It is critical to recognize when funds are needed, whether for capital investments or regular operations. This funding requirement and the funding choices available affect the cost of capital and the required rate of return.

## Exercise 7–2: Estimating Financing Requirements

*Assumptions:*

1. All income statement lines (in 000's) are variable and dependent on sales.
2. Accounts receivable equal 60 days' sales.
3. Inventory turnover is 4 times (based on cost of sales).
4. Assume that sales growth necessitates an additional investment in fixed assets of $150,000, to be funded by long-term debt already arranged.
5. Taxes are 50 percent.
6. Accounts payable equal 3/4 of a month's cost of sales.

| | |
|---|---:|
| Sales | $1,200 |
| Cost of sales | 800 |
| Gross profit | 400 |
| Operating expenses | 200 |
| Earnings before interest | 200 |
| Interest | 80 |
| Earnings before taxes | 120 |
| Taxes | 60 |

| | |
|---|---|
| Earnings after taxes | 60 |
| Preferred stock dividends | 18 |
| Change in retained earnings | $ 42 |

**Step 1:** Calculate accounts receivable.

**Step 2:** Calculate inventory.

**Step 3:** Assume a 20 percent growth in sales. Compute the new income statement.

**Step 4:** Calculate new accounts receivable.

**Step 5:** Calculate new inventory.

**Step 6:** Compute the incremental assets assuming all other assets remain constant.

**Step 7:** Identify sources of funds to pay for these incremental assets.

## Calculating the Cost of Capital

Exhibit 7–2 shows a sample Balance Sheet relating to Exercise 7–2.

The cost of capital will be determined after weighting the sources, recognizing the costs of the different funding sources, and by recognizing the effect of tax rules.

The Balance Sheet is set up in order of descending liquidity and therefore, in order of ascending risk. Logically, then, as we descend the liability side of the Balance Sheet, we encounter increasing cost for each type of capital. In this example, notes payable, which are not considered part of long-

---

**E** **xhibit 7–2**

**Balance Sheet for Exercise 7–2**

*Assets*

| | |
|---|---|
| Cash | $ 20 |
| Accounts receivable | 200 |
| Inventory | 200 |
| Current assets | 420 |
| Fixed assets | 750 |
| Total assets | $1,170 |

*Liabilities*

| | |
|---|---|
| Accounts payable | $ 50 |
| Notes payable | 200 |
| Accruals | 10 |
| Current liabilities | 260 |
| Long-term debt (15%) | 400 |
| Preferred stock (18%) | 100 |
| Common equity | 410 |
| Total liabilities/equity | $1,170 |

---

**xhibit 7-3**

Calculation of Weighted Average Cost of Capital

|  | Weighting | Cost | Tax Effect | Net Cost |
|---|---|---|---|---|
| Long-term debt | 400/910 = .44 | .15 | 1 − .5 = .5 | .033 |
| Preferred stock | 100/910 = .11 | .18 | No adjustment | .020 |
| Equity | 410/910 = .45 | .20 | No adjustment | .090 |
| Weighted average cost of capital |  |  |  | .143 |

The weighted average cost of capital in this case is 14.3 percent.

term funding because they will be paid in less than one year and are therefore excluded from the cost of capital computation, carry an interest cost of 10 percent. The interest rate on long-term debt is 15 percent, higher than for notes payable because the long-term debt is riskier than the short-term. The dividend rate on the preferred stock should be higher than the interest rate on the long-term debt because the preferred stock is riskier than the long-term debt. At a dividend yield of 18 percent, the cost is higher. Although there is no dividend rate for the common equity, the cost, in this case the expected return on equity (defined as earnings after tax and preferred stock dividends divided by equity) is expected to be higher than the yield on the preferred stock, again because the investment in equity is riskier. For this example we would estimate the expected return on equity to be 20 percent. In this case, the company's profit after taxes and preferred dividends is not equal to the expected return. This does not reduce the stockholders' expected return.

Let's look at the computation, in Exhibit 7-3.

A capital project must yield at least this rate of return in order to satisfy the current funding sources. If new funds are necessary, unless competitive rates have declined, it is reasonable to expect new funds to be more expensive and the cost of capital to rise. This is even truer with our sample company because the equityholders' requirements were not met in the previous year.

Let's look at some additional points. In the Balance Sheet in Exhibit 7-2 we simply assumed the financing would be long-term debt. Obviously, a company could also use short-term debt or equity. If we were to compare these alternatives, we would identify other planning concerns. The same Balance Sheet could be constructed to include the additional financing first as short-term notes payable, second as long-term debt, and third as equity. Computing the weighted average cost of capital with each option would highlight the importance of financing choice.

Even with only this minimal amount of additional funding the ratios will change noticeably. If an additional investment in fixed assets or a more significant increase in accounts receivable and inventory had occurred, the effect on financial measurements could have been dramatic.

This whole discussion of cost of capital and choices in funding method leads to considerations of return on investment and calculations of payback period, net present value, and internal rate of return. We will discuss these topics in detail later in this chapter. For now, be aware that decisions regarding funding sources affect the cost of capital computation for the company, and in turn, affect the required rate of return for an investment to be satisfactory. In the discussion of capital budgeting later in this chapter and in Chapter 8, investment project acceptability alludes to satisfying the company's required rate of return.

## CAPITAL BUDGETING

By assessing rate of return on a project, company management is able to evaluate the contribution that such an investment will make to overall performance. Many companies undertake formal investment evaluation programs that identify the amount of investment required, including working capital, and the cash flows that will result. The comparison of the present value of the cash flows to be received and the amount of the investment enables management to assess the acceptability of the project. Computing the payback period tells management how long it will take to return the investment funds committed. Calculating the net present value of the project using the company's cost of capital as a discount rate enables management to identify acceptable projects. Computing the internal rate of return in projects enables the company to rank projects of dissimilar size and life. However, the internal rate of return computation is more complicated and many companies, particularly smaller ones, do not use the technique. Later in this chapter the specific computational procedures will be detailed.

Capital investments involve:

- large amounts of money
- long periods of time
- delayed receipt of income
- complex tax treatments
- careful planning

The investment analysis process we have just discussed provides an introduction to the whole area of business investment decision making and the management of long-term assets, considered in more depth in Chapter 8. As a starting point let's consider the reasons for making capital investment decisions. These choices will lead to an assessment of the risks involved as well as to the modification of required rates of return.

## TYPES OF CAPITAL INVESTMENT PROJECTS

Businesses make capital investments for many reasons, nearly all related to improving the competitive position of the company. Therefore, the assessment of these investments should be predicated on the need to deliver an appropriate reward to the shareholders of a corporation or owners of other business types as well as to pay the other providers of the needed funds their expected rate of return. We can identify six classes of capital investments:

*Replacement*—enabling the company to continue to do what it has done in the past. These investments do not involve new technologies or capabilities, but merely replace worn out or destroyed capacity.

*Expansion*—increasing the capacity of the company, permitting the company to take advantage of additional volume opportunities. These investments often take longer than replacement projects to become fully utilized and involve, in many cases, taking market share from competition, which is more difficult than merely retaining existing volume.

*Rationalization*—undertaking efforts to improve technology, lower cost, or increase productivity, often requiring changes that have not been fully proved. These projects frequently also include expanded capacity.

*Development*—advancing the company through new products, new markets, or new technologies. These projects often incorporate elements of all of the above options plus significant changes in company operations.

---

[This line denotes the separation between those projects that generate a return and those that do not.]

*Mandatory*—required investments to satisfy legal or contractual requirements. These projects may result from changes in legislation (such as the environmental protection laws or the Americans with Disabilities Act) or from safety requirements (required by insurance companies or the Occupational Safety and Health Administration) or from negotiations (such as actions required as a result of collective bargaining). These investments do not offer any return but must be made.

*Other*—upgrading or changing assets deemed necessary or desirable by management but offering no measurable financial return to the company. These investments might include upgrades to the computer systems to satisfy Y2K or other concerns, refurbished office décor that will improve employee morale or provide the appropriate image to visiting customers and others, or executive perquisites needed to attract and retain key corporate executives. In this listing, the top four investment purposes are presented in order of increasing risk. As a consequence of this progressively higher risk, expansion projects require a higher rate of return than do replacement projects; rationalization projects require a higher rate of return than expansion; and development projects require a still higher return.

Mandatory and Other projects, both of which often have no return at all, must be paid for through the return earned by the profitable projects, because shareholders, who are rewarded through the profitability of the company's performance, including the capital investments, require an adequate return regardless of how their money is utilized.

The consequence of this is to require the profitable projects to also pay for those projects that are deemed necessary but do not offer a return on

## xhibit 7–4
**Required Rate of Return for Various Project Types**

| Type of Project | Required Rate of Return |
| --- | --- |
| Replacement | 10 percent |
| Expansion | 12 percent |
| Rationalization | 14 percent |
| Development | 16 percent |
| Mandatory | 0 percent |
| Other | 0 percent |

their own. This is important, because the investors who provide the funds for these capital investments are not willing to forgo any return just because the company must make investments that do not offer a return.

Therefore, we can see the following effect on the required rate of return for a project. Let us assume that the cost of capital is 10 percent. Therefore, the required rate of return on a replacement project, being least risky, must offer a rate of return equal to the cost of capital. All other profitable projects must offer higher rates of return, and the greater the risk, the greater the return must be. Let's assume that the incremental risk raises the required rate of return 2 percent for each step.

We can build a table to demonstrate this, as shown in Exhibit 7–4.

Because the profitable projects must pay for the others, we need to adjust the required rates. If we assume that 80 percent of our capital budget is for profitable projects and 20 percent of our capital budget is for the nonprofitable projects, we must increase the required rates of return by 25 percent (20/80) to accommodate the shareholders' requirements. Therefore, we can recalculate the table, as shown in Exhibit 7–5.

These higher required rates of return shown in Exhibit 7-5 will adjust for risk and also for the funding of the nonprofitable projects.

## xhibit 7–5
**Recalculating the Required Rate of Return**

| Type of Project | Required Rate of Return | Adjusted Required Rate of Return |
| --- | --- | --- |
| Replacement | 10 percent | 10 percent × 1.25 = 12.5 percent |
| Expansion | 12 percent | 12 percent × 1.25 = 15.0 percent |
| Rationalization | 14 percent | 14 percent × 1.25 = 17.5 percent |
| Development | 16 percent | 16 percent × 1.25 = 20.0 percent |
| Mandatory | 0 percent | |
| Other | 0 percent | |

## Applying Cost of Capital

There are almost always more alternative investment opportunities available than there are funds available to pay for them. The cost of capital provides a basis for evaluating these investments and determining which are most beneficial, at least from a financial perspective. The assessment of the various projects raises several other issues to consider.

In order to judge among the investment opportunities, the manager must recognize several decision criteria. Financial return is one, and we will examine the financial assessment in the next few pages. But before considering the financial evaluation, it is important to understand some other aspects of the capital budgeting landscape.

The decisions relating to project choice are complicated by a number of factors beyond the financial ones. For example, some projects may be mutually exclusive. That is, the decision to fund one immediately eliminates the other. Sometimes, these are alternative ways to solve the same problem. Other times, they represent corporate decisions to move the business toward one market and away from another. The decision to choose one over another often involves favoring the project of one manager over the project of another, setting up internal conflicts and competitions that have nothing to do with financial management.

Another area of concern relates to the interdependence of potentially separate projects. In some cases parts of a project are distinct, but the funding of one requires the funding of another. However, because managerial authority often has financial limits, such projects may be separated in an effort to gain approval in pieces of a project that might not get approved as a single investment. Consider for example, the building of a research laboratory on a particularly attractive piece of property, access to which would require building a road. Perhaps the road cost, as a single project, would fit within the discretionary authority of a manager. Similarly, the cost of the laboratory would also fit within that individual's authority. However, combined the cost would exceed the manager's authority. In some instances, the manager might seek to fund the road as one project and the laboratory as another, exercising his or her authority separately for the two parts of what is really one project. The financial manager will often recognize the interdependence of two or more projects and intervene in the best interests of the shareholders. This does not necessarily mean that the project will not be funded, only that a larger group of decision makers will evaluate the project.

In most companies, the fact that the capital budget is limited restricts the number and size of the investments. This limitation is described as capital rationing, the restriction of overall investment and the requirement that investments be evaluated to assure that the best ones are chosen. This in turn leads to the careful financial and operational evaluation of the investment options.

In order to accomplish this careful financial evaluation, the financial manager needs to determine the true cost of the project as well as the appropriate revenues and operating expenses that will yield the profits from the investments that will be the basis of the computed return on investment. The next section addresses these issues and sets a framework for calculating the investment cost.

## Determining Investment Cost

Determining the cost of a fixed asset is often much more complex than looking at the invoice. For this discussion we will focus on the acquisition of a piece of productive equipment, but you can extrapolate these issues to include real property or even the acquisition of another company. While it may seem that the examples are focused on manufacturing companies, these concepts are equally applicable to service companies, to not-for-profit organizations, and governmental agencies, without regard to size. In addition to the acquisition cost, the investment includes site preparation, installation and training, and incremental working capital. This last item creates confusions and misunderstanding, but it represents a very important aspect of capital investment funding.

The acquisition cost is fairly straightforward. It includes the invoice cost of the asset as well as the transportation to bring it to the site. In the minds of many people, investment is only acquisition. It is not!

Site preparation costs obviously include the costs of making the location ready, but they also include the financial consequences of removal and sale or disposal of anything being replaced. Sometimes this requires expenditures to remove the old asset, receipts from its sale, adjustment of depreciation to assure that the value of the old asset has been accounted for, and computed tax consequences of the actions. The tax computations involve recognition of depreciation expense recaptured if the asset is sold, accounting for depreciation not yet recorded if the asset was not fully depreciated, and computation and separate taxation of any capital gains resulting from the sale of the asset.

Installation costs include the physical installation of the asset, connection and testing of all related services, and training personnel and management in the proper use or operation of the asset. Among the challenges associated with these and the other costs of acquiring an asset is the recognition that all costs included in the determination of the cost of the asset will be included in the accounting basis for the asset and will be depreciated or amortized over the life of the asset. While this increases the value of the investment, which will impact the rate of return percentage, it also delays the recognition of the cost of the asset in the financial results of the company. This means that all costs considered part of the cost will be capitalized, recorded as part of the asset on the Balance Sheet. This cost, subject to depreciation, will be recovered by the company through depreciation expense recorded in the Income Statement over several years. If these investment costs were treated as expenses of the accounting period in which they were spent, they would pass through the Income Statement immediately, reducing profit and therefore reducing the taxes of the current period. The choice to **capitalize** these expenditures has implications for the company and for the shareholders because of the time value of money as discussed in Chapter 6.

Working capital as part of asset cost is also hard for many managers to understand. The working capital involved includes the incremental accounts receivable resulting from the new sales that represent the revenues associated with the project. It also involves the incremental inventory required to support the operation of the asset and to support the incremental sales. When an asset involves increases in accounts receivable and inventories, these additional assets add to the capital required to finance the acquisition. This amount needs to be included in the project cost to be evaluated. In some cases, a new piece of equipment results in improved efficiencies and actually reduces the inventory required, but generally such a reduction is not deducted from the asset cost. This is one example of conservatism in investment evaluation. The understanding of the working capital requirement is complicated by the assumption that when the investment is terminated, the working capital investment will be recovered. As we will see, the difference between the working capital investment at the beginning and the working capital recovery at the end is a function of the time value of money.

The cost of the investment is the sum of the acquisition cost, the site preparation cost, the installation cost, and the incremental working capital required. The return on investment related to the asset will be computed based on this total project investment cost.

## Determining the Cash Flows of a Project

For all of the years of the capital project evaluation, usually six or seven, all of the income and expenses associated with the project activity need to be determined. The evaluation is concerned only with the incremental activity, not the already existing fixed costs that will be allocated to the sales and operations involved. The choice of a useful life limited to six or seven years recognizes the difficulty of estimating results too far into the future. It also recognizes that the present value interest factors beyond six or seven years are sufficiently low that the present value of cash flows then is probably modest.

In many cases incremental revenues are easy to determine. The analyst needs to be aggressive in seeking out the costs because they are much more difficult to identify.

This difficulty is compounded by the fact that the manager who is recommending the project is usually optimistic and positive about all aspects of the project; he or she may leave out expenses and other costs, generally inadvertently. Nevertheless, determining the cash flows associated with a project, and taking all elements into account, may be difficult. The consequence will be optimistic projections of profits and cash flows resulting from the investment.

For each year, the revenues and costs are computed and structured into an Income Statement format, accounting for depreciation as an expense before computing the after-tax profit associated with the project. The depreciation is then added back to the after-tax profit because it is a noncash expense and we are concerned with cash flows. These cash flows are then adjusted for time in computing the return on investment, as we will see shortly.

## Determining the Terminal Cash Flows

As noted above, the normal time frame for evaluation is generally six or seven years, even though the equipment or other acquisition will last longer than that. The time value of cash flows after the six or seven years, when the discount rate is applied, will be relatively small, and the uncertainty that far out is substantial. Therefore, for evaluation purposes, the assessment is terminated at the end of this time.

On termination of the investment, whenever it occurs, the company may incur removal and disposal expenses. If the environment has been changed, there may be restoration costs. Additionally, there are salvage or sales values that may be significant and may involve recovery of some portion of the original investment. And the working capital will be recovered as well. All of these cash flows as well as the projected cash flows of this final year must be taken into account in computing the terminal cash flow.

# EVALUATING CAPITAL INVESTMENT PROJECTS

In order to evaluate the capital project, you must relate all of the costs and cash flows of the project into an evaluation model so that management can judge the attractiveness of the investment. There are several methods used to assess the attractiveness of a project. The most frequently used are payback period, net present value, and internal rate of return.

## Payback Period

**Payback period** is the time elapsed from the start of the project until the investment dollars have been recovered by the project's cash inflows. This method of evaluation is very easy to calculate and to understand. As a result many companies use it, even though it does not address the time value of money and does not take into account any cash flows subsequent to the recovery of the initial investment. When someone proposes an investment, the first question asked is often, "What's the payback period?"

While many textbooks suggest that there is no risk assessment in the payback method, in fact the sooner you recover your investment, the lower is the risk. However, the payback method is really not a good way to evaluate projects, particularly dissimilar ones competing for limited investment funds.

To compute the payback period, deduct cash flow amounts from the original investment until the entire initial investment has been recovered. The process is very simple and easy to understand.

## Net Present Value

**Net Present Value** recognizes the time value of money, which was discussed in the last chapter. In capital investment evaluation, the time value of money takes on additional importance. Because the investment in the asset takes place and recovery of the investment depends on future cash flows that have to not only recover the value of the investment but also provide an acceptable return to the providers of the funding, incorporating the time value into the assessment provides a much more realistic assessment of the project.

The Net Present Value methodology applies the present value factors to the annual cash flows, comparing the present value of the future cash flows to the cost (where the present value interest factor is 1) to determine whether the sum of the present values of the future cash flows exceeds the investment cost.

The discount rate used to determine the factors is the required rate of return identified based on the cost of capital, the adjustment for risk, and the adjustment for the nonprofitable investments. If the sum of present values of the future cash flows exceeds the investment cost, the investment is deemed acceptable. It provides a rate of return that exceeds that required by the investors.

Computing the net present value is relatively easy, and many academic writers like it, believing that it enables a manager to assure the greatest dollar return to the shareholders. However, because there are limited capital investment funds available, and because businesses are more concerned with rate of return than absolute dollars, the net present value calculation is less attractive to business analysts than to the academics. The net present value computation makes it difficult to compare projects of different sizes. A costly project that offers a few more dollars of net present value may not really be as attractive as a less expensive project that leaves funds for other investments.

## Internal Rate of Return (IRR)

The **Internal Rate of Return** method of evaluating capital investment projects utilizes the time value of money assessment tools to relate the cash flows to the original investment. It determines that rate of return that exactly equates the present value of the future cash flows with the cost of the investment, thereby determining the rate of return of the project. Using this IRR method permits the analyst to rank projects based on their rate of return, permitting the analyst to choose those projects that maximize the overall rate of return offered to the shareholders. With IRR, projects of differing sizes may be effectively compared and ranked.

Before the arrival of financial calculators, computing IRR was difficult, requiring multiple iterations to determine the right rate of return. Today, with more sophisticated and powerful calculators and computers, computing the IRR is primarily a function of collecting the right data and entering it correctly into the calculator. The calculator or computer applies the time value of money factors, just as the manual process does, but it does do automatically, arriving at the result very rapidly, even for the most complex projects.

One problem with IRR is that, when the IRR is very high, it may be misleading because it assumes that the cash flows in the early years are reinvested at the same rate as is determined overall. If the computed rate is high, it may not be possible to reinvest those cash flows at comparable rates, resulting in a lower overall return rate. In most cases this is not crucial, but if you recommend investment projects, it is information you should know. Finance textbooks offer an alternative called the modified internal rate of return that assumes reinvestment at the corporate cost of capital, a more conservative approach.

**xhibit 7-6**

**Comparing Two Investments**

Consider two alternative investments that will accomplish the same purpose. These investment alternatives are mutually exclusive.

|  | Investment A | Investment B |
|---|---|---|
| Initial Investment | $100,000 | $125,000 |
| *Cash Inflows* | | |
| Year 1 | $40,000 | $10,000 |
| Year 2 | $30,000 | $20,000 |
| Year 3 | $30,000 | $30,000 |
| Year 4 | $20,000 | $40,000 |
| Year 5 | $11,000 | $50,000 |
| Year 6 | $10,000 | $60,000 |
| Total Cash Inflows | $141,000 | $210,000 |
| Payback Period | 3 Years | 4.5 Years |
| *At a Required Rate of Return of 14%* | | |
| The Net Present Value is | $509 | −$3,610 |
| A is acceptable, B is not | | |
| The Internal Rate of Return is | Slightly over 14% | Slightly over 13% |

The exercise in Exhibit 7-6 offers an opportunity to compare the processes and results of the different evaluation methods.

### Exercise 7-3: Calculate the Rate of Return

*INSTRUCTIONS:* ☛ Determine the payback period, the net present value at a 15 percent required rate of return, and the internal rate of return for the following investment.

Investment: $12,222
Earnings: $4,444 per year for 4 years.

Payback _____

Net Present Value at 15% _____

Internal Rate of Return _____

- Risk raises the required rate of return on a capital project. How much depends on the risk. The assessment of projects and alternatives is a critical part of managing the financial results of a company.
- Risk is the uncertainty of result more than the potential of loss. The uncertainty is evident in the range of possible outcomes. The wider the range, the greater the risk.
- Evaluating projects is a function of relating:
  - present value
  - future value
  - term
  - rate

If we know any three of these variables, we can solve for the fourth.

- Evaluation of capital projects is most often done by measuring:
  - payback period
  - net present value, using the cost of capital as the discount rate
  - internal rate of return, determining the interest rate that equates the present values of the outflows and the inflows
- If the rate of return exceeds the Weighted Average Cost of Capital, the project is financially acceptable.

## ANSWERS TO EXERCISES

### Exercise 7–1

Compute the Weighted Average Cost of Capital following the model in Exhibit 7–1, except use for the weighting: 50 percent for long-term debt, 10 percent for preferred stock, and 40 percent for common stock and retained earnings.

### Computing the Cost of Capital

| Funding Type | Cost | Rate | Tax Effect | Weight | Cost of Capital |
|---|---|---|---|---|---|
| Long Term Debt | Interest | 10% | .6 | 50% | $.1 \times .6 \times .5 = .030$ |
| Preferred Stock | Dividends | 12% | 1 | 10% | $.12 \times 1 \times .1 = .012$ |
| Common Stock and Retained Earnings | Earnings | 14% | 1 | 40% | $.14 \times 1 \times .4 = .056$ |
| Weighted Average Cost of Capital | | | | 100% | .098 or 9.8% |

What are the implications of the result you have just determined?

The use of additional debt reduces the weighted average cost of capital. The will make it possible for the company to identify more projects that will increase the wealth of the shareholders. The increased use of debt is known as leverage.

## Exercise 7–3

Investment = $12,222
Earnings = $4,444 for 4 years
Payback − $12,222/$4,444 = 2.75 years
The Net Present Value at 15 percent = $12,687.62 − $12,222 = $465.62
The Internal Rate of Return = $12,222/$4,444 = 2.75, the present value interest factor of an annuity falls between 16% and 17%, slightly closer to 17%.

**Review Questions**

1. The cost of capital is:                                                           1. (d)
   (a) the price you pay to be an investor.
   (b) the fee required to sell stock through an investment banker.
   (c) the amount needed to finance a particular purchase.
   (d) the return required to satisfy the provider of a particular type of
       capital to be used in the business.

2. The weighted average cost of capital, WACC, is:                                   2. (a)
   (a) that rate of return which will satisfy all of the investors.
   (b) the lowest interest rate in the market.
   (c) the higher of the interest rate on debt or the dividend rate on
       preferred stock.
   (d) the amount needed to finance a particular purchase.

3. The dividend rate on the preferred stock should be:                               3. (c)
   (a) lower than the interest rate on the long-term debt.
   (b) equal to the interest rate on long term debt.
   (c) higher than the interest rate on long-term debt.
   (d) indeterminate from the information provided.

4. A replacement project:                                                            4. (a)
   (a) enables a company to do that which they have done in the past.
   (b) enables a company to expand its market share.
   (c) causes a company to seek acquisition candidates.
   (d) permits a company to grow in an orderly fashion.

5. Mutually exclusive investments are investments which if you do one:  5. (b)
   (a) you must do the other.
   (b) you will not do the other.
   (c) has no affect if you do the other.
   (d) you cannot afford to do the other.

Do you have questions? Comments? Need clarification?
Call Educational Services at 1-800-225-3215, ext. 600,
or email at ed_svcs@amanet.org.

# Managing
# Long-Term Assets

*focus*

## Learning Objectives

By the end of this chapter, you should be able to:

- Distinguish between long-term and short-term assets.
- Explain how depreciation relates to the valuation of fixed assets on the Balance Sheet.
- Identify those investments that may adversely affect financial performance.

## OVERVIEW

**Long-term assets** are the productive assets of a business. They are generally more expensive and complex than short-term assets and require several levels of approval before acquisition. Their management comes under the scrutiny of senior management and the operating manager needs to understand how performance is judged. This chapter will tie into Chapter 6 relating to Risk and Return, as well as to the discussion in Chapter 7, relating to Capital Investment Decision Making.

### The Basis for Investing in Long-Term Assets

"Bob, I've been checking our company financials every month on the intranet and also looking at the annual reports of some of our competitors on the Internet as well as looking at the budget for my department every week. It seems to me that the company has pretty low depreciation amounts on the Income Statement compared to some of our competitors. And my department has almost no depreciation charges assigned to it. Wouldn't we save a lot on taxes if we bought a couple of new machines in the finishing area?"

"Let me ask you a question, Pam. How well are the machines you've got working? Do you need any more capacity, or can you keep up with the work that's coming to you? Are you having problems with breakdowns or excessive maintenance?"

"Well no, Bob. The machines we have are old, but they never break down and they can handle all the work we give them. I just thought you could raise your earnings by taking more depreciation."

"Pam, do you remember the figures we calculated for Hang Tan at the last meeting? A new machine has to cover a lot more than depreciation. It needs to bring in more return than anything else we might invest in."

## CONSIDERING ASSET CLASSIFICATION

The Balance Sheet is divided into sections. The sections relate to the expected life of the elements contained within the section. For example, the **current assets** of a company are those assets that individually are expected to be turned into cash within a year. Similarly, the **current liabilities** are those obligations that are expected to be paid within one year. The long-term assets of the company, by contrast, are those assets that are not expected to be converted to cash within the next twelve months.

When we refer to long-term assets, we generally focus on the fixed assets of a business: land, buildings, equipment, furniture and fixtures, vehicles. However, the term "long-term assets" relates to these plus investments, intangibles, and any other assets that will not or may not be turned into cash within one year.

Managing these assets is different from managing the more liquid assets. In many books, these assets are described as the "earning assets" because they generate the revenues of the company. Therefore, we are concerned with how to make them productive and how to keep them productive. Some of these answers relate to maintenance management and the assurance that the productive equipment is kept in good working order. This is not the focus of this chapter.

An issue of consequence in the management of these fixed assets relates to how productive they can be; that is how much revenue they can generate. In Chapter 3, when we considered the Asset Turnover Ratio, we showed that investments in fixed assets that do not generate enough revenue serve as an early warning of financial difficulty. In his "Z-formula" work, Altman[1] demonstrated that a low Asset Turnover in a business with significant asset investment was a clear predictor of bankruptcy. Many companies today reward their managers in part on managing the investment in assets.

In this chapter, we are particularly concerned with identifying which assets to keep and use and which to replace or discontinue using. We are also concerned with tying up resources in these expensive assets if we cannot utilize them effectively.

---

[1] Edward I. Altman, a professor at Stanford University, in 1968, identified through scenario analysis, a ratio based formula that provides a prediction of business distress and failure. See also Chapter 4.

# The Investment in Fixed Assets

The decision to invest in fixed assets is based on the expectation that this investment, which is intended to last a long time, will result in the continuous production of positive income and cash flows. The application of the principles of time value of money discussed in Chapter 7 provides the basis for evaluating these investment choices and making the actual investment decisions. Businesses make capital investment decisions for the reasons identified in the last chapter:

- replacement
- expansion
- rationalization
- development

- mandatory
- other

These choices must fit into the strategy of the company and within the capabilities of the company. Then, the judgment as to which are attractive and which are not will be based on the financial and operational benefits to be derived from the investment. Bearing in mind that some investments (Mandatory and Other) do not offer a return, the other investments must pay for the nonreturn choices because the stockholder will not forgo return just because an investment is attractive or required.

We demonstrated in the last chapter how to evaluate these investments for financial return and therefore, how to compare alternative investments. In this chapter we are more concerned with other ways to evaluate the investments and the management of the assets.

Because capital investment decisions frequently require more money than can be generated through operations, the decision to invest in a certain way requires additional consideration as well. For example, the decision to invest in a particular piece of equipment may mean that the company will follow one business track and abandon another. They may choose one product line and give up on another; favor one manager's ideas over another; favor one group of potential customers at the expense of another. Over the years there have been many such choices, some good and some very bad. One such example is the decision by Digital Equipment Corporation to limit the technology its computers could use to that developed as proprietary to DEC machines. There are many such decisions in business history.

We can see the consequences of investment decisions in the financial statements and ratios of a company. Remembering that in our system of accounting there has to be "another side," we can evaluate these investment decisions in terms of their impact. The investment must be paid for. If we pay for it by reducing our cash position, we will save ourselves financing costs, improve our negotiating position (because we are paying cash), and adversely affect our current ratio and similar measurements of financial liquidity and strength.

Similarly, if we choose to pay for the asset by extending our accounts payable or even borrowing short-term, we can complete the transaction fairly quickly, but we hurt our current ratio, decrease our apparent liquidity, and decrease our interest cost, when compared to borrowing long term, increasing our profit and return to the shareholders.

If we pay for the asset by borrowing long-term, we match the life of the debt with the life of the asset, often deemed to be sound business management. However, we incur a higher interest cost than had we borrowed short term, reducing the potential income. Such a decision may weaken the company's debt-to-equity position, making the ratio unattractive to the lender. At the same time, the increased debt, called leverage, may increase the potential return to the stock investor.

A decision to pay for the investment through issuance of additional common stock will reduce the riskiness of the company but will also reduce the per share earnings that reward the stockholder. As you can see, each of these choices has advantages and disadvantages. The final decision is based on which choice most nearly satisfies managements' concerns for risk, return, and shareholder satisfaction.

A closer look at these fixed assets will help us understand the decision choices that are represented by their presence on the Balance Sheet. For example, investments in land and buildings in nonreal estate companies reflect a conservative management position. The investment in these high cost assets puts additional pressure on performance to generate sufficient return to make these investments attractive. They also reflect a management philosophy that favors the comfort and security of owning your own resources and being, therefore, less dependent on others and less vulnerable to increases in operating costs introduced by others.

Contrast the investment in land and buildings with an investment in machinery and productive equipment. Here, the investment has a clear impact on revenues and earnings. Therefore, we will see, in the more aggressive companies, focused investment in equipment and a reluctance to invest in "bricks and mortar." In the 1970s Colgate-Palmolive undertook a concerted effort to sell and lease back its factories in an effort to increase their liquidity and reduce the concentration of real estate on the company's Balance Sheet.

Today, companies are concentrating their investment in high technology types of investments, recognizing that these investments generally translate into higher productivity, generating strong return on investment performance. These higher technology investments often have limited life, due to the rapid changes in technology being presented to the marketplace. This causes the companies to seek to depreciate or amortize their investments over shorter and shorter useful lives, reflecting more of the cost in the Income Statement every year. In the next section we will discuss depreciation and amortization more specifically.

**Depreciation** is a cost allowance that permits a company to recover the dollars of investment in an asset over its useful life. The longer the depreciation life, the longer it takes to recover the cost.

The opportunity to depreciate these assets quickly enables the company to recover the cost by reducing the operating income. One impact of such an action is to lower the taxable income and therefore the tax expense to the company in that year. Some people suggest that investment in fixed assets is wise because it offers higher depreciation and therefore lower taxes. This logic is flawed in that to save on taxes requires the earlier disbursement of cash or commitment to a liability (debt) in an amount far greater than the taxes that will be saved.

The only sound basis for investing in fixed assets is that the investment will generate a rate of return that significantly exceeds the risk adjusted required rate of return and is therefore attractive to the shareholders. Then the benefits of depreciation or amortization will increase the cash flow resulting from the investment, making it even more attractive.

Other fixed assets that appear on the Balance Sheet generally represent things needed to make the company work effectively, such as vehicles and furniture and fixtures, or to provide better working conditions for the employees such as leasehold improvements. These investments are harder to justify based on return on investment and, as a result, fall into the "Other" category for capital investment decision making, requiring that the necessary return on investment be provided through the profitable investments.

## Depreciation

There has been much written about depreciation and its attractiveness or negative consequences to the performance of a business. The most important point about depreciation, and amortization for intangible assets, is that it enables the company to recover the cost of the asset over its useful life. It is important to recognize that depreciation and amortization are not guaranteed. For example, to recognize depreciation or amortization deductions, the company needs to make a profit. Otherwise, the benefit (if there is one) of deductibility for tax purposes loses its appeal. In addition, an examination of the legislative history of depreciation suggests that it represents more a reflection of Congressional objectives than of business requirements. Over the past few decades Congress has approved several changes to depreciation rules, modifying the impact of depreciation on reported business performance and on tax revenues. There is every reason to believe that there will be similar actions in the future.

Under the current tax laws, businesses may follow a range of options for depreciation for reporting purposes and are expected to follow some specific rules for tax reporting purposes. Over the years, depreciation rules and practices and related taxation rules have been changed to respond to impact of taxation, international competition, and other economic forces. Depreciation methods have ranged from the very simple to understand to complexity that requires specialists to decipher. Depreciation rules are part of the Internal Revenue Code. Examples of depreciation methods include:

- *Straight line*—dividing the cost of the asset by the years of its useful life and recognizing depreciation expense equally each year.
- *Sum-of-the-years'-digits*—adding the numbers of the years of useful life (10 years = 55) and depreciating in reverse (the first year is 10/55 of the total asset cost, the second year is 9/55 of the total asset cost, etc.).

- *Double-declining balance*—taking twice the straight line rate, but applying it only to the remaining asset value (for a 10 year asset, using 20 percent, yielding a decreasing expense [.2 × 100 percent of the cost in the first year, .2 × 80 percent of the cost for the second year, .2 × 64 percent of the cost in the third year, etc.]).
- *Accelerated Cost Recovery System* (ACRS)—applying twice the rate over half the traditional useful life (40 × 100 percent the first year, 40 × 60 percent the second year, etc.).
- *Modified Accelerated Cost Recovery System* (MACRS)—similar to ACRS except that it requires the inclusion of a half year convention, that is, only one-half the otherwise allowable depreciation may be recorded in the first year.
- Many variations including crossover from double declining balance to straight line, 150 percent declining balance, and others.

The consequences of such are differences between financial reporting and tax reporting that result in complex reporting of book-tax differences, appearing on Balance Sheets as deferred tax obligations. This program will not delve into these issues further than to alert the student to be aware of such reporting requirements.

## Fixed Asset Accounting

Because companies have these assets that remain on the books for a long time, it is important that management be able to assure the shareholders that these assets and the value they represent are correctly reported on the Balance Sheet. Therefore, the fixed asset records are very detailed and must be reconciled every year. Companies maintain records by asset showing the acquisition date, cost, depreciation expense, accumulated depreciation (both book and tax), remaining book value, remaining life, and often information such as location and classification. Because of the complexity of fixed asset accounting, many companies set a policy limit of the minimum value require for an asset to be capitalized. For small companies this limit may be $500; for larger ones it may be $1,000 to $2,500; and for even larger ones, it will be much larger. One requirement is that whatever the policy adopted, it must be administered consistently within the year and from year-to-year.

The decision as to which fixed assets to capitalize—to put on the Balance Sheet rather than expense through the Income Statement—is in part a reflection of company management. The decision to capitalize assets will occur when management wishes to report higher profits. The consequences will also include higher income taxes. The decision to expense these asset purchases reflects a willingness to report lower profits, a desire to pay lower taxes, and less concern with the market valuation process, which often is based on earnings per share calculations. Because the effect of these decisions can be significant, accounting conventions require a policy that is consistent from year-to-year. It is not deemed appropriate to decide on your capitalization policy based on the rest of your performance.

Some fixed assets, such as computers, other office equipment, and some machinery, are attractive. Therefore, keeping track of these assets and taking extra precautions to protect them is important. Many companies conduct physical inventory counts of the fixed assets just as they do of the inventory.

## Acquisition of Fixed Assets

The most frequent and obvious method for acquiring fixed assets is to purchase them. However, because many fixed assets represent very significant investments, the purchase requires financing. Traditional financial management education emphasized the "matching principle," that the life of the financing should be consistent with the life of the asset. Therefore, a long-term asset should be paid for using long-term financing, either debt or equity.

However, long-term financing is harder to get than short-term financing. It is more expensive than short-term financing. And, it is often more restrictive than short-term financing. As a result, the importance of matching is sometimes lost on management. The recession of the early 1990s was, in part, made more difficult because many companies had financed their long-term assets with short-term bank loans, acquired when the banks were aggressively seeking more business, but containing a clause that required immediate repayment if there were any difficulties in the company, or, as it turned out, in the bank. As a consequence, when the banks encountered difficulties, loans were called that could not be replaced in time to protect the companies, causing or aggravating financial problems for the companies, and deepening the recession.

In more recent years, we have again seen an increase in the use of short-term notes and lines of credit being used for the acquisition of fixed assets, raising the possibility of similar challenges again if the economy should falter. It is important for management to understand the risks that go along with the benefits of using short-term debt.

## Other Long-Term Assets

One category of "Other Assets" that is often present on a Balance Sheet is "Goodwill," the excess of the purchase price for an acquisition over the market value of the assets acquired. Goodwill pays for the value attributed to a business' success and is amortized over a time long enough to reflect the long-term benefits of the acquisition. The amortization of goodwill is a charge to income (often over as long as twenty years) and may depress the performance and market value of the company. The decision to pay a premium over the intrinsic value of the assets being acquired has real consequences for the rate of return offered to the shareholders.

Other assets that are included in the long-term assets section of the Balance Sheet include such items as Cash Surrender Value of Life Insurance, Organization Costs, Patents and Trademarks, and Investments. Each represents a disbursement of company cash for an asset that may be difficult to liquidate or to liquidate for full value. Therefore, it behooves management to think carefully about these assets.

Cash Surrender Value of Life Insurance is an asset, found particularly in small, privately-held companies, that on the surface seems reasonable, but may not be a particularly valuable investment. The asset occurs when the company has purchased a life insurance policy on a key manager or owner and that policy is accumulating value. The value that accumulates, however, may assume a much lower interest rate than would be available if the company were to purchase term life insurance and invest the difference. However, it may be even more advantageous to the company to purchase term life insurance and use the remaining cash in the business itself. After all, we have demonstrated the possibility, particularly in companies with accounts receivable and inventories, that it will be necessary to borrow funds to provide working capital. The major point here is that management should consider carefully the utilization of its resources.

Organization expenses are capitalized because they are considered to have value over at least the early years of the company. While they often are not significant, they also represent cash outlays that take a long time to recover through amortization.

Patents and trademarks are similar in that they often represent cash outlays that can only be recaptured over an extended period of time. The capitalization of these costs moves expenses to future periods and brings profits forward. It is, therefore, important to account for such expenses very carefully.

Investments may be very valid and important assets, committing current resources for future gains. However, in some cases, investments are made for reasons that are personal to the owners and managers. In some companies, particularly those that are privately held, assets such as boats, airplanes, and artwork, or loans to shareholders or officers or investments in children's companies appear on the Balance Sheet. In these cases investments may be draining resources that are or will be important to the company.

These assets often do not generate a return and may represent a drain on company resources. All of these assets fall into a Miscellaneous Assets classification for financial analysis purposes. The relationship of these assets to net worth, calculated in a ratio known as "Miscellaneous Assets to Net Worth (Equity)"[1] may be an indication that resources important for the company's future may not be available when they are needed. If this ratio is increasing, owners and managers may be using the company's resources in a way that limits future profitability. This ratio is not evaluated as frequently as it probably should be, and unfortunately, some companies that could be successful do not succeed because the financial resources were diverted to less valuable assets.

---

[1] This ratio, identified by James MacDonald and Wallace Davidson in *Financial Statement Analysis: Basis for Management Advice*, is a measure to identify increasing investment in nonearning assets, highlighting the potential for future financial difficulties.

Long-term assets, which appear on the Balance Sheet in the lower section of the asset side, represent assets that have a useful life longer than one year. These assets, which generally are more expensive than short-term assets, require special accounting and record keeping.

Depreciation, which is the means by which the company recovers the cost of the asset over its useful life, is an allowance permitted by the government, but which requires careful computations and records as well.

There are many methods of depreciation, all of which will affect the Income Statement and the Balance Sheet. Businesses will choose based on the laws and the impact that the depreciation expense will have on financial results. Faster depreciation will recover the asset's cost sooner, but will depress the profit. It will also decrease the taxes the company must pay. However, to benefit from depreciation expense, both in terms of taxes and cash flows, you first have to spend money for the asset or commit to long-term financing, both of which requires commitment of cash, so depreciation itself is not a reason to invest in an asset.

Other long-term assets also require cash expenditures, so the decisions should be based on the potential return to be generated. Examination of the other long-term assets may provide an insight into management's philosophies.

## Review Questions

1. Long-term assets are:
   (a) those assets expected to be turned into cash within one year.
   (b) those assets not expected to be turned into cash within one year.
   (c) those assets that actually belong to someone else, but we are using.
   (d) only those assets not subject to depreciation or amortization.

   1. (b)

2. Depreciation is important because it:
   (a) increases the cost of a capital project.
   (b) enables a company to recover the cost of an asset over its useful life.
   (c) reduces the cash flow resulting from an investment.
   (d) guarantees that a project will have a positive cash flow.

   2. (b)

3. Capitalizing assets rather than expensing them within the year of acquisition:
   (a) increases income after taxes for profitable companies.
   (b) decreases income after taxes for profitable companies.
   (c) assures constant income for profitable companies.
   (d) cannot be determined without additional information.

   3. (a)

4. Measuring Miscellaneous Assets to Net Worth may provide useful information because miscellaneous assets:
   (a) often offer a return less than other fixed assets.
   (b) indicate the company has excess cash to spend.
   (c) make a higher return than other fixed assets.
   (d) is a general account for recording all capital investments.

   4. (a)

5. The decision to finance the acquisition of a long-term asset with current liabilities will:
   (a) dramatically increase the current ratio.
   (b) increase the current ratio.
   (c) decrease the current ratio.
   (d) not affect the current ratio.

   5. (c)

Do you have questions? Comments? Need clarification?
Call Educational Services at 1-800-225-3215, ext. 600,
or email at ed_svcs@amanet.org.

**9**

# Managing Liabilities

## Learning Objectives

By the end of this chapter, you should be able to:

- Explain the role of debt in the growth of a business.
- Analyze bank loan pricing.
- List and explain the criteria used to evaluate a credit application.

Neither a borrower nor a lender be;
For loan oft loses both itself and friend,
And borrowing dulls the edge of husbandry.
This above all: to thine own self be true,
And it must follow, as the night to day,
Thou canst not then be false to any man.

William Shakespeare, *Hamlet:* Act I, Scene 3

## OVERVIEW

This quotation, among the most famous in literature, may have been useful advice in its day, but today's business success frequently depends on the judicious and profitable use of other people's money. As we saw in Exercise 7–2, Chapter 7, and will see when we look at it again as Exercise 9–1, a growing business may not be able to survive, let alone prosper, on its profits alone. It may have to borrow money to finance its resource requirements. The borrowing of money creates business liabilities.

Many people, heeding the Shakespearean admonition, do not want to borrow money for any reason. They recognize borrowing as when it involves notes and interest and guarantees, failing to acknowledge that any purchase on credit really reflects borrowing and debt obligation.

### Rethinking Liabilities

"Hi, Bob. You said that we should analyze the company's financial statements and bring any of our concerns to this meeting. I'm concerned about the increase in liabilities. I know that sales are growing and that we've had to invest a lot of money in a new building and new equipment to keep up with the demand, but shouldn't we be reducing our liabilities when business is this good? If you can't pay off your debts in the good times, what's going to happen when things get tight?"

"Chris, that's an excellent question. I know a lot of people feel that way. They just don't like debt. Is there anyone else who shares Chris's concern?"

Bob notes several raised hands and then calls on one of the others.

"Chris, a company can't sustain the kind of growth we're experiencing out of current income. And think about your own finances. You're incredibly disciplined—you're one of the few people I know who's never carried a balance on your credit cards. Yet you financed your first home with a mortgage. When you sold it last year, you really made a bundle. That was an excellent investment, and you couldn't have made it if you hadn't financed the house.

"Increasing our liabilities in the company is like that in a lot of ways. As long as we're financing things that will bring in more revenue over the long term, we're better off."

## THE LIABILITIES OF THE BUSINESS

Liabilities are the obligations of a business. They may be long-term or short-term. They evolve from management actions, creating commitments to pay money to vendors, employees, and others in return for goods or services or in compliance with laws and obligations. The decision to purchase has a payment consequence that must be recognized and managed by the operating managers as part of their operating responsibility. This chapter explores what short-term liabilities are, how they are managed, and the impact on the company as a whole of the decisions the manager makes. We'll also cover long-term liabilities, primarily long-term debt, recognizing the differences in risk and return related to these short- and long-term financing choices.

We have already discussed the importance of debt as part of the funding for a business, recognizing that the use of borrowed funds limits the amount of investment required of the shareholders. We have examined the effect of debt on cost of capital and on the investment decision-making process. To make this point one more time, consider example of the effects of leverage shown in Exhibit 9–1.

## xhibit 9–1

### The Effects of Leverage

*Assumptions:* A company has an operating profit of $100,000. The tax rate is 50 percent and the interest rate is 10 percent for all relevant levels of earnings and borrowings. Finally, the total capitalization of the company, that is, the sum of debt plus equity, is $500,000. We can build a table of these values along with a couple of key ratios, Net Profit Margin and Return on Equity, as follows:

| Net Profit Margin | Debt | Equity | Return on Equity |
|---|---|---|---|
| $50,000 | $0 | $500,000 | 10.00% |
| $45,000 | $100,000 | $400,000 | 11.25% |
| $40,000 | $200,000 | $300,000 | 13.33% |
| $35,000 | $300,000 | $200,000 | 17.50% |
| $30,000 | $400,000 | $100,000 | 30.00% |

Notice in Exhibit 9–1 how as the relative levels of debt and equity, making up the total capital, change, increasing the debt and decreasing the equity, for a given level of capitalization and operating profit, the result is an increase in the return to the shareholders who remain. This consequence recognizes the increased risk undertaken by the equity holders, whose investment is subordinated to the debt.

## SHORT-TERM OR CURRENT LIABILITIES

The current liabilities section of the Balance Sheet shows all the obligations of the company that will be due within the next year. These obligations include accounts payable, notes payable, taxes payable, accruals, and the current portion of long-term debt.

### Accounts Payable

**Accounts payable,** also known as trade payables, reflect obligations undertaken by the company in the normal course of business. Vendors will generally offer credit terms to qualifying customers in order to entice them to do business. Because these credit terms are so prevalent in industry today, it is rare for a company not to offer credit, and those that do not are often very limited in their opportunities to do business. Vendors expect that their customers will pay their obligations according to the terms established. However, some customers must be reminded to pay their bills. We have discussed the management of accounts receivable, the other side of accounts payable, in Chapter 5.

Bearing in mind that we have suggested in our discussion of cash management that we want to hold our cash as long as we can, if we make sure our accounts receivable are paid on time, we in effect, manage our customers' accounts payable, at least with respect to us. Only if our vendors are relaxed in their enforcement of credit can we manage our obligations and use vendor funds to support our business. Nevertheless, because most vendors do not charge interest for delinquent accounts, it may be advantageous to delay payment of our payables if our cash is tight. The risk is that, if we are routinely delinquent in our payments, we will become known as a slow pay customer and the availability of credit will be restricted.

The general rule for managing accounts payable is to "hold our cash as long as we can, subject to never jeopardizing our credit rating." Our credit rating is our ticket to borrowing from our vendors. If our access is limited, whether in business or personally, it restricts our flexibility and our opportunities. It also may necessitate additional bank borrowing, incurring interest costs, which decrease profits, and make it harder to grow our company.

The use of accounts payable to grow our business, therefore, is a critical managerial decision. The choice of vendors, the items and quantities purchased, the terms we seek and agree to, and the payment practices we follow all combine to describe our business management. Too many companies operate without understanding the interrelationship of these elements and end up buying more than they need, buying items that are not needed, managing the credit they have poorly, and sacrificing profits, growth, and overall business success simply because they did not understand how important and how interrelated these decisions really are.

## Notes Payable

The account, **Notes Payable,** generally reflects short-term funds borrowed from banks either as a one-time loan or as a revolving line of credit. The choice is often made without understanding the difference, resulting in a use of credit that does not fully meet the company's needs.

A one-time loan, the borrowing of a specific amount of money for a specific, limited period of time, makes sense when the need is just that, a specific amount of money required for a specific purpose with a specific termination when the money can be paid back. Unfortunately, many companies agree to a limited loan when what they need is the flexibility of a revolving line of credit that will fluctuate with cash flows but be available to extend the capabilities of the company as the business grows. A review of the situation presented in Chapter 7 will demonstrate this.

Look at the example and complete Exercise 9–1. In the process of determining the required funding, think about how the funds you need will be paid back.

### Exercise 9–1: Initial Exercise in Estimating Financing Requirements

*INSTRUCTIONS:* ☛ Knowing how much we need and why we need it is essential if we are to negotiate our borrowing successfully. In redoing the following exercise, think about the "why and how much" as well as the "how long" aspects of the borrowing that results.
*Assumptions:*

1. The Income Statement presented represents an annual Income Statement.
2. All Income Statement lines (in 000's) are variable and dependent on sales.

3. Accounts receivable equal 60 days' sales.
4. Inventory turnover is 4 times (based on cost of sales).
5. Assume that sales growth necessitates an additional investment in fixed assets of $100,000, to be funded by long-term debt already arranged.
6. Taxes are 50 percent.
7. Accounts payable equal 3/4 of a month's cost of sales.

| | |
|---|---:|
| Sales | $1,200 |
| Cost of sales | 800 |
| Gross profit | 400 |
| Operating expenses | 200 |
| Earnings before interest | 200 |
| Interest | 80 |
| Earnings before taxes | 120 |
| Taxes | 60 |
| Earnings after taxes | 60 |
| Preferred stock dividends | 18 |
| Change in retained earnings | $ 42 |

**Step 1:** Calculate accounts receivable.
**Step 2:** Calculate inventory.
**Step 3:** Assume a 20 percent growth in sales. Compute the new Income Statement.
**Step 4:** Calculate new accounts receivable.
**Step 5:** Calculate new inventory.
**Step 6:** Compute the incremental assets assuming all other assets remain constant.
**Step 7:** Identify sources of funds to pay for these incremental assets.

In Exercise 9–1, the Company will use the money it receives to finance part of its increase in working capital, classified as short-term or current assets. However, in a growing business, the working capital assets, as long as they are controlled, won't decrease because every time you receive payment of an account receivable, it is replaced with another one from a subsequent sale. Similarly, every time you sell a unit of inventory, you replace it with another one, and actually more than just one for one, because the demand will require continuous stocking of merchandise. This portion of current assets is referred to as "permanent" current assets and may be reasonably considered as fixed and long term as some of the long-term assets discussed in Chapter 8.

Therefore, the credit you will require, while generally classified as a note payable on the Balance Sheet, must be continuous. You don't want to have to pay it off or pay it down. If the need is only seasonal, then the required clearing of the note is reasonable, but if the note is a result of year-to-year growth and the growth is expected to continue, you'll face a continuous need for available credit. As long as the company continues to grow, the need will continue; when, or if, the company's growth slows or ceases, the company should be able to pay the money back and clear the note payable.

Later in this chapter we will examine the considerations surrounding the extension of credit, most of which apply whether you are a vendor extending trade credit or a bank offering loans, long or short term.

## Taxes Payable

As part of our economic system, many of our activities generate obligations to pay taxes to the various levels of government. When we recognize these obligations, we record them as tax expenses and as taxes payable. We pay property taxes on the land and buildings we occupy as well as on the value of other fixed assets and inventory that we own. Sometimes, these taxes are paid to municipal governments to provide funding for the local services we utilize; sometimes, they are paid, as excise taxes or income taxes, to state governments for statewide services; and sometimes, they are paid, as income taxes, to the federal government.

The obligation to pay taxes is mandated by law and we cannot choose whether or not to pay. However, we are only obligated to pay the minimum amount of tax the law stipulates. Therefore, many companies expend a great deal of effort seeking to lower the taxes they must pay, in some cases by improperly accounting for expenses. The consequence of that type of action is to mislead anyone who reviews the company's financial statements and seeks to establish value or understanding of the operations of the company. Not only do companies that "cook their books" to evade taxes face many consequences in the courts and in the investment market, they no longer have good information to serve as a basis for decision making. They become less able to manage their business.

Many people hold the philosophy that paying taxes diminishes our income. However, since we are obligated to pay these taxes, another way to look at them is to recognize that, under our current system, for every dollar we pay in taxes, we keep between one and one-half and two or more dollars after taxes. Therefore, to maximize the wealth of the shareholders, we should manage the business to be strongly profitable and we should pay in taxes the minimum necessary in accordance with managing the business in that profitable manner. To summarize, evasion of taxes is against the law, but avoidance of taxes, that is, minimizing that which we owe, is sound business practice and should be followed.

That said, we should never undertake any action solely to reduce our taxes. Under our current system, to avoid one dollar in taxes means we must spend at least two-and-a half dollars. Given the importance of cash in a business, any decision to spend merely to reduce taxes needs to be examined very carefully.

## Accruals

As discussed in Chapter 2, there are two methods of accounting, cash and accrual. In cash accounting, transactions are only recorded when cash actually moves. There are no accounts receivable or payable and revenue is recognized only when the sale is paid for. In accrual accounting every effort is made to record activity in the period in which it occurs. Sometimes, in order to do that, it is necessary to record transactions that relate to the period, even though they are determined after the period is over and were not really obligations until the period was over. Accruals, which is what accounting for these transactions is called, are predominantly accrued payroll, accrued taxes, and accrued expenses.

Accrued payroll occurs when the payroll due date falls into the next period, or more likely, year. For example, a company pays its employees on Thursday for the period that ended on the previous Sunday. In 2000, July 1 was a Saturday. For a company with a June 30 year-end, the last payroll paid during the fiscal year was paid on June 29 for the period that ended on June 25. The payroll for the last 5 days of June, not payable until July 6, needs to be accrued in order for the company to match the expenses and the revenues through June 30. Similarly with taxes—both payroll taxes, and more particularly income taxes—the tax obligation cannot be calculated until all the other accounting has been completed. The taxes that would have been owed as of June 30, but which are not due until September 15, will be accrued as of June 30. A final calculation and adjustment of the tax expense will occur later.

Accrued expenses are similar, but because accounting for business activity cannot wait until all the bills relating to the prior period have been received and entered, after a few days, the accounting department records those bills relating to the prior period as a journal entry to bring the expenses back into the proper period. Because in most companies the amounts accrued are not significantly different from one month to the next, accruals are really only important at the end of the year. At that time, accruals are computed carefully and journal entries are made that are only reversed at the end of the next fiscal year, when the new year-end accruals are prepared. The reversing process makes it possible to record only the expenses appropriate for the period in the last accounting period of the year.

## Long-Term Debt

**Long-Term Debt,** usually bank debt, reflects money borrowed for longer than one year. In some cases when a company borrows long-term money, a portion is due to be repaid each year. The amount due within twelve months is recorded and reported as a current liability, Long-Term Debt Due within One Year, while the remainder of the obligation is reported as Long-Term Debt below the current liabilities on the Balance Sheet.

All debt, whether funded by a bank or not, is loaned based on the credit worthiness of the borrower, as assessed by the lender. While all lenders and vendors go through different credit assessment procedures, all attempt to determine how likely it is that the borrower will be able to pay for the loan. The extension of credit as part of the sales process is as much a loan as is a formal note presented to a bank. In the following pages we will examine the criteria for credit, considering the kinds of concerns that a lender will evaluate. While we will use a bank as an example, trade credit and borrowing from a bank are very similar. As part of this assessment, we will also look at how a bank determines its interest rate, so that when you negotiate for a loan, you will understand the issues as well as the lender does.

When you establish a borrowing relationship with a bank, it is wise to initiate the process long before you need the money, so that you can choose your bank as well as your banker, the form of funds as well as the source. Many business people do not realize that they do not have to accept the "banker of the day." If you begin the borrowing process when the need is imminent, your negotiating power and your options are severely limited. There is real truth to the old saying, "The best time to borrow money is when you don't need it." Being well prepared gives the borrower the most power.

Similarly, when seeking leasing funds or equity capital, do not settle for the first choice to present itself. Rather, shop around for compatibility as well as price. To settle for less than the most appropriate available resource is to open the company up to relationship problems that only aggravate the other challenges facing businesses today. The Internet today increases the options available significantly.

As with everything else, the more control business people maintain, the more likely they are to be successful. If they delay application until the last moment, all of the negotiating power and all of the options rest with the banker. The borrower becomes a supplicant rather than an applicant.

## Choosing a Bank Lending Officer

If your needs are, or are likely to be, reasonably significant, it is desirable to seek out a high-ranking officer to be your primary contact. This individual will be your representative throughout the approval process. In today's banking environment, it is unlikely that the loan officer who works directly with the borrower will have the authority to approve a large loan. Similarly, investment decisions generally require several reviews and approvals. Other officers will approve the funding, or a loan or investment committee will judge the application. The higher your lending officer's rank, the less complicated and time consuming the approval process will be, providing the officer endorses and advocates the application.

# THE "C's" OF CREDIT

Because there are so many words beginning with "C" that apply to the credit process, every discussion of credit includes a presentation of the "C's" of credit. Identification of these terms provides an easy way to remember the issues and criteria involved in a credit decision. The following list includes the traditional "C" words, as well as some that are less frequently used. The key terms are:

- character
- capacity
- capital
- cash flow
- collateral
- conditions

- competition
- credibility
- competence
- communications

Not all of these terms are relevant to all credit situations, and not all of those utilized have the same level of importance in all circumstances. However, borrowers and lenders should address each of these issues when considering any arrangement. The resulting evaluation will be thorough and surprises will generally be avoided.

Authors of programs, articles, and credit management textbooks focus on some of these differentiable criteria. However, all of these elements come into play either directly or indirectly. It is important to recognize that lenders consider a broad range of assessment and evaluation bases when reviewing a loan application. In the following discussion of these criteria, the focus will be on borrowing and lending; they are, however, equally applicable to soliciting and investing. The standards are no less stringent in an investment situation.

## Character

The assessment of **character** is the evaluation of the borrower's predisposition to repay an obligation. It is an attempt to measure integrity, the commitment to repay that will motivate the borrower even if a problem arises.

Character involves the borrower's reputation in business and personal dealings. It recognizes the borrower's personal attributes, including historic behavior.

Included in the character assessment are considerations of:

- **Business reputation**—The reliability of one's word, measured through references, credit history, and reputation.
- **Management experience**—What the borrower has done in the past and how well it has been done. The age of the borrower or the organization and the extent of the time reflected in the experience are included in this part of the evaluation, recognizing that past achievements may be a predictor of future accomplishments. While a previous failure is not necessarily a knockout, it will raise major concerns in the mind of a lender.
- **Risk orientation**—An assessment of the attitude that the borrower has toward financial resources. Conservatism will be valued in this consideration.

Today a high character rating is essential if you want to get a loan approved. In times past character was often considered necessary and sufficient to permit the approval of a loan. If the lender knew the borrower personally and had high regard for the borrower's character, the loan was approved, based on the borrower's word. Now, the character assessment is necessary, but it is not sufficient. Without a satisfactory character assessment, a loan will generally not be approved. Other criteria must also be met.

Early in 1993, President Clinton suggested that lenders should increase the level of "character lending" as part of the effort to improve the national economy. While this suggestion received extensive media coverage, there has been no indication that lenders plan to change their evaluation process. In light of the recent credit problems and regulatory scrutiny, lenders will continue to require that borrowers satisfy many other evaluative criteria. One change, however, was the establishment of the "low doc" and MicroLoan programs under the auspices of the Small Business Administration (SBA). These programs, which involve modest-sized business loans, acquired through banks but partially guaranteed by the SBA, require far less paperwork and impose fewer restrictions than do conventional bank loans.

Even though many other criteria are involved, the character assessment is the most important evaluation of all. In every case, the character of the borrower will be considered and only those applicants who satisfy the character criterion will be given further consideration.

## Capacity

**Capacity** measures the ability of the borrower to utilize the amount of credit sought. This measure is important because funds committed by a bank to one borrower cannot be committed to another, even if the first has not utilized them. The lender, therefore, wants to make sure that funds committed have some likelihood of being used, providing interest income to the lender.

Another aspect of the assessment of capacity is the evaluation of the borrower's ability to use the credit effectively. If the funds cannot be used effectively, there is a much greater risk that the loan will not be repaid. Funds that are used—or are "available"—for nonproductive purposes, will not generate a return. Numerous instances of this type of bad loan were publicized at the height of the banking crisis. Time after time lenders did not assess the capacity of a borrower to utilize the credit sought or offered for a business application.

Often the company's financial statements, particularly if confirmed either through audit or review, provide the evidence of capacity that a lender requires. Eighty-five percent of the bankers surveyed in a bankers' study[1] identified financial statements as the most important information a borrower provides.

In a similar vein, capacity assesses the business's ability to utilize an equity investment effectively and to generate an appropriate return on the investment. Very often, a business will seek too much or too little funding, resulting in an unsuccessful financing arrangement.

## Capital

**Capital** as a consideration refers to the level of owners' equity in the business. The lender is attempting to assess the level of owner commitment to the borrower organization. If the bank is going to be the primary source of funds for a business, the loan should be conservative, or the bank may deny the loan request.

If there is a substantial amount of equity (net worth) in the business, it indicates that there will be value in the assets to protect the bank even if the assets are not specifically identified as collateral for the loan. Remember that

---

[1] Study conducted by the Massachusetts Bankers Association in 1993.

in liquidation debt is paid off before the shareholders receive any payments: the level of equity provides security for the lender.

In the case where the loan is sought to provide funds for an acquisition or for some purpose other than the direct support of operations, the bank may insist on additional equity to preserve the existing debt/equity ratio. Bankers have expressed this requirement as, "If this investment is such a good idea, why are you asking me to take all the risk?"

The assessment of a borrower's capital is not so much a measure of creditworthiness as it is a measure of lender protection. It has become more important in last few years as the banks have experienced a widespread banking crisis.

Capital is often evaluated through ratio analysis. Bankers benchmark leverage and liquidity ratios such as debt/equity, current ratio, and inventory and receivables turnover.

## Cash Flow

**Cash flow** is generally defined as the net income of the business plus any noncash expenses such as depreciation, depletion, amortization, and extraordinary additions to reserves.

The estimate of future cash flows helps the bank to assess the borrower's ability to service the debt being evaluated. The issues relate first to meeting the interest requirements and then to the repayment schedule. If the company's cash flow projections do not indicate comfort in covering these requirements, banks will not make the loan.

Banks evaluate financial statements even when both the lender and the borrower know that the projected growth of the business will consume all of the cash generated. Cash flow analysis assesses the company's ability to project the generation of cash that will permit the company to return the funds to the lender. Because of this requirement, companies often make unrealistic projections of working capital or underestimate the need for supporting assets. Otherwise, it requires assumptions such as funding all incremental fixed assets with externally generated funds.

In some cases this last assumption suggests that the company will have to return to the bank for more funds for asset acquisition. This criterion may be satisfactorily addressed within a strategic plan that identifies an exit strategy—a plan to bring substantial new equity into the business some years later. This topic will be discussed in greater depth later.

Again, bankers benchmark using cash flow ratios such as cash flow adequacy, operating cash index, mandatory cash flow index, and debt coverage.

## Collateral

**Collateral** is an asset or a group of assets pledged to secure debt. The security assures the lender that, in the event of failure to make contractual payments on the debt (default), the lender may take possession or control of the asset(s) and dispose of them to recover the value of the loan.

To be good collateral, the assets must have recognized value in the market. During the early 1990s, the markets for many assets used for collateral, notably real estate and machinery, declined in value, resulting in an under-protected position for many banks. The subsequent foreclosures (claiming the assets for the lenders), put a number of companies out of business and further depressed the markets. This, in turn, created wider losses for the lenders and exaggerated the economic recession.

Good collateral is never a substitute for a bad loan. In the late 1990s many bankers learned this lesson the hard way. Collateral that they thought would provide more than adequate value should the borrower not meet the loan obligation was not marketable at a sufficient price or at all. This was particularly true of real estate in the Northeast and California, and, to a lesser extent, in other parts of the country. Similarly, equipment collateral lost much of its value as the used machinery markets softened.

Even though collateral will often be required, a well-trained banker will never make a loan based principally on the perceived value of collateral.

## Conditions

The strength of the economy and of the specific industry of the borrower also influences the availability of credit. In a weak economic period credit is harder to obtain because lenders are concerned that the business will be adversely affected and the loan will be jeopardized. Similarly, if the borrower's industry is suffering, the borrower will have a harder time, even if the company is actually doing well. And the reverse is true, too. A strong economy and a strong industry will ease the availability of credit. It is said that "a rising tide lifts all boats."

A banker recently noted[1] that **"Conditions"** has, for his bank, become an overriding criterion. If the economic conditions of the industry and the general marketplace are not positive, credit will not be offered. This particular bank, which is an aggressive small business lender, has become very sensitive to the tenor of the marketplace and the overall economy as indicators of loan success.

## Competition

As included in credit criteria, **competition** can be viewed in two different ways. The competition may be related to the lender or to the borrower.

The lender's competitors will have an influence on the availability of loan funds from the chosen lender. If one competitor is lending aggressively to increase market share, the other lenders in the same market will become more aggressive, and funds will be more readily available, even for marginal loans. Conversely, if previously aggressive competitors tighten up or encounter difficulties, the entire lending community will limit the availability of credit.

When considered in relation to the borrower, the evaluation of competition takes into account the borrower's position in the market and its ability to compete with others in the same market. For example, a company seeking funds may have a good application from every consideration, but if it is

---

[1] A discussion between the author and Tim Fahey, Vice President of Middlesex Savings Bank, Natick, MA.

seeking to compete with very strong and aggressive market players, the amount of credit extended may be restricted or controlled more tightly than if the competition is weaker, less well organized, or fragmented.

## Credibility

**Credibility** is not one of the "C" words normally presented, but the credibility of the borrower is becoming more and more a critical part of the assessment. Often borrowers have only limited financial and operational history. With the fluidity of banking relationships more the norm than the exception, lenders are finding it necessary to rely on the information provided or confirmed by others.

Credit references are very important, but references are not particularly indicative of creditworthiness. Even in those instances where a company is virtually insolvent, it is likely that there are three or four vendors with whom the company has maintained a good payment record.

These are the credit references the company provides. The information garnered from these references will be positive and, in the absence of any conflicting reports, would indicate that the potential borrower is a good risk. If all of the references are small and local, their value as corroborators of company-provided information may be limited. On the other hand, if the references are larger firms or are national in scope, these references may be more useful.

Similarly, financial information provided by the applicant that includes financial statements audited by a CPA will carry more weight than will statements without such confirmation. The reputation of the CPA will reflect positively on the applicant, particularly if the CPA firm is well known and well respected by the lender. In some instances an audit opinion by a highly regarded local firm will be much more valuable in establishing the credibility and the creditworthiness of the applicant than will a similar audit opinion by a much larger regional, national, or even "Big Five" firm. On more than one occasion, bankers have gone on record as preferring a local firm's evaluation. In a study of banks' lending to small businesses, presented by the Massachusetts Bankers Association (1993), 76 percent of all lenders stated that they would like to see the company's accountants or attorneys when making a loan to a company.

Another way that creditworthiness is evaluated is through one of several credit rating organizations such as Dun and Bradstreet, Fitch, Moody's, and Equifax. These agencies gather credit experience information relative to many companies from many of the vendors in the marketplace. They also gather financial statements, legal filings, and other information, all of which they report to subscribers and use to establish credit ratings on companies. Many vendors rely on these ratings when making their own credit decisions.

## Competence

Lenders first defined **competence** as the managerial ability of the people who own and run the business. Very often, the founders of entrepreneurial enterprises start their businesses because they have a good idea, a solution for a real business problem, or a better way to achieve some technological objective. However, they do not have substantial managerial experience and are not equipped to direct their business successfully as it moves beyond the very basic levels. The provider of funds is very concerned that the additional resources that he or she is being asked to provide will be managed properly and the additional business size and strength that the money will enable will be handled effectively. Many companies grow much faster than their management can handle, but the entrepreneurs often do not recognize this or are unwilling to relinquish management control to an outsider, fearing they will simply not "understand" the business to the extent necessary. Frequently, even if they do recognize and acknowledge the need, they do not have the hiring and selection skills to choose the proper manager to handle the task. This is the competence measure.

The mezzanine lender mentioned in the last chapter included the following paragraph in their announcement brochure:[1]

> The single most important factor in our investment decision is the quality of the people who make up a company's management team. We expect them to have both the requisite technical expertise for their industry as well as the broad managerial skills required to grow the company.

## Communications

The same lender also added **communications** to the list of criteria. He noted that a customer who has established a relationship with the bank before seeking funds and who has a reputation for keeping the bank informed is a much more attractive borrower than someone who only comes to the bank when funds are needed. The extension of this is that an application will be more successful if it includes the structure and frequency of communications, whether it involves reviews, submission of financial reports, periodic updates on the business situation, or other opportunities for the lender or investor to see and understand what is happening. There is a general fear of the unknown, and if what is being done with the money is unknown, the fear on the part of the provider is substantial.

## BANKING RELATIONSHIPS

The nature of the banking environment is changing rapidly. In the late 1980s bank financing was fairly accessible, even for marginal borrowers. The credit market was more restrictive a few years later. Today, it is relatively easy, but more restrictive than in the late 1980s and it varies as conditions change. Also, where, in the past, banks offered free services to attract clients, today nearly all services carry fees that necessitate a cost/benefit analysis before agreeing to them.

---

[1] Brochure issued by Citizens Bank introducing their mezzanine lending subsidiary, 1997.

In the past a loan generated sufficient income for the bank that it could stand on its own. With today's relatively low interest rates, a bank cannot earn a sufficient return from a loan by itself. As a result, all bank credit decisions are based on the entire banking relationship and whether or not the entire relationship produces a sufficient yield to make a loan attractive. As you read the next few pages, keep in mind that at the time of this writing (April 2000), the prime interest rate is 8.25 to 8.5 percent.

It is important, therefore, for a bank customer to understand the bank's perspective and perform the same analysis that the bank does. It is as essential for a bank customer to get a proper return for its funds as it is for the bank to get a proper return for its funds.

This analysis draws on the same information presented in the preceding pages. It is important to continuously ask the question, "How does this strengthen the financial position or results of the company?"

## Defining Debt

As noted earlier, the most common source of funding for a business is debt financing. The definition of debt includes such terms as *obligation to pay*, *owing*, and *amount owed*. All of these terms signal that money or some other item of value is due from the borrower to the lender. Debts are not incurred and things are not loaned without an expectation of return of the original plus some added value, which may or may not be tangible, in accordance with some agreement and, generally, a timetable.

For our purposes we will focus on monetary debt, incurred either because money was borrowed and needs to be returned or because some other resource or product was acquired in return for an obligation to pay for it.

Because accounts payable reflect an obligation and a commitment to pay (just as much as a formal note does), we will look at vendors as sources of debt financing. Vendors, along with banks and all other funding sources, expect to be paid or paid back in accordance with a plan or a schedule.

## Bank Structure Dictates Loan Interest Rates

A bank is a business. Therefore, its management has a responsibility to earn a return for the bank's shareholders, just as a business' management has that responsibility toward the business' shareholders. Therefore, the bank must charge a rate on the loan that will enable it to make such a profit.

For the following example, we will use as a basis the financial statement of a fictitious but typical small regional bank we will call the Composite National Bank. Its most recent Balance Sheet and Income Statement are presented in Exhibits 9–2 and 9–3 and are referenced in the following sections.

The rate that a bank charges for a loan is a function of the costs that the bank has to cover and the profit it wishes to make. To understand how a loan is priced, we must understand the cost structure of the lending institution.

## The Cost of Bank Funds

Recognizing that banks can only generate income by lending money, either to borrowing customers or to the government or by charging fees for its services, it is important to understand the costs and expenses that must be

## xhibit 9–2

**Balance Sheet for Composite National Bank (in millions)**

*Assets*

| | | |
|---|---:|---:|
| Cash and due from banks | $ 133.31 | 9.3% |
| Federal funds | 306.58 | 21.4% |
| Investments | 120.91 | 8.4% |
| Loans | 820.71 | 57.2% |
| Allowance for credit losses | −19.53 | −1.4% |
| Net loans | 801.18 | 55.8% |
| Property, plant and equipment | 47.91 | 3.3% |
| Other assets | 25.48 | 1.8% |
| Total assets | $1,435.37 | 100.0% |

*Liabilities and Equity*

| | | |
|---|---:|---:|
| Deposits | $ 970.26 | 67.6% |
| Purchased funds | 346.10 | 24.1% |
| Other current liabilities | 7.41 | 0.5% |
| Long-term debt | 24.68 | 1.7% |
| Total liabilities | 1,348.45 | 93.9% |
| Contributed capital | 36.04 | 2.5% |
| Retained earnings | 50.88 | 3.6% |
| Total equity | 86.92 | 6.1% |
| Total liabilities and equity | $1,435.37 | 100.0% |

covered by the yield from those loans. Since the loan is an asset, it is obvious that the most meaningful performance measures for a bank relate to return on their assets, loans, rather than revenues.

Funding, regardless of source, comes with a cost. The cost may be measured as interest expense, as dividends, as fees (requirements imposed as conditions for the funding), or as earnings that belong to the shareholders. Cost is a critically important consideration in determining the type of funding to choose. Funding that is too expensive defeats the purpose of seeking funding. When we understand how rates are determined, we will be better prepared to negotiate rates and requirements.

The first cost area to consider is the cost of funds because this expense to a bank is comparable to cost of goods sold in other industries. Those expenses that are directly related to the generation of income helps to determine the cost of funds.

Remember that the yield on a loan includes both the interest income and the fees that are part of a borrowing relationship. Determine the bank's gross profit by relating interest expense to total income. By comparing interest expense to interest and other income, you can readily see the relationship between revenues and gross profit. Further, by comparing interest expense to total deposits and borrowed (or purchased) funds, you can begin

## xhibit 9–3

**Income Statement for Composite National Bank**

| | | |
|---|---|---|
| Interest income | $122.70 | 75.82% |
| Other income | 39.13 | 24.18% |
| Total income | 161.83 | 100.00% |
| Interest expense | 71.97 | 44.47% |
| Operating expenses | 55.44 | 34.26% |
| Operating income | 34.42 | 21.27% |
| Provision for loan losses | 10.57 | 6.53% |
| Earnings before taxes | 23.85 | 14.74% |
| Taxes | 8.58 | 5.30% |
| Earnings after taxes | $ 15.27 | 9.44% |

to understand the yield that the bank must achieve on its loans, its productive assets.

Looking at the Composite National statements (rounded to simplify the computation), we can see that

Interest income  =  $123 million
Other income  =  39 million
Total income  =  $162 million

Remember that other income includes fees and other charges that the bank imposes for the services it offers.

Total deposits  =  $970 million
Purchased funds  =  346 million
Total resources  =  $1,316 million
Interest expense  =  $72 million

Therefore, for Composite National, cost of funds ($72 ÷ $162) equals 44.4 percent of revenues, not too different from the percentage relationship that cost of sales bears to sales in many product-based businesses. Cost of funds may also be described as ($72 ÷ $1,316) or 5.5 percent of loanable funds. This approach gives us a way to relate costs to the pricing of a loan.

While 5.5 percent may seem high, remember that a bank's loanable funds are not only short-term demand notes and savings deposits that carry a low interest rate. They are also borrowed funds, individual and commercial CD's, longer-term deposits, and "jumbo" certificates, all of which carry negotiated (generally higher-than-market) rates.

Cost of funds may be presented in equation form as

$$\text{Cost of Funds (CF)} = \frac{\text{Interest Expense (IE)}}{\text{Deposits (D)} + \text{Purchased Funds (PF)}}$$

$$\text{CF} = \frac{\text{IE}}{\text{D} + \text{PF}}$$

For Composite National, CF = 72 ÷ (970 + 346) = 5.5%

## Operating Expenses

We can assess operating expenses in the same way. The bank's operating expenses may be compared to other business' selling, general, and administrative expenses (S, G, & A). Just as S, G, & A represent the costs of operating a business, so, too, these operating expenses reflect what it costs the bank to provide services. On a relative scale the bank's operating expenses may be higher than the S, G, & A expenses of, for example, a manufacturing company, because of the high cost of personnel, facilities, and security. Also, bear in mind that the cost of funds to a bank is similar to only the cost of raw materials in a manufacturer.

Veribanc, Inc., a bank rating company, commented that bank operating expenses continue to rise, spurred on in part by increasing regulatory demands. They concluded that operating costs would not routinely decline in the future, providing impetus for the current bank merger trend. This is clearly a significant contributor to the bank consolidation movement of recent years and will continue to be a focus of bank management effort, as operating expenses are most controllable by management. As you continue this analysis, you should recognize that this is the only area that the bank can manage directly.

The merger activity is one way in which banks can decrease the percentage of revenue devoted to S, G, & A expenses. With each merger of banks serving the same area, layoffs and branch closings reduce the amount of overhead expense in the surviving institution. Furthermore, because revenues are additive, the percentage for S, G, & A is also reduced, enabling the surviving bank to price its loans more competitively.

Examining Composite National's statements, we can see that

Operating expenses = $55 million.

As a percentage of revenues ($162 million), this translates to 34.0 percent. As a percentage of loanable funds ($1,316 million), the operating costs equal 4.2 percent. Expressed as an equation:

$$\text{Cost of Operations (CO)} = \frac{\text{Operating Expenses (OE)}}{\text{Deposits (D) + Purchased Funds (PF)}}$$

$$CO = \frac{OE}{D + PF}$$

For Composite National, CO = 55 ÷ (970 + 346) = 4.2%

An examination of operating expenses as a percentage of loanable funds will often identify a bank that will be an attractive takeover target. When you borrow money for your business, you would like to borrow from a bank that will continue to be your lender. Banks that are targets for takeover add an additional area of concern for the manager.

## Loan Losses

Because loan losses are a significant concern and because loans outstanding are so much greater than annual revenues, banks include a separate recognition of the risks inherent in their business. In predicting their performance they specifically estimate loan losses and incorporate this risk element into their planning and their pricing.

In Composite's case, the loan loss provision was $11 million, equal to 6.5 percent of revenues and equal to 0.8 percent of loanable funds. Recognize also that the Balance Sheet allowance for credit losses ($20 million) represented 2.4 percent of all outstanding loans. The allowance reflects loans considered in jeopardy but not yet written off. In fact, early in the 1990s during the banking crisis, the provision for loan losses exceeds the remaining loan loss reserve, meaning that a significant loan volume was recognized as problematic and also deemed truly uncollectible in the same year.

It is important to note here that as you assess the strength and security of banks, whether for deposits or for loans, you should examine the footnotes to the annual report as well as the financial statements. Included in the footnotes is an analysis of the loan loss provision and the loan loss reserve. Also included is a statement relating to the total volume of loans considered at risk. If the loan loss reserve is not adequate to cover all of the loans considered to be problem loans, you can reasonably conclude that the bank may be faced with additional loan write-offs. Additional write-offs will apply more pressure to the bank's Balance Sheet, perhaps requiring that the bank call some outstanding loans to increase its liquidity, seek an increase in equity to strengthen its Balance Sheet, or take some other action that will affect bank customers.

As we have with the other measures, we can present the loan loss provision in equation form.

$$\text{Cost of Loan Losses} = \frac{\text{Provision for Loan Losses (PLL)}}{\text{Deposits (D)} + \text{Purchased Funds (PF)}}$$

$$\text{CLL} = \frac{\text{PLL}}{\text{D} + \text{PF}}$$

For Composite National, CLL = 10.57 ÷ (970 + 346) = 0.8%

## Profit Criteria

Banks are expected to be profitable just as other businesses are, but, as noted earlier, the measurements are somewhat different because of the great disparity between assets and revenues. In manufacturing companies, for example, a statistic widely used to assess performance is total asset turnover (sales ÷ total assets). Such a measure relative to a bank is meaningless. Banks consider a profit equal to or greater than 1 percent of assets to be acceptable or even good. Composite National's profit of $15 million is equal to 1.1 percent and would, therefore, be acceptable.

To arrive at profit after tax, the measurement basis, we must accommodate taxes, which will differ from bank to bank. In Composite's case, the profit before taxes as a percentage of revenues equals 14.74 percent. As a percentage of loanable funds it equals 1.8 percent. Taking taxes into account, the after-tax result of this pre-tax profit level is 1.1 percent of assets.

$$\text{Profit before Tax (PBT)} = \frac{\text{Profit before Tax}}{\text{Deposits (D)} + \text{Purchased Funds (PF)}}$$

$$\text{PBT} = \frac{\text{PBT}}{\text{D} + \text{PF}}$$

For Composite National, PBT = 24 ÷ (970 + 346) = 1.8%

## COMPARISON TO TRADITIONAL BUSINESS COST STRUCTURE

Let's compare the traditionally formatted Income Statement results of Composite National Bank to a similarly structured Income Statement developed from the average results of several publicly held industrial companies. We will see that the two statements are not wildly different.

Exhibit 9–4 is intended to assist you in relating bank operations to business results that are more familiar. It highlights the fact that banks' financial results may be viewed comparably to those of other businesses. This fact is important because banks use their anticipated financial results to determine

### xhibit 9–4

**Comparison of Bank and Company Income Statements**

|  | Composite National | Composite Industries |
|---|---|---|
| Sales | 100.0% | 100.0% |
| Cost of sales | 44.4 | 63.6 |
| Gross profit | 55.6 | 36.4 |
| Operating expenses | 34.3 | 26.9 |
| Operating profit | 21.3 | 9.5 |
| Interest/other | 6.5 | 3.7 |
| Earnings before tax | 14.8 | 5.8 |
| Taxes | 5.3 | 2.6 |
| Earnings after tax | 9.5% | 3.2% |

their loan pricing. Stated in another way, the results we have presented above for the Composite National Bank may be presented in terms of the loanable resources of the bank and used as the basis for loan pricing.

| | |
|---|---|
| Cost of funds | 5.5% |
| Cost of operations | 4.2 |
| Cost of loan losses | 0.8 |
| Profit before tax | <u>1.8</u> |
| Required average loan yield | <u>12.3%</u> |

It is true that some classes of loans, such as credit cards for example, will carry higher interest rates, subsidizing the yield required on less risky loans. However, these high rate loans are much riskier than the average loan for the bank. Therefore, in estimating the required yield on a loan relationship, this required rate build-up is a reasonable overall estimate.

Composite National represents a sound bank of modest size with an average mix of clients. Other institutions may have somewhat different costs depending on their size, financial strength, loan risk, or other characteristics. For example, a bank that is perceived to be unstable, perhaps because of higher than average loan losses, will have a higher cost of funds and a higher risk adjustment. It may also have higher operating costs for loan management and collection expenses. On the other hand, a bank that serves only a commercial clientele may reduce its operating costs below those other banks by offering only business transactions and providing fewer retail services.

## Bank Debt Pricing

Just as with other businesses, a bank must price its products to cover its costs and to yield an acceptable profit. When we looked at Composite National Bank, we recognized a cost structure that required a loan yield of 12.3 percent.

It is important that a borrower, before entering into any negotiations with a bank or anyone, determine the provider's required yield. This knowledge will make it much easier to reach a mutually satisfactory outcome.

Clearly, any pricing mechanism must cover the costs and satisfy the profit objectives of the selling entity. Otherwise, the entity cannot survive. Although we are using a bank to represent all lenders, we must recognize that a bank is confronted with some regulatory, as well as some convention-based, interpretations. Specifically, if a bank makes a commitment to provide funds to one borrower, it may not commit those same funds to another borrower. Therefore, the bank must, for pricing purposes, assume that the borrower will utilize all the funds that are committed.

From both the lender's or the borrower's perspective, the measurement of loan pricing is the yield divided by the funds actually loaned:

$$\text{Computed Yield} = \frac{\text{Revenues Generated}}{\text{Funds Actually Provided}}$$

But pricing a loan is not easy. Every borrower has an idea of what rate he or she is willing to pay, usually related to the "prime rate," which is the rate that a bank charges its more creditworthy customers. Therefore, comparing a borrower's actual borrowing rate to the prime rate has become synonymous with creditworthiness. As a result a borrower, when offered a loan at several percentage points above prime, generally interprets such an offer as an insult. When market interest rates fall below the costs that a lender must cover, the lender must find creative ways to increase the loan yield to the required levels.

## Loan Pricing Example

Consider the loan pricing example in Exhibit 9–5 to see this situation.

How can we make the loan arrangement in Exhibit 9–5 more palatable to the borrower without asking the banker to compromise significantly on the yield required by the bank, a request that cannot be satisfied?

As should be obvious from the example in Exhibit 9–5, even though the bank explains compensating balances as added security, they really do not represent any security at all because the amounts required to be kept on deposit for compensating balances are really not loaned at all. Rather, the compensating balance serves to increase the effective yield on a loan to the level the bank needs in order to meet its financial requirements. Therefore, it should be negotiable as long as it serves that purpose.

Borrowers often focus on the nominal interest rate rather than the effective cost of a loan. In the example in Exhibit 9–5, once the nominal interest rate barrier has been overcome, a mutually acceptable arrangement can be established.

If the borrower has done the proper analysis, he or she will understand the bank's cost structure and will, therefore, recognize the yield that satisfies that cost structure. While a rate that works out to approximately three points over prime seems high for a creditworthy account, the costs dictate that rate. Acknowledging that, the borrower may negotiate a trade-off, offering to pay a higher stated rate in return for relief from one of the compensating balance requirements.

The rate in Exhibit 9–6 is much more attractive and clearly the best that the bank can do considering its costs.

When interest rates fall much below the levels outlined in Exhibit 9–6, the bank will find it very difficult to structure a loan that will meet its yield requirements. As interest rates fall, the bank pays out lower interest rates and its cost of funds is lower, but all other elements remain the same. Therefore, if we assume a cost structure consistent with Composite National's, with the cost of funds reduced from 5.5 to 3.5 percent and with all other information kept the same, the required yield for a loan will be 10.3 percent.

However, if the prime rate is very low, such as the 6.0 percent it was in 1993, the borrower, seeking a rate of half over prime, would be willing to pay a rate of 6.5 percent, but the banker would be unable to suggest any scenario that would meet the bank's needs, even at a modestly higher rate. This helps to explain why, in a recession, interest rates may be very low but there may still be a credit crunch, with little availability of loans, even in a depressed market.

# E | xhibit 9–5

**Bank Debt Pricing Computation**

*Consider the following situation:*

A borrower with a seasonal business anticipates a working capital need that will average $400,000 and peak at $800,000. It is possible that the requirements could reach $1,000,000. Assume that the current prime rate is 9.5 percent and the borrower, recognizing that his company isn't really equal to the bank's very best customers, estimates that the loan rate should be half a point over prime, or 10 percent. The Composite National Bank loan policy committee, recognizing its cost structure, has established a minimum yield of 12.0 percent and a target, or average, yield objective of 12.5 percent.

In order to meet the bank's requirements and accommodate the borrower's expectations of a loan at "half over prime," the banker must insist on a combination of compensating balances, commitment fees, origination fees, and additional services to increase the total yield.

Since bankers must assume that all funds committed are loaned out, an interest rate of 10 percent on a line of $1,000,000 must really have an effective loan amount of only $800,000 or must generate additional income beyond the interest.

In this example, the banker might insist on compensating balances equal to 10 percent of the line plus 10 percent of the loan. This would result in an effective yield of 12.5 percent, satisfying the bank's target yield.

Interest yield:  $1,000,000 × .10 = $100,000

Loan amount:
$1,000,000 Nominal loan
 −100,000 10% compensating balance on the line
 −100,000 10% compensating balance on the loan
 $800,000 Effective loan amount

$$\frac{\text{Revenue}}{\text{Net Loan}} = \frac{100,000}{800,000} = 12.5\%$$

Before continuing, compute what the borrower sees, using the average loan balance of $400,000.

*The borrower calculates:*

Interest yield:  $400,000 × .10 = $40,000

Loan amount:
$400,000 Average outstanding balance
 −100,000 10% compensating balance on the line
 −40,000 10% compensating balance on the loan
 $260,000 Effective loan amount, which is inadequate

$$\frac{\text{Revenue}}{\text{Net Loan}} = \frac{40,000}{260,000} = 15.38\% \text{ or 5.9 points over prime}$$

Revising the computation to provide sufficient funds:

Interest yield:  $560,000 × .10 = $56,000

Loan amount:
$560,000 Average outstanding balance
 −100,000 10% compensating balance on the line
 −56,000 10% compensating balance on the loan
 $404,000 Effective loan amount

$$\frac{\text{Revenue}}{\text{Net Loan}} = \frac{56,000}{404,000} = 13.86\% \text{ or 4.4 points over prime}$$

In either case the borrower becomes very distressed by the rate, and in the case of lower amounts, doesn't get all the funds he or she needs. The nominal rate of the loan is the desired half-over-prime, but the effective rate is far higher.

## xhibit 9–6

### Continuing the Bank Debt Pricing Computation

We can recompute the banker and borrower positions if the stated rate of interest is raised one percentage point, to one and one-half points over prime, equal to 11.0 percent, and the compensating balance of 10 percent of the line is eliminated. Since in the bank computation each of the compensating balances is equal, it should be possible to negotiate the compensating balance on the line of credit so that it is no longer part of the agreement.

*The Banker's Computation*

Interest yield:    $1,000,000 × .11 = $110,000

Loan amount:    $1,000,000 Nominal amount of the loan
　　　　　　　 −100,000 10% compensating balance on the loan
　　　　　　　 $ 900,000

$$\frac{Revenue}{Net\ Loan} = \frac{110,000}{900,000} = 12.22\%$$

This rate is slightly lower but within the bank's acceptable range.

*The Borrower's Computation*

Interest yield:    $400,000 × .11 = $44,000

Loan amount:    $400,000 Nominal amount of the loan
　　　　　　　 −40,000 10% compensating balance on the loan
　　　　　　　 $360,000

$$\frac{Revenue}{Net\ Loan} = \frac{44,000}{360,000} = 12.22\%$$

or, more likely,

Interest yield:    $450,000 × .11 = $49,500

Loan amount:    $450,000 Nominal amount of the loan
　　　　　　　 −45,000 10% compensating balance on the loan
　　　　　　　 $405,000

$$\frac{Revenue}{Net\ Loan} = \frac{49,500}{405,000} = 12.22\%$$

Once this loan pricing issue is understood, the borrower and the lender can often arrive at a mutually agreeable arrangement. This is true for all liabilities management issues. As long as both the borrower and the lender understand the same things, it is generally possible to reach a deal acceptable to both parties.

Liabilities are accounting recognition of obligations we have undertaken. They represent amounts of money that must be paid back to lenders, either within one year (Current Liabilities) or beyond one year (Long-Term Liabilities). Managing these obligations is a critical task, helping to assure that resources will be available as the company needs them.

Liabilities include accruals, those accounting transactions that assure that the financial results reflect the activities of the period, but which may not yet be completed. The handling of accruals is a critical part of assuring the validity and usefulness of the financial statements.

The choice of whether to use short-term debt or long-term debt to fund the business is in part a decision by the management to follow a higher risk, higher profit path or a lower risk, lower profit path.

Short-term debt is:

• easier to get, because it is less risky to the lender
• less expensive, because it is less risky to the vendor
• riskier to management, because it must be repaid or renegotiated within a year

Long-term debt is:

• more difficult to negotiate, because it is riskier to the lender
• more expensive, because it is riskier to the lender
• less risky to management, because it does not need to be repaid as soon as short-term debt

## ANSWERS TO EXERCISES

### Exercise 9–1

*Assumptions:*

1. The Income Statement presented reflects an annual Income Statement.
2. All Income Statement lines (in 000's) are variable and dependent on sales.
3. Accounts receivable equal 60 days' sales.
4. Inventory turnover is 4 times (based on cost of sales).
5. That sales growth necessitates an additional investment in fixed assets of $150,000, to be funded by long-term debt already arranged.
6. Taxes are 50 percent.
7. Accounts payable equal 3/4 of a month's cost of sales.

| | | |
|---|---|---|
| Sales | $1,200 | $1,440 |
| Cost of sales | 800 | 960 |
| Gross profit | 400 | 480 |
| Operating expenses | 200 | 240 |
| Earnings before interest | 200 | 240 |

| | | |
|---|---:|---:|
| Interest | <u>80</u> | <u>96</u> |
| Earnings before taxes | 120 | 144 |
| Taxes | <u>60</u> | <u>72</u> |
| Earnings after taxes | 60 | 72 |
| Preferred stock dividends | <u>18</u> | <u>18</u> |
| Change in retained earnings | <u>$ 42</u> | <u>$ 54</u> |

**Step 1:** Calculate accounts receivable.    $200

**Step 2:** Calculate inventory.    $200

**Step 3:** Assume a 20 percent growth in sales. Compute the new Income Statement.

**Step 4:** Calculate new accounts receivable.    $240

**Step 5:** Calculate new inventory.    $240

**Step 6:** Compute the incremental assets assuming all other assets remain constant.

A/R $240 − $200 = $40    INV $240 − $200 = $40    $40 + $40 = $80

**Step 7:** Identify sources of funds to pay for these incremental assets.
$10 comes from Accounts Payable, $54 comes from Change in Retained Earnings
The remaining $16 must be borrowed or invested.

## Review Questions

1. Borrowing money:
   (a) reduces the amount of money required to be invested by share-holders.
   (b) increases the amount of money required to be invested by share-holders.
   (c) has no effect on the amount of money to be invested by share-holders.
   (d) provides additional money for use by shareholders.

2. Stretched or extended accounts payable means that a company:
   (a) is using vendor funds to help finance the company.
   (b) recognizes its obligation to pay its bills on time.
   (c) does not collect its receivable on time.
   (d) does collect its accounts receivable on time.

3. A revolving line of credit with a bank:
   (a) is a note payable for a fixed amount for a fixed time.
   (b) involves paying a note payable when funds are received and bor-rowing again when funds are needed.
   (c) is a continuous deposit that earns money at the bank's prime rate.
   (d) is limited to the amount needed the day the note is signed.

4. We are required to pay:
   (a) only the minimum tax stipulated in the tax laws.
   (b) as much tax as we can afford.
   (c) the amount of tax we think is appropriate.
   (d) enough tax to fund our fair share of government services.

5. In a cash accounting system credit sales:
   (a) transactions are recorded when the sale is made.
   (b) transactions are recorded only when the cash is collected.
   (c) cannot occur.
   (d) are called something else.

1. (a)

2. (a)

3. (b)

4. (a)

5. (b)

Do you have questions? Comments? Need clarification?
Call Educational Services at 1-800-225-3215, ext. 600,
or email at ed_svcs@amanet.org.

# *10*

# The Equity in the Business

*focus*

## Learning Objectives

By the end of this chapter, you should be able to:

- Describe the components of the equity section of the Balance Sheet.
- Distinguish between different forms of business structure.
- Explain the characteristics of the different types of equity.

## OVERVIEW

The equity component of the Balance Sheet contains the information relating to company ownership. While we have focused almost entirely on the corporate form for our discussion, the structure of the Balance Sheet and the Income Statement are consistent across all business forms. In today's marketplace, increasingly, there are variations on the basic business form based on a broad range of needs. Where there used to be only Proprietorships, Partnerships, and Corporations as business forms, today there are also Limited Partnerships, Limited Liability Partnerships, Limited Liability Companies, Real Estate Investment Trusts, S Corporations, Section 1244 Corporations, Trusts, Associations, and other entities structured to meet particular needs or situations. While each of these entity types has different characteristics, the generalized financial statement formats we have discussed are applicable to them all. Each will have an Income Statement, a Balance Sheet, and a cash flow statement, and while they may or may not be available to the public, they will be interpreted consistently and will respond to the same management actions.

When we deal with other than the corporate form, the Equity section will take on a different appearance, describing the ownership's financial interests with terms such as Owner's Capital, Partners' Capital, and similar words. These correspond to Common Stock and Additional Paid-in Capital. Retained Earnings will be consistently interpreted.

### The Rewards for Success

"As you all know, the board of directors met last week. They're thrilled with the results we've posted for the year, and they've asked me to talk to you about the stock purchase plan they're putting in place. This year for the first time you'll be able to purchase company stock as part of the company savings and investment program."

"That's great, Bob, but why are they making us purchase the stock? If we're doing so well, why don't they just distribute stock along to us?"

"There are a couple of reasons, Aleksei. If it were a gift, you might not value it so highly. And some people might not want to hold a lot of stock in the company. It's very risky to have all of your resources dependent on one source. So we think some people will want to stick with the large, professionally managed mutual funds that are already available"

"I understand what you're saying, Bob, but why are they making this offer? Won't it lessen the control of the current owners?"

"It will do that, Enrique. But it will make owners out of a lot of people in the company. Do you remember when we started these sessions, Enrique, that the purpose of a for-profit business is to maximize the wealth of the shareholders of the long run?"

"I do. And that's why I'm asking: Why would they want to share the wealth?"

"They want to share the wealth, so to speak, so that the people who work here have the same long-term objectives as the other shareholders. It's the people who work here—managers and staff and line workers—who really determine how well the company does. By giving you a piece of the company, the board hopes that your interests will be the same as theirs. Everyone will strive their hardest to make sure the company increases in value.

"Let's spend some time talking about this, so that you can go back and share the news with your department. People are going to have a lot of questions about why this is happening and whether it's good for them. You need to be prepared to answer those questions. We'll post an outline of the plan on the intranet at 11:30. People can check out the mechanics and the details there. But be sure you meet with everyone in your department today."

## EQUITY AND BUSINESS STRUCTURE

While there are several forms of business structure and more being developed almost daily, the principal structures are Proprietorships, Partnerships, and Corporations as described in Chapter 1. The differences in form appear in financial statements primarily in the equity section of the Balance Sheet. All of these businesses have traditionally structured Income Statements with revenues and expenses, interest, and tax computations. All of them have current assets and fixed assets, current liabilities and, at least potentially, long-term debt. When it comes to equity, the terminology changes and some of the treatment changes as well. Additionally, and more importantly, each of these business types have distinguishing characteristics that make them more or less attractive under differing circumstances.

Proprietorships are businesses with one owner who is responsible for everything. The proprietorship form does not really distinguish the business from its owner, as the owner takes on all responsibility for the obligations of the business, the management decisions for the business, and the financial control of the business. The proprietorship is easy to form, requiring minimal registration and legal filings. In fact, there may be no filing required at all unless the business is subject to some local tax reporting, such as sales or meals tax reporting. All of the income and expenses of the business are considered to be an extension of the proprietor, who includes the financial activities of the business in his or her personal income tax returns. The owner undertakes personal liability for the obligations of the company and its existence continues only as long as the proprietor chooses to continue it. A proprietorship technically does not survive the proprietor although the owner may transfer the business to another proprietor. There are many, many more proprietorships in the United States than any other business form, but they represent only a very small percentage of the business volume and business wealth.

A partnership, belonging to two or more partners, often has more strength and more flexibility than a proprietorship because it draws from the financial and managerial resources of more than one person and can, therefore, achieve greater size and complexity than most proprietorships. General partnerships involve all the partners in the obligations of the business, and in most general partnerships, each partner is responsible for all of the obligations of the business. Therefore, if one partner is unwilling, unable, or unavailable to pay for obligations of the business, the other partner or partners are obligated to cover them. This has led to a number of problems, which have been addressed by creating limited partnerships (LPs) and limited liability partnerships (LLPs). These entities, based on their structures, provide for protection for partners who are, in the first case, only financial partners, not active in the business, and, in the second case, partners who were not involved in the situations that led to the liabilities. The establishment of limited partnerships and limited liability partnerships has defined special rules and characteristics that dictate the way these entities are treated for legal and tax purposes. Partnerships are taxed only at the partner level, with the profits of the partnership assigned to the partners on the basis of their partnership agreement. Generally, there is a carefully constructed partnership agreement detailing the management relationships as well as the financial participations of all the partners. A partnership technically does not survive the departure of a partner, although the major partnership entities have defined the procedures for automatic reestablishment if a partner leaves or dies.

Corporations represent a relatively small percentage of the business entities in the United States, but they are responsible for the vast majority of all economic wealth and activity. In recent years tax considerations as well as issues related to Congressional desire to foster economic development have resulted in a number of variations to the traditional corporate form and structure. The basics remain, however. A corporation is considered an entity unto itself, separate and distinct from its ownership. Therefore, its life is not limited by the lives of its owners; the ownership may be transferred without any effect on the corporation. As a consequence, the capacity of a corporation to borrow money, for example, is not limited by the financial strength of the owners, a problem that faces proprietorships and partnerships. The liabilities of the corporation are the responsibility of the corporation; the owners' obligations are limited to the amounts of money they have invested and if the obligations of the corporation exceed the capabilities of the corporation to pay, the owners are not responsible for them.

Because corporations are not limited the way other business types are, they offer more ways to reward managers, notably through the opportunity to achieve an ownership position, making it easier for a corporation to fill out its management staffing. In today's marketplace, with the dramatic rise in high-tech start-up companies, the use of stock as compensation has become very popular. Similarly, corporations have more access to debt capital because the entity can be expected to continue, without a limit imposed because of the owners.

Corporations are taxed on their earnings. The owners are not taxed on these earnings unless the earnings are distributed as dividends. The owners are taxed on the dividends they receive and which are generally paid out of the after-tax earnings. This is often referred to as the problem of "double taxation," and it is one of the characteristics that differentiates corporations from other business forms.

## Preferred Stock

We will continue our discussion of equity focusing on corporate form, so the discussion that follows will look at the owners' equity specifically from a corporate perspective. In some corporations, the first line of the Equity section is Preferred Stock. Corporations, whose management wishes to distinguish owners from other investors who may not have an ownership role, issue Preferred Stock.

Preferred Stock is so named because it has certain preferences under special circumstances. For example, preferred stock does not generally have a vote on corporate matters or actions. However, under certain circumstances, such as if the company has not paid any preferred stock dividends for a specified number of periods, preferred stock owners may not only have votes but control the voting process. This preference for ownership of the interests of the preferred stockholders gives these investors some control over the management of their investment.

Other preferences include the right to receive cash dividends before any cash dividends may be paid to common stockholders. If the preferred stock is "cumulative," preferred shareholders have the right to receive all back dividends that were not paid before any cash dividends may be paid to common stockholders; and the right to receive repayment of invested amounts before any such redemption payments may be made to common stockholders if the management decides to liquidate the company. Unlike common stock dividends, dividend amounts for preferred stock are generally specifically defined, providing a clear value for each share. These preferences are really not very important, except if there is some prospect of financial difficulties.

However, some investors are interested in specific and predictable cash flows, and the dividends for preferred stock are generally higher than is interest on debt, because preferred stock, falling below debt in the repayment hierarchy, is riskier than debt, even subordinated debt. Therefore, the predictable dividends offered by companies through their preferred stock may be attractive to investors. Another reason for investing in preferred stock is a tax preference offered to corporations that invest in the stock of other corporations. The Internal Revenue Code offers a "dividends received deduction" equal to 70 percent of the value of such a dividend to the receiving corporation, increasing the after-tax value of such dividends. As a result, corporations with excess cash that they expect to be able to hold for at least 46 days, to satisfy a qualification rule, may choose to invest in the preferred stock of other corporations, purchasing the preferred stock so as to qualify for the dividend, holding the stock for the requisite time period, and selling the stock to reestablish the cash position in advance of its requirement. Thus, we can see how the marketable securities investment practices of one type of company relate to the capital funding needs of another.

Some preferred stock issues offer another type of opportunity for investors. **Convertible preferred stock,** in addition to the preferences identified above, may also offer the shareholder the opportunity, if desired, to convert the preferred stock into common stock at a defined rate. Often, this conversion privilege is offered when the stock price is low but expected to increase. The shareholder has the option to convert or not as he or she chooses, but will receive the higher dividends as long as the investment is held in preferred stock form. Therefore, if the common stock price is well below the conversion price, preferred stock will be held. If the common stock price rises, the shareholder has the choice, but can continue to hold the preferred stock and receive the dividends. If, at some point, the common stock price rises enough, the shareholder may opt to convert the preferred stock into common stock and then may choose to sell all of the common stock for cash that will be significantly higher than the original investment, or sell some of the common stock in order to recover the investment while continuing to hold some of the common stock in order to continue to benefit from the rising market price.

As you can see, understanding how finance works contributes to the shareholder's ability to judge investment alternatives. Obviously, the investor's ability to anticipate what will happen to the company and to its stock also helps. This ability comes from understanding financial management and financial reporting and being able to interpret the information contained in the financial statements and explanatory information provided by the company.

## Common Stock

Common stock represents the actual ownership of the company. The shares of common stock, if there is only one class, each signify an equal portion of the company. There may be a few shares, each with a relatively large portion or millions or billions of shares outstanding, each of which owns an infinitesimal part of the ownership. However, in widely held companies a relatively small percentage may represent a substantial and influential position.

Common stock may be issued for cash investment or as a reward for effort on behalf of the company. In the stock market of 1999, for example, there were numerous examples of companies entering the public market through an Initial Public Offering (IPO) and instantly making employees of the company, who received part of their early pay in stock, extremely wealthy overnight. These employees, who own a very small percentage of the company are benefiting from the sale to the public of a large number of shares, resulting in a significant dilution of their ownership position, but also translating into their wealth in terms of the market price of the shares after offering multiplied by the number of shares they hold.

Common stock ownership conveys certain rights to the owner, including the right to vote on certain corporate matters including the membership of the Board of Directors, the right to vote on the number of shares to be issued, the right to vote on matters that will guide management, and sometimes the right to preserve their ownership position in the event the company issues additional stock. This last right, included in the by-laws of some corporations and mandated by law in some states, is called a **pre-emptive right,** and assures that a shareholder cannot be diluted from a position of influence to one without influence without his or her consent. Perhaps the most important ownership right is to vote for the Board of Directors and through that vote to influence the direction of the company.

The value of the common stock shown on the Balance Sheet reflects only the par value of a share of common stock multiplied by the number of shares outstanding. It does not represent the amount paid for the common stock unless either the par value and the amount paid per share are the same or there is no par value for a share. The par value represents the minimum per share value that a share owner would be responsible for if the company fails. If the shareholder has already paid that amount, then the entire amount that he or she could lose is the amount already invested. This differs from the exposure to risk of proprietors or general partners in the other principal forms of company organization structure.

## Additional Paid-In Capital

The difference between the par value and the issue price of a share goes into the line identified as "Additional Paid-in Capital." This represents the rest of the capital invested by the shareholders that was received by the company. It has nothing to do with the price of a share paid on any stock exchange, over the counter, or between shareholders. For example, if a company issues shares having a par value of $1.00 for $25.00 each, the $24.00 difference between issue price and par value would be Additional Paid-in Capital. If these shares were issued in a public stock offering, and after the initial sale, a second investor purchased the shares from the first shareholder (through a broker) for $40.00 per share, the difference between the issue price, $25.00, and the purchase price, $40.00, goes to the seller of the shares (net of commissions and fees), and no additional money goes to the company.

## Retained Earnings

The amount of profit that the company earns and retains in the business, that is, does not pay out in dividends, is recorded as Retained Earnings. These amounts, adjusted each period for the profits after taxes and dividends, reflect the perceived success of the company and enhance the "shareholders' wealth."

The section of the Balance Sheet made up of Common Stock, Additional Paid-in Capital, and Retained Earnings represents the **book value** of the shareholders' ownership. The relationship of the book value to the market value is determined by the price-earnings ratio. While it has less to do with the book value of the shares than the current market atmosphere, it is generally felt that those corporations that are performing well and increasing the book value of the shares are also going to perform well in the market. Therefore, the measures of performance and financial success generally focus on Balance Sheet and Income Statement based performance measures.

## THE INVESTMENT MARKETPLACE

Companies that are looking for equity, whether for the first time or the umpteenth time, often look to the public for funding. The sale of common stock is the most frequent method of raising substantial capital. The first time stock of a particular company is sold to the public is called the **Initial Public Offering (IPO)** and it often occurs with substantial publicity. Because these companies are often unknown to the investing public, there are a complex series of meetings and presentations to bring the company to visibility in the investment community. The IPO process is a very exciting and challenging time for the company, and provides a unique opportunity for the management to tell its story to the investment press and the investment bankers and brokers who will help make the offering successful. There is a lot written about the IPO process, a very specialized marketing effort.

Subsequent offerings, to add more equity and provide funding for expansion or acquisitions, generate less publicity and are managed carefully to provide capital and not disrupt the orderly market for the stock. In some cases the additional equity is marketed to one or a limited number of institutional investors in a **private placement** that effectively brings substantial capital into the company and limits the disruption to management inside or the existing market outside.

When companies go public, that is issue stock in a public offering, they often seek to be listed in a stock market that provides a place or a system for the orderly purchase and sale of the company's stock from shareholder to shareholder. These markets do not directly involve the company at all, although the management is very aware of the value placed on the shares in the market. There are a number of organized exchanges where company shares are traded. The largest and most well known of these is the New York Stock Exchange (NYSE). Here approximately 3,700 major companies have their stock issues listed and traded daily. Approximately 900 additional companies are listed on the American Stock Exchange and several hundred more companies are listed on several smaller regional exchanges in Boston, Philadelphia, Cincinnati, San Francisco, and elsewhere. In recent years a new and very vibrant market, the Nasdaq (National Association of Securities Dealers Automated Quotation) market has become the center for much stock market activity. More than 5,100 companies have their stock traded through the Nasdaq, which operates entirely over-the-counter, that is without a formal exchange location, through telephone and electronic communications between brokers buying and selling on behalf of customers. Daily trading volume on Nasdaq is comparable to that on the NYSE and is increasing. More recently, an alternative marketplace has arisen through the Internet and it is likely that electronic stock trading will become the predominant means of exchanging shares in the years to come. In fact, there have been a number of smaller companies that have issued their shares to the public over the Internet, by-passing the traditional markets entirely.

## ACCOUNTING FOR EQUITY

One of the ways to consider the accounting effect of different transactions is to consider what will happen to equity as a result. For example, if a company incurs a loss, the ultimate effect, through the closing of the Income Statement into retained earnings will be a reduction in shareholders' equity. Similarly, if a company increases its sales, the ultimate effect will flow through the Income Statement to affect the owners' wealth. While many analysts focus on the effect on cash of different actions, the real concern should be directed toward the net worth of the company.

Consider this flow: Assume that the sales department wants the company to carry more inventory in order to satisfy customers' desires for faster delivery. To purchase more inventory, the company will either have to use its cash or borrow funds from a bank. If it uses the cash, the company will reduce its ability to invest the cash and increase its income. If the company borrows money, it will incur interest expense, lowering both profits and retained earnings. The cost of carrying the inventory, as we saw, results in higher expenses and therefore will have a depressing effect on profits. The test of the suggestion, therefore, must be to assess whether the higher investment in inventory will add to or detract from the profits of the company, ultimately affecting the equity on the Balance Sheet.

To complicate this analysis a bit, consider whether the impact will be to lower profits this year, but increase them in future years. Now we must add time value of money considerations as well as assessment of the likelihood of the forecast to the assessment. These kinds of considerations are a significant part of the financial management of a business and require that the managers understand the financial implications of such decision making.

The equity on the Balance Sheet reflects the ownership of the company. Whether the company is a proprietorship, partnership, or corporation, or some variation on one of these, the equity remains the reflection of the ownership values.

The principal forms of business structure are:

1. Proprietorship
   - single owner
   - general liability
   - limited access to capital
   - ease of establishment and dissolution
   - single level of taxation
2. Partnership
   - multiple owner
   - general liability
   - somewhat limited access to capital
   - partnership agreement usually required
   - automatic dissolution when partner leaves
   - single level of taxation
3. Corporation
   - one or more owners
   - limited liability
   - required legal documentation for establishment
   - easier access to capital
   - unlimited life
   - double taxation of earnings on distribution

Common Stock represents ownership and has certain rights, such as voting for directors and on major corporate actions.

Preferred stock is investment that may include an ownership interest under certain circumstances and provides certain preferences, predominantly related to the distribution of corporate assets.

Most accounting transactions eventually have an impact on equity, generally through the Income Statement, where the net income after taxes and dividends becomes the change in retained earnings.

## Review Questions

**1.** A corporation is characterized by:                                  1. (a)
  (a) limited liability for the owner, unlimited life of the entity, and
      double taxation.
  (b) unlimited liability for the owner, limited life of the entity, and
      single taxation.
  (c) limited liability for the owner, limited life for the entity, and sin-
      gle taxation.
  (d) unlimited liability for the owner, unlimited life for the entity,
      and single taxation.

**2.** Preferred stockholders receive certain preferences related to their   2. (a)
  ownership including:
  (a) a priority claim on dividend payment and priority over common
      stock shareholders in the event of liquidation.
  (b) first chance to vote for management.
  (c) priority claim on assets ahead of everyone else.
  (d) guaranteed protection for their investment.

**3.** The Common Stock line on the Balance Sheet represents the:            3. (b)
  (a) total market price paid for the stock shareholders own.
  (b) total par value of the stock the shareholders own.
  (c) the accumulated earnings of the company.
  (d) the net worth of the company.

**4.** The profits of a corporation are recorded in the Balance Sheet       4. (c)
  each period when the books are closed into:
  (a) common stock.
  (b) additional paid-in capital.
  (c) retained earnings.
  (d) long-term debt.

**5.** The ownership of the business is reflected in the:                   5. (d)
  (a) current assets on the Balance Sheet.
  (b) total assets on the Balance Sheet.
  (c) total liabilities on the Balance Sheet.
  (d) equity portion of the Balance Sheet.

Do you have questions? Comments? Need clarification?
Call Educational Services at 1-800-225-3215, ext. 600,
or email at ed_svcs@amanet.org.

# Financial Planning

*focus*

## Learning Objectives

By the end of this chapter, you should be able to:

- Differentiate between strategic or long-range planning and annual or operational budgeting.
- Describe the similarities and the differences in the planning process resulting from company size and ownership.
- Identify the differing roles of different managers in the planning and budgeting process.

## OVERVIEW

This chapter puts the financial management information previously presented into the context of business financial planning. The structure of the planning continuum, from the business plan to the strategic plan to the operative plan to the detailed components of the departmental budget, is discussed. The chapter will include specific discussion of departmental budgeting and relating the departmental budget to the larger entities of which the department is a part. At the end of this chapter the student will understand the whole process and how his or her responsibility fits into the whole picture. The operating manager will recognize the effect the department or the project has on the company results.

Before beginning the discussion of specific aspects of planning, a brief look at the different types of plans and planning is appropriate. A company's planning includes several parts, some major and some less so. The major parts are the *business plan*—an overview of the company, its people, products, markets, customers, and competitors; the *strategic plan*—the long-range view of the company; the *annual budget*—a detailed prediction of revenues, expenses, and results; the *capital budget*—the identification and evaluation of major investments in equipment and resources; and the *cash budget*—the prediction of cash flows and cash needs including magnitude and timing.

### Planning and Replanning

"Good morning, Bob. How's it going?"

"Things are great. I just want to remind you that it's time to update the strategic plan and to confirm this year's budget."

"Why do we have to confirm the budget, Bob? We've been analyzing our results—and our financial statements—all year long. Everything should be under control."

"We've all kept our eyes on a number of financial measures this year, Pat. But when we pull together all of the information for the strategic plan, we may find that something in the environment has changed. If it has, we should revise our thinking as early as possible to avoid any nasty surprises. Don't you remember earlier in the year when we put together the proposal for a new machine for the A600s. We hadn't accurately forecast how much capacity we'd need to keep up with orders when we prepared last year's budget. It's always a good idea to reconfirm the plan at the beginning of the year."

"Will we be using the same forms we used in the past, Bob?"

"No. We revised the forms this year. You'll get a call from the budget department and one of the analysts will set up an appointment to meet with you. After all you've learned about our accounting system and financial analysis over the past year, you shouldn't have too many questions."

## THE ESSENCE OF FINANCIAL PLANNING

Every company does some planning because, even if there is nothing formal, the manager or managers have a reasonable idea what to expect in the months to come. However, if there is no formal planning and budgeting process, the projected results for next year are only "guestimates" and little can be done to assure that the expected results will become real.

It has been said that, in reference to a managerial choice, the decision not to decide is a decision. Similarly, the decision not to plan in effect is a plan. Such a plan is to let "the chips fall where they may." This is akin to the ship's captain, in the heat of battle, ordering the crew to "Ready!" "Fire!" "Aim!"

A business, any business that intends to be successful, is too important to leave to chance. Planning and budgeting permit management to control the results, to avoid surprises. In a well-managed business there will be no surprises. Planning enables business management to anticipate what the business will do and to identify the resources necessary to assure that what is desired is possible.

Consider the numerous popular sayings that relate to planning. Here are a few, all of which convey the same message.

- Failure to plan is planning to fail.
- If you don't care where you are going, it doesn't matter which road you take.
- Plan your work and work your plan.
- A plan provides the means to differentiate between managing and reacting.

### Exercise 11–1: A Planning Exercise

*INSTRUCTIONS:* ☛ As we begin this chapter, think about planning a family vacation that will involve driving to a place you've never visited before. You pull out a road map of the United States. As you begin your planning, where do you look first?

_____

_____

_____

_____

Your first reaction in Exercise 11–1 is to find your home city, a touchstone, the comfort of familiarity. But. almost immediately, you look to find your destination and you plan your trip back from the destination to the starting point.

Business planning is very similar. We start with what we know, the most recent financial and operational results, but quickly move to consider our objectives. We then build a plan to get there. Some companies extrapolate the future from the past and trends, but that is like planning your trip without looking at your destination. You might get where you want to go, but it may be by accident. We can all think of companies that predicted their future based on past achievements.

One such example is IBM, which planned its future predicated on its dominance of the mainframe computer market, ignoring the direction that the market was taking, the movement toward minicomputers and personal computers. Only because they recognized soon enough that the road had changed and then only because they had enough resources to withstand the dramatic change of business direction did they succeed in redirecting the company. The cost to the company to achieve this recovery was staggering, in both money terms and people terms.

### Exercise 11–2: When a Business Loses Its Focus

*INSTRUCTIONS:* ☞ Look at newspapers and periodicals, such as *The Wall Street Journal, Business Week, Industry Standard* and other business publications and think about business news you remember from past years. Can you find examples of companies that lost their strategic focus? What were the consequences?

_____

_____

_____

_____

_____

The essence of financial planning is to recognize the factors that will influence your company's success and to prepare to exploit or respond to them, whichever is appropriate.

## BUSINESS PLANNING—A CONTINUOUS PROCESS

Planning and budgeting can be described as the coordination of information inside the business to predict future results. This chapter describes briefly a continuous planning process that keeps planning current rather than letting it become a once a year interruption to be completed as quickly as possible, often without regard for validity or congruence with corporate objectives. Planning should be continuous, current, and comprehensive—involving all levels and all functions of the organization. The process depends on the commitment of the people who have to deliver the results if the company is to meet its objectives.

Strategic planning and operational budgeting are not difficult, per se, but many companies do not do a particularly effective job of either. As a result, their planning documents do not provide accurate plans, and this, in turn, discredits the process and leads to the deterioration of subsequent efforts.

The most effective planning system is a comprehensive planning process involving people at all levels that converts the planning effort from a once-a-year interruption of business activity to a continuous update of what's going on. As a result, planning and budgeting becomes an integral part of the management of the business.

Therefore, the soundest source of sales forecast information will be the salespeople, as long as they understand the purpose of the information. Similarly, the staffing and expenditure requirements to deliver the projected products, revenues, and profits are best predicted by those who have to deliver the results. The people who are continuously in the market should generate the best competitive information. In a similar vein, the sales force, the people in the organization closest to the marketplace, will often identify the new products most likely to succeed.

## Roles of the Key Players

In the planning process within a company, everyone has roles and responsibilities. Most important, the manager who coordinates the budgeting and planning activities, often a financial manager, is *not responsible* for, nor does he or she *do* the budget or plan. Rather, the budget manager's role is to facilitate and coordinate.

Top management sets the rules for the planning, defines the overall strategy, and establishes the overall objectives. They also approve the budgets and plans and retain overall responsibility for the process and its results.

Operating managers are responsible for the specifics related to their areas. They provide the detail, determine what actions are to be taken, identify what resources they will need in order to be successful, and communicate, often through the budget manager, to the other parts of the company the needs and expectations as well as their contributions to the operations of other managers.

The budget manager oversees the process and provides the interface that assures that all managers receive the information they need. Among the budget manager's duties are the setting of the timetable, development of the planning assumptions, coordinating organizational communications, assuring the avoidance of conflicts between departments and disciplines, and assurance that the final plan document, whether it is the budget or the strategic plan update, is internally consistent and clear in its projections and requirements.

## Overview of the Financial Planning Process

It's easy to incorporate a comprehensive financial planning program into the regular activities and responsibilities of the various functions within a company. By doing so, the managers of the company recognize the integrated relationship between historic experience, current activity, and future growth and success. The most knowledgeable people regarding any aspect of the business operations are the people who have to perform in the function. The integrated nature of business operation means that business planning and financial planning are virtually synonymous.

## Planning Sequence

Because business planning information builds on the information that precedes it, a company that follows a comprehensive planning process, will develop its plans from the general to the specific, from the longest range to progressively shorter time periods, taking advantage of the accumulated knowledge.

Therefore, after the closing of the financial books for a year, early in the new fiscal year, the planning for the next cycle begins. Bear in mind that plans already exist for the current fiscal year. We will assume for this discussion that the fiscal year and the calendar year coincide, although, obviously, there is no need for that to be true.

The first step is to review the business plan that is already in existence to be sure that it still applies. If it does, that is good. If it does not, management should confirm the company vision and its mission statement or modify them as required. Management then updates the other sections of the business plan, delineated in the next section, to reflect the new or revised corporate direction.

The updated or confirmed business plan serves as the starting point for the strategic plan, the five-year guide to business development that defines the expectations for each of the five years and the steps necessary to reach the strategic goals established. The strategic plan is updated every year: the first year of the plan drops off, as it is history; each succeeding year is updated; and a new fifth year is added.

This updating usually occurs in the first half of the year. The capital budget is generally initiated in conjunction with the strategic plan and sometimes adjusted as part of the annual budget when, during the assessment of capacity, other near-term investment needs are identified. The capital budget decisions are incorporated into the cash budget. The **cash budget** focuses attention on the availability of the cash resources needed to meet the business's requirements.

## DIFFERENT KINDS OF PLANS

As noted earlier, there are five primary parts to the planning process: Business Plan, Strategic Plan, Operative Plan or Budget, Capital Plan, and Cash Plan. Other planning elements are of lesser importance and are really components of the other plans. For example, the advertising budget and the media plan detail the timing and the costs of the year's advertising program, one element of the annual budget. The advertising program may also be an important part of the strategic plan and may significantly affect the cash budget, particularly with regard to timing. Similarly, the product development plan is an integral part of the strategic plan and will also have an effect on the annual budget and the cash budget. It could also contribute to the capital budget.

It should be noted that once prepared and approved, the budget remains in place for the entire year. If management chooses to update or revise the budget as the year progresses, doing so creates another comparison basis, but does not replace the "original" budget.

As a structure for this chapter, we will look at each of the major planning types and tasks, beginning with the business plan.

### Business Plan

The business plan is frequently prepared as an overview of the company, often as a basis for attracting financing. And it is often the first effort at planning because it provides a good starting point and usually exists even for entities that have no formal planning process. Business plans are updated annually, most easily at the time the strategic plan is prepared. Because some of the information and some of the structure of the business plan differ from the strategic plan, keeping the business plan current should be a separately assigned task.

In today's marketplace there is a great deal of talk about business plans. Most companies seeking financing must submit a business plan. Many prospective employees ask to see the business plan before deciding whether or not to join an organization. Vendors and customers, asked to become parts of a strategic alliance, ask for a copy of the business plan. There are many, many books and pamphlets on how to write a business plan. The American Management Association offers seminars and self-study courses on how to write a business plan.

A business plan is the first step to formalized strategic planning. As noted earlier, it describes the company, its people, its products, its markets, its customers, and its competitors. Most of the time a business plan is written to satisfy a specific purpose and, therefore, very specifically addresses the requirements of the audience to whom it is directed.

A business plan can also serve the business itself well. As such, perhaps it should be written first with the internal organization as its audience in mind and then edited to satisfy an outsider. When management looks at the business plan as a necessary evil, they will write it for the outsider; when management looks at the business plan as the first guide to internal development, they will write it to satisfy the inside organization. With either audience, the structure of the business plan will be basically the same. In the annotated outline that follows, drawn from requirements presented by a venture capital provider, a plan organization is suggested that will serve any audience.

Obviously, the business plan, often originally written to attract financing, will serve as a very thorough starting point for the continued strategic and operative planning that follow from it. Keeping the business plan up-to-date is a part of the strategic planning effort that the company should be pursuing.

## Strategic Plan

The strategic planning process is the long-range look at the company's future. The most commonly used time frame is five years, but it really should be reflective of the product life cycle for the business. For this reason, the strategic planning period for an aircraft manufacturer would be significantly longer than five years and for a software developer significantly shorter.

The strategic plan is updated annually, removing the year just completed, adjusting and modifying the remaining four years (including the year currently underway), and adding a new fifth year. Thus, in the 2000 renewal period, January through June 2000, 1999 would be dropped off (it is now history), 2000–2003 would be updated based on the 1999 experience, and 2004 would be added. Note that the first period being updated, 2000, is the same period for which a detailed budget has been prepared. Therefore, the strategic planning process provides an initial confirmation of the budget and its

## Exhibit 11–1

### A Business Plan Outline

**A. Cover Sheet**
This first page identifies the company, its location, its telephone number, and its principal contact person.

**B. Executive Summary**
This first section, no longer than two pages, identifies the essential information about the company, its products, and its markets. It provides a very brief history of the company, including a summary of business accomplishments and its current financial condition. Because it is so short, it is probably the most important section of the entire plan. It requires the author/manager to focus on the most important aspects of the business, to concentrate on that which will make the company stand out and which will provide the appropriate return to the investor. This focus will also provide the strongest push toward company success.

**C. The Company**
This section describes the company, its history, and its plans for the future. It provides more detail than the Executive Summary and provides a lead-in for the sections that follow. Included in this information will be a statement of the general philosophy of the management and its approach to the marketplace. Management has the opportunity here to provide a general discussion of strategy and tactics. Elements of this section will be expanded in the Product, Market, and Competition sections.

**D. The Product**
This section describes the company's product(s) and the characteristics that make it special. Performance information and comparison to competitive items are essential. Technical details may be included or presented in an appendix depending on complexity and specific characteristics. Often this section describes in general the future generations of the principal products, providing some guidance for the development of the strategic plan content.

**E. The Market**
The description of the market focuses on customers and the way that the marketplace functions. Of specific interest is how the market is defined. Does the company focus on a narrow niche or on a larger, more general market? The key elements here are how the company gets its product to its customers and the marketplace mechanism itself. Is the market driven by demand or by supply? Is the market well-defined or is the company trying to establish a new or next-generation product?

**F. The Competition**
With whom is the company competing? What are the relative strengths and weaknesses of the competition? What are the market shares of the competitors? How well does the company compare to its competitors? If the company is seeking to establish a new approach to the market and therefore has no competition, how and by whom is the market currently being served?

**G. The People**
This section describes the key people in the company. Resumes or biographical information is presented in sufficient detail that a reviewer can assess the technical competence, the experience, and the disciplinary balance of the organization. It is important to remember here that different reviewers have different motivations but, among the outsiders, none wants to be involved in the operations of the company and so wishes to be sure that the people are sufficiently strong that direct managerial involvement will not be necessary.

Exhibit continued on next page

**Exhibit 11–1** continued from previous page

## H. The Financial Picture

Financial statements and analysis are presented in this section. Not only is historical financial information included, generally covering three years or more, but projected future results are also included. Commentary covers what happened, why it happened, and what was done about what happened. It also covers what is expected to happen, why it is expected, and how the company expects to assure that it does happen. If no history exists, the financial projections must be clear enough that the reviewer can understand and accept these as reasonable.

## I. Appendix

In this section additional detail covering any and all of the topics included in the body of the plan is presented. Being a supplement it can be separated from the body and distributed only to those who have a need to know. This section can present more detailed product, market, and competitive information. It can include copies of brochures and promotional material as well as more detailed biographical information on the principals and more detailed financial information.

The body of the business plan should not exceed 30 to 40 pages, but should be complete enough that any reader has a clear understanding of all aspects of the company. The appendix to the business plan can be as long and as detailed as is necessary.

achievability. Furthermore, the detailed expectations of the first strategic plan year are known and form a well-constructed starting point for the five-year plan.

If, perhaps, the business' situation has changed, this is the first opportunity to revise the plans and expectations. Many companies review their operations periodically and issue revised estimates to keep management informed. Therefore, included in the update process is a review, reassessment, and revision of the action steps and benchmarks that make up the essence of the strategic plan.

### Defining Strategy

*A company's strategy is the basic business approach it follows to meet its goals.*
Strategy has been described in many ways. Among them are:

- A plan of action intended to accomplish a specific goal.
- A carefully devised program for achievement of objectives.
- Skillful management to attain an end.
- Guidelines for making directional decisions.

The strategy defines the methodology for accomplishing goals, strategic objectives. The tactics the company employs are chosen to move the company toward its goals while adhering to the overall strategy. Often, the strategy of a company can be summarized in a single word or short phrase.

**xhibit 11–2**

**Corporate Strategies Defined**

Here are some specific words and phrases often used to identify corporate strategy:

- Innovation
- Market leadership
- Low price—high volume
- High price—specialty products
- Me too
- Second source
- Price leader
- Service leader
- Quality leader
- Demand pull—market image
- Supply push—promotion oriented
- Product range breadth
- Universal product—one size fits all
- Distribution strength
- Technological leadership
- Exploitative

Take a moment to think of companies that exemplify some of these strategies. More than one word may apply to a company.

---

### The Difference Between Strategy and Tactics

The terms used to define business strategy are generally drawn from military analogies. **Strategic objectives** describe what we want to accomplish, the **strategy** itself defines the approach we plan to take to achieve the objective, and the **tactics** are the explicitly identified action steps that will be employed to succeed.

Therefore, to achieve $10 million in sales is not a strategic objective any more than to destroy 10,000 enemy soldiers is a strategic objective. To be the recognized leader in the industry based on product quality may be a valid strategic business objective in the same way that controlling the entrance to a valley, or surrounding an enemy army on a particular battlefield, may be a valid military objective.

To achieve such an objective the company will undertake action steps keyed to quality and reliability. Steps targeting market share and lowest cost will not be appropriate. The military commander may undertake a flanking maneuver or rush the ridge overlooking the valley. Damming a river running through the valley will not help the military leader succeed.

Carrying this analogy a little further, consider the following scenario.

Our strategic objective is to surround the enemy army, containing and capturing their large force, while minimizing our casualties.
    We will undertake a flanking strategy.

Therefore, Unit 1 will circle to the east following the river. Unit 2 will circle to the west along the ridge. Unit 3 will confront the enemy from the south to permit Units 1 and 2 to succeed.

If all units complete their action steps, the strategy will be successful and the strategic objective will be accomplished. An examination of the strategy and the tactics employed by the allied forces in the Gulf War in 1991 demonstrates the successful military implementation of such a strategy and the related tactics.

## The Operative Plan or Annual Budget

Consider this scenario:

Tom has managed the specialty light production at Bright Brites for five years now. Every year top management asks his unit to submit their budget figures for the next year—based on sales projections provided by the company's large sales force. It's budget time again, and Tom is meeting with his top people to finalize their budget figures.

Tom:    Listen up, team. These figures are way too high. I've checked the sales forecasts and this year's production numbers. There's no way that we'll need to spend this amount on inventory or on labor. What gives?

Janice:    Well, I've been the business manager here for three years now, and every year we give management our best estimate . . . and every year they come back to us and ask us to reduce the number. Usually they want us to give back about 18 percent. I'm tired of having to cut corners when I see other units getting more than enough in their budgets. I just bumped up all the numbers by 20 percent.

Tom:    I can see why that approach is tempting, Janice, but how can top management—or any of the rest of us, really—get a good handle on what's going on if they don't start with good numbers?

Do you think the behavior of top management at Bright Brites encourages managers to submit accurate budgets and plans? Or, is it more likely that managers will inflate their needs so that they will have the resources to meet their functional obligations? Is management's strategy an effective tool for getting everyone in the organization committed to striving for the corporate objectives?

Long-range planning and annual budgeting enable management to establish goals and define expectations. They also identify benchmarks for evaluating accomplishment in the financial and measurement periods that follow.

By itself a strategic plan or a budget is nothing more than some papers containing words and numbers. For the planning process to be successful, all members of the organization for which the budget or plan is written must accept and acknowledge as valid the objectives established. The achievement of this buy-in by the people who must deliver the results is one of the most important points in this entire program. The active participation and commitment by the operating organization is essential to the successful planning of the business and achievement of the plans established.

When we examine the process, the same conclusions apply whether we speak of the strategic plan or the budget. For example, a strategic plan develops goals and expectations both in financial and in operational terms. A well-constructed plan includes a clear set of actions that, when completed, achieve the objectives. The same will be true, in more detail, for the annual budget.

The action steps in all planning activities must include time frames and criteria for measurement. The result is a set of benchmarks, or evaluation points, that enable the manager to assess progress toward the goal.

## PROJECTING THE FINANCIAL FUTURE

Planning uses the analysis of what has happened in the past to guide the projection of future results. It helps answer questions like: Do we like the results of the past? What can we do to improve them?

In the projection of future performance, the starting point is the past. If the manager and the organization feel that the past performance was satisfactory or exemplary, then it is used as the basis for the next expectation.

If, on the other hand, the performance was not satisfactory, some significant change must be incorporated into the projection. Planners must look at past performance to see how it must be altered. In a properly prepared plan, the projected results, whether of some major revenue or expenditure item or of a less important element, must identify those factors that will make the result differ from the past.

Review the following exercise which was presented in Chapters 7 and 9. Continue to follow its development. Think about the benefits of knowing early in the planning process how much additional financing your business will require.

### Estimating Financial Requirements

### Exercise 11–3: Initial Exercise in Estimating Financing Requirements

*INSTRUCTIONS:* ☛ The forecasting of financing requirements is both an out growth and an input to the planning process. In this exercise, the need for funding, which has an impact on the projected balance sheet may also have an impact on the final estimate of interest expense that ties back to the operating budget.

*Assumptions:*

1. The Income Statement presented is an annual Income Statement.
2. All Income Statement lines (in 000's) are variable and dependent on sales.
3. Accounts receivable equal 60 days' sales.
4. Inventory turnover is 4 times (based on cost of sales).
5. Assume that sales growth necessitates an additional investment in fixed assets of $150,000, to be funded by long-term debt already arranged.

6. Taxes are 50 percent.
7. Accounts payable equal 3/4 of a month's cost of sales.

| | |
|---|---:|
| Sales | $1,200 |
| Cost of sales | 800 |
| Gross profit | 400 |
| Operating expenses | 200 |
| Earnings before interest | 200 |
| Interest | 80 |
| Earnings before taxes | 120 |
| Taxes | 60 |
| Earnings after taxes | 60 |
| Preferred stock dividends | 18 |
| Change in retained earnings | $ 42 |

**Step 1:** Calculate accounts receivable.

**Step 2:** Calculate inventory.

**Step 3:** Assume a 20 percent growth in sales. Compute the new Income Statement.

**Step 4:** Calculate new accounts receivable.

**Step 5:** Calculate new inventory.

**Step 6:** Compute the incremental assets assuming all other assets remain constant.

**Step 7:** Identify sources of funds to pay for these incremental assets.

| **Assets** | |
|---|---:|
| Cash | $ 20 |
| Accounts receivable | 200 |
| Inventory | 200 |
| Current assets | 420 |
| Fixed assets | 750 |
| Total assets | $1,170 |

| **Liabilities** | |
|---|---:|
| Accounts payable | $ 50 |
| Notes payable | 200 |
| Accruals | 10 |
| Current liabilities | 260 |
| Long-term debt (15%) | 400 |
| Preferred stock (18%) | 100 |
| Common equity | 410 |
| Total liabilities/equity | $1,170 |

In projecting the Income Statement and Balance Sheet, the budget manager sets up the means to project financial resource needs. As you know from the earlier versions of Exercise 11–3, this company can project a financing need of $16,000 in addition to the cost of the new fixed asset. The new fixed asset is part of the capital budget that was discussed in Chapters 6, 7, and 8.

## Capital Budgets

The capital budget is a separate task for two reason: it is affected by the strategic planning effort and is confirmed and may be modified by the annual budgeting process, and it often involves substantial funding, more than is available through normal business operations.

## Cash Budgets

The operating budget just described focuses on operations. What we sold and what we made are measured as current activities. However, as we all know, the activities of today do not represent the cash flows of today. The cash picture may be entirely different from the daily activity.

The cash budget presents only cash activities, and it presents them as they are expected to occur. For example, the raw material we need to manufacture our product may be purchased several months before it is to be used. Such a transaction in normal accrual accounting would appear as:

| | | |
|---|---|---|
| Inventory | 1,000 | |
| Accounts payable | | 1,000 |

This same transaction has, at the time it occurs, *no* cash effect at all. While the company has an obligation, there has been no effect on cash availability per se.

When the bill comes due and is paid 30 days later, there is another bookkeeping transaction:

| | | |
|---|---|---|
| Accounts payable | 1,000 | |
| Cash | | 1,000 |

This obviously has a cash effect that must be recognized. The important point here is that the cash transaction, if planned, would be planned for 30 days after the inventory acquisition date.

Similarly, when a sale is recorded, the transaction appears as:

| | | |
|---|---|---|
| Accounts receivable | 1,500 | |
| Sales | | 1,500 |

Again, no cash transaction has occurred, and no cash recognition takes place. When the customer remits payment, the bookkeeping transaction is recorded as follows:

| | | |
|---|---|---|
| Cash | 1,500 | |
| Accounts receivable | | 1,500 |

As with the purchase above, if the cash transaction had been planned, it would have been planned for a date significantly after the date of the sale.

When the bookkeeping transaction does not have any cash effect, it is not included in the cash budget. Therefore, accruals, depreciation, and amortization entries, and other noncash records do not enter into the cash budget.

Cash inflows result from receipt of sales revenues, generally a significant time after sales have been recorded and long after payments have been made to cover the costs of the products or services have been sold. Other sources of cash inflows are financing actions, recovery of prior year tax overpayments, and other similar nonrepetitive items.

To determine the appropriate schedule of cash receipts, the budget manager will refer to prior years and develop a pattern of customer payments. The sales are then converted to receipts following the pattern of the company's experience in prior years. If management decides to change its receivables management policy, perhaps increasing the collection effort in order to improve the time of cash receipts, such a change can easily be accommodated.

## Exercise 11–4: Cash Management

INSTRUCTIONS: ☛ Prepare a cash budget for Testco Extra Company for the first quarter of 20X2, based on the following assumptions.

The budgeting session of the corporate finance department of Testco Extra has received the following sales estimates from the sales department:

|  | Total Sales | Credit Sales |
|---|---|---|
| December Year 1 | $1,000,000 | $800,000 |
| January Year 2 | 630,000 | 490,000 |
| February Year 2 | 640,000 | 580,000 |
| March Year 2 | 720,000 | 600,000 |

The company has found that, on average, about 25 percent of its credit sales are collected during the month when the sale is made, and the remaining 75 percent of credit sales are collected during the month following the sale. As a result, the company uses these figures for budgeting.

The company purchases raw materials equal to 50 percent of the next month's sales, and payments for those purchases are budgeted to lag the purchases by one month. Various disbursements have been estimated as follows:

|  | January | February | March |
|---|---|---|---|
| Wages and salaries | $200,000 | $300,000 | $150,000 |
| Rent | 47,000 | 20,000 | 34,000 |
| Other expenses | 12,000 | 14,000 | 16,000 |

In addition, a tax payment of $200,000 is due on January 15, and $40,000 in dividends will be declared in January and paid in March. Also, the company has ordered a $100,000 piece of equipment. Delivery is scheduled for early January, and payment will be due in February. The company's projected cash balance at the beginning of January is $100,000, and the company desires to maintain a balance of $100,000 at the end of each month.

After developing a cash budget, compare these two alternative scenarios:

1. The company's collection pattern is 15 percent in the month of sale, 45 percent in the following month and the remainder in the second month after sale. For these parts, assume that November's sales were $600,000, of which $500,000 were credit sales.
2. Purchases are 60 percent of sales instead of 50 percent. Assume a collection pattern that follows the original scenario.

There are several major planning activities in a business. Therefore, planning should be continuous rather than conducted as a stop and start process.

Planning includes:

- Business Plan—updates as business needs change
- Strategic Plan—updated annually
- Operative Plan (Annual Budget)—prepared carefully every year
- Capital Plan—Prepared every year and drawn from the strategic plan and the annual budget
- Cash Plan—prepared annually, drawn from the annual budget, and the capital plan

Planning involves all managers. It is not the responsibility only of the budget manager. All managers have major responsibilities if the budgeting and planning process is to be successful.

## Review Questions

1. Planning in a business should be done:
   (a) as quickly as possible, so not to interfere with work.
   (b) continuously throughout the year.
   (c) using as few people as possible.
   (d) whenever the bank asks for it.

   1. (b)

2. The strategy of a business is:
   (a) the detailed revenue and spending plan for the year.
   (b) the action steps a company undertakes to achieve its goals.
   (c) the basic business approach it follows to meet its goals.
   (d) an overview of the company.

   2. (c)

3. Successful planning requires:
   (a) good guesses about the future.
   (b) active commitment and buy-in by the operating organization.
   (c) a good friend who works for your competitor.
   (d) a superior spreadsheet program and someone who can use it.

   3. (b)

4. The cash budget should be prepared:
   (a) first, so everyone knows how much cash the company will have.
   (b) whenever the bookkeeper has time, since it is independent of the rest of the process.
   (c) as early as possible, so the banker will have time to get the company the money it needs.
   (d) last, because it depends on the information in the operating budget and the capital budget.

   4. (d)

5. A strategic plan develops goals in:
   (a) both financial and operational terms.
   (b) in financial but not operational terms.
   (c) in operational but not financial terms.
   (d) in neither financial nor operational terms.

   5. (a)

Do you have questions? Comments? Need clarification?
Call Educational Services at 1-800-225-3215, ext. 600,
or email at ed_svcs@amanet.org.

# Relating Departmental Performance to the Big Picture

## Learning Objectives

By the end of this chapter, you should be able to:

- Relate the principles of finance and accounting to your functional responsibility.
- Apply financial management principles to personal financial activities.
- Explain the financial relationship between your functional activities and the company as a whole.

## OVERVIEW

Throughout this course we have looked at financial and accounting information from the perspective of the company as a whole, without considering the relationship of the responsibilities of a manager to the financial effects on that company. In this chapter we want to summarize this relationship and consider the various levels within the company and how they are interrelated. To do so, we will begin at the highest level, the company, and progress to more specific and detailed levels, through subsidiary, division, department, group, and individual. In doing so we will summarize the material that we have examined throughout the first eleven chapters.

### Financial Management Is Everyone's Responsibility and It Is Continuous

"You've all learned so much over the past year, I think you could come to work in accounting and finance—except that we need you right where you are. The fine work you did as part of the planning process really demonstrates how much you've accomplished."

"Does that mean we won't be having these meetings anymore?"

"No, Les. I think it's important to talk about company performance with people throughout the company. You all know how your department fits in and where it has an impact on financial results.

"This year we'll continue to see how we can improve results and we'll talk about some other performance measures that can help us monitor the internal and external environments. When the marketplace is changing so fast, we don't want to get caught with our radar down."

"Bob, I want to thank you for all the time you've given us this year. It's great to know how we measure up financially, and it's given all of our employees better tools for making this a stronger and more efficient place to work. I'd really miss these meetings if we gave them up."

## THE INVERTED TRIANGLE: FINANCE FROM BROAD TO SPECIFIC

In the consideration of financial management topics, the discussion has looked at all aspects of assets, liabilities, revenues, and expenses and at all aspects of managerial responsibility. As early as Chapter 1, it was clear that the rules of finance apply equally well at the broadest level of business management and at the individual level, whether in your business role or in your personal role. The essence of financial management is the same throughout. The conclusion to this course will reiterate this general applicability.

### The Company

In all of our discussion thus far we have looked at issues from a company standpoint. The company produces financial information derived from all of the activities of its different parts. The financial information, in the form of standardized financial statements, summarizes financial performance and conditions in a manner and following a format that can be understood by most readers.

Obviously, the performance of the various subsidiaries, divisions, departments, groups, and individuals that make up the company, in aggregate, yield the results that are reported. As we consider these subparts of the company, we will see where each impacts the company as a whole. By understanding what each part does and how it contributes to the whole, you should see where your efforts and actions appear in the financial performance of the company and should, therefore, be able to understand how you will influence the results.

This discussion will also enable us to consider another concept that affects the **consolidation** of the company as a whole. In some cases the work of one segment serves as an input to another. The results may not always be a situation of simple addition. Consider a subsidiary that sells to another subsidiary of the same company. The selling entity is expected to make a profit on its efforts so it charges a profit on top of its costs. However, since the two subsidiaries are within the same company, there is no real profit to the company as a whole. Therefore, when two parts of the same company sell to each other, the accountants must eliminate the **intracompany profit**. This **elimination** assures that the consolidated company results are correct.

The consolidation process takes place outside either subsidiary so that the managements of both are in a position to assess the performance of their own company. This, too, is important because companies reward their managers on the basis of performance and should not penalize one management group because it assisted another management group to meet its goals. The whole area of eliminations and consolidations is an area of contention and misunderstanding and needs to be managed very carefully.

## Subsidiary

Each subsidiary of a company is generally treated as if it were independent. Each such company has its own goals and objectives, budgets and plans, and all are expected to perform according to their budgets. They are measured against their plans, against last year, and sometimes against their competition, in all cases using the financial information they produce.

All of the detail we have covered in these chapters applies to a subsidiary in exactly the same manner as it applies to the parent company. In most cases a subsidiary has all the assets of an independent company. Sometime, the parent company will take on responsibility for credit and accounts receivable management. More frequently, it will control the cash of the entity, metering it out on an as-needed basis. If the parent does control the cash, the cash manager will maintain clear records as to the source of the cash under management, making it possible to create records that show, on the books of the subsidiary, a "Due from Parent" account in lieu of cash. A comparable "Due to Subsidiary" account will reflect the same balance, but on the liability side of the parent. It is accounts such as these that will be eliminated in consolidation and that will permit the subsidiary to measure its performance just as the parent company measures the performance of the company as a whole.

Because subsidiaries will be competing with each other for capital investment funds, all recommended projects for capital investment will require return on investment computations. Those projects, from among all the divisions, that offer the highest return will generally get the most favorable attention. Sometimes, projects are deemed critical that may offer less return than other projects in other subsidiaries. The decision to fund one of these is part of the prerogative reserved for top management. Such decisions, however, do not detract from the validity of the capital investment decisions criteria.

## Division

A division is a part of a company. As such, it may not have a Balance Sheet. The division often uses assets that are shared, so attempting to construct a full Balance Sheet will not be meaningful. However, we are still able to report on the performance of the division and to focus attention on several critical aspects of the division's financial situation.

It is certainly possible to construct a divisional Income Statement, measuring sales, costs, and expenses, and comparing these results to budget, to prior years, and to other companies in the same field. Annual budgets for divisions of companies are usually focused on the Income Statement and the management of accounts receivable and inventories. If the division is generating increasing sales, at higher margins, is controlling its inventories and its accounts receivable, its management will receive high marks from the parent company's executives.

The performance of the division, reflected in the divisional Income Statement, will be measurable in all of the operating lines of the parent company's Income Statement: sales, cost of sales, and the individual lines of the operating expense section. It will be harder to attribute interest expenses to a division because of the shared expenses that remain at the parent level and because of the shared assets used to generate the sales. For example, if a company uses one manufacturing plant to produce the products for three divisions, it may be very difficult to separate out responsibility for the cost of the production equipment. Company cost accountants will compute standard, or expected, product costs and will charge the division for those costs, absorbing variances at the plant and corporate level. If one division sells more than was anticipated and another sells less than planned, there may or may not be an adjustment to costs, but such adjustment will be arbitrary.

However, it will be possible to measure the use of and cost of working capital. Divisional management will generally be held accountable for the investment in accounts receivable and inventory related to the division's customers and products. There may be a "capital consumption" charge, an attempt to have divisional management recognize the cost of carrying its working capital assets. The management will also be expected to track average collection period and inventory turnover because these assets are specifically related to the divisional activities.

Divisional capital investment evaluations are generally prepared in conjunction with other functional areas, such as operations. The division is generally responsible for sales, while the operations function is responsible for production and distribution. Therefore, in a company with a divisional structure, production is often designated as a separate division, the "manufacturing" division, and capital investment analysis will involve input from both entities.

## Department

Departments are often responsible for only a small segment of one or a few lines on an Income Statement. Nevertheless, the specific responsibilities of the department are visible in the Income Statement of the division, the subsidiary, or even the whole company. If it is the sales department, it is responsible for the top line of the Income Statement—or part of it at least. There will be sales budgets and forecasts, as well as expense budgets to guide the costs of generating those sales. Individual managers take on responsibility for specific aspects of the departmental activity, whether individual products or sales functions or support tasks to help achieve the goals. These functions are visible in the composition of the operations and expectations of the area.

Departmental budgets and measurements are more likely to be expense focused, with particular attention directed to key expense lines. For example, the advertising department will concentrate on the costs of advertising production and placement, on personnel costs, and on directly related support costs. There will be little or no attention paid to administrative expense, product cost, or development expense. On the other hand, the research and development department will focus on laboratory and testing costs, development expense, and technical research and will be only tangentially interested in selling costs or logistics.

Some departments or groups of departments may be considered cost centers, if they only involve expenses, or profit centers, if they have responsibilities for revenues as well. Cost centers and profit centers provide another breakdown of the detail within a company, permitting management to understand how the company results have been achieved.

## Group

As we focus on smaller and smaller economic segments, we look at finer and finer designations of cost and contribution. The media buying group of the advertising department is really only interested in the cost of media and the number of placements or contacts established, and measures its performance on the basis of these, often nonfinancial, measurements. Success depends on achieving benchmarks tied to the activities of the narrowly defined group. But here, too, the financial effects of the group are visible in the financial reports of all the entities above it. The consequences of overspending at the group level will be evident at the department levels and so forth. It really does not matter where you see yourself, it will be possible for you to identify how you affect the results of the larger and larger entities within the company.

## Individuals

Obviously, this tracing can be taken all the way to the individual working within a group. It is very important that each member of the group recognize that he or she has a real impact on the results of the segments to which he or she belongs. If everyone is aware of the effect brought to the entity, the overall performance would be better, wherever it is measured. This is the essence of a managerial program called "Open Book Management."[1] Open book management is built on the premise that each person has an impact on the financial success and condition of what ever entity is involved and the more that each person knows about this the better off the entire organization is. Open book management is operated on the assertion that if an individual, on any level and of any rank, understands how financial systems work and where they fit in the organization, they will respond by doing their job

---

[1] Open Book Management is an approach to financial management where a company provides detailed financial information to all employees and helps them understand how their actions and efforts affect company results.

better and paying more attention to necessary compared to discretionary or even careless expenditures.

It is certainly possible to assign each person within a group or department responsibility over some spending or some task. It is asserted that given such responsibility, the individual will do a better job of controlling costs and delivering results and it will be more likely than not that the people and the entity will deliver the results predicted in the budget. The more you know, the more likely you are to use the information effectively.

## THE RELATIONSHIP BETWEEN BUDGETS AND ACTUALS

When the budget has been conscientiously prepared, it will generally be a good predictor of the results the company will achieve. Therefore, a well-constructed and carefully prepared budget provides an excellent basis for evaluating the performance of the organization. The budget should be prepared in exactly the same format as the financial statements that are produced and disseminated.

On a regular basis periodic financial statements should be produced and compared to the budget that was established. The budget should not be changed during the year; it was the best estimate of what was expected and it should stand up all year long. The comparison that is thus produced will permit management, at all levels, to identify the changes from the budget assumptions, permitting management to develop responses when they are necessary as well as informed input to the next planning cycle.

Financial management is important at all levels within a company as well as at all levels outside the company. The principles are the same whether you are in a large company, a small company, an individual proprietorship, or a family setting.

It is important to recognize the interaction of revenues and expenses, assets and liabilities, and to recognize how your actions affect them.

It is important to recognize the relevance of financial reporting to management information and to recognize that financial reporting is not a foreign language. Everyone can understand it. Everyone can do it. Everyone can manage with it, and can do so better than without it.

## Review Questions

1. Intracompany profit is the profit that is earned on sales:  1. (b)
   (a) to end use customers.
   (b) between parts of the same company.
   (c) from the subsidiary of one company to the subsidiary of another company.
   (d) from one company to another.

2. It is possible to measure the consumption of working capital at the:  2. (a)
   (a) divisional level.
   (b) departmental level.
   (c) group level.
   (d) individual level.

3. Departmental budgets are:  3. (b)
   (a) revenue focused.
   (b) expense focused.
   (c) asset focused.
   (d) liability focused.

4. The budget should:  4. (c)
   (a) be changed whenever a significant change occurs in the market.
   (b) be changed every time the accounting period closes.
   (c) not be changed during the year.
   (d) not be changed from year to year.

5. As an individual financial manager, the principles developed for a company:  5. (a)
   (a) apply at all levels.
   (b) do not relate at all.
   (c) work only if you are in a large company.
   (d) are only relevant at the most detailed levels.

# Appendix: Time Value of Money Tables

**Present Value Table**

| | 1% | 2% | 3% | 4% | 5% | 6% | 7% | 8% | 9% | 10% | 11% | 12% | 13% | 14% | 15% | 16% | 17% | 18% | 19% | 20% |
|---|---|---|---|---|---|---|---|---|---|---|---|---|---|---|---|---|---|---|---|---|
| 1 | 0.990 | 0.980 | 0.971 | 0.962 | 0.952 | 0.943 | 0.935 | 0.926 | 0.917 | 0.909 | 0.901 | 0.893 | 0.885 | 0.877 | 0.870 | 0.862 | 0.855 | 0.847 | 0.840 | 0.833 |
| 2 | 0.980 | 0.961 | 0.943 | 0.925 | 0.907 | 0.890 | 0.873 | 0.857 | 0.842 | 0.826 | 0.812 | 0.797 | 0.783 | 0.769 | 0.756 | 0.743 | 0.731 | 0.718 | 0.706 | 0.694 |
| 3 | 0.971 | 0.942 | 0.915 | 0.889 | 0.864 | 0.840 | 0.816 | 0.794 | 0.772 | 0.751 | 0.731 | 0.712 | 0.693 | 0.675 | 0.658 | 0.641 | 0.624 | 0.609 | 0.593 | 0.579 |
| 4 | 0.961 | 0.924 | 0.888 | 0.855 | 0.823 | 0.792 | 0.763 | 0.735 | 0.708 | 0.683 | 0.659 | 0.636 | 0.613 | 0.592 | 0.572 | 0.552 | 0.534 | 0.516 | 0.499 | 0.482 |
| 5 | 0.951 | 0.906 | 0.863 | 0.822 | 0.784 | 0.747 | 0.713 | 0.681 | 0.650 | 0.621 | 0.593 | 0.567 | 0.543 | 0.519 | 0.497 | 0.476 | 0.456 | 0.437 | 0.419 | 0.402 |
| 6 | 0.942 | 0.888 | 0.837 | 0.790 | 0.746 | 0.705 | 0.666 | 0.630 | 0.596 | 0.564 | 0.535 | 0.507 | 0.480 | 0.456 | 0.432 | 0.410 | 0.390 | 0.370 | 0.352 | 0.335 |
| 7 | 0.933 | 0.871 | 0.813 | 0.760 | 0.711 | 0.665 | 0.623 | 0.583 | 0.547 | 0.513 | 0.482 | 0.452 | 0.425 | 0.400 | 0.376 | 0.354 | 0.333 | 0.314 | 0.296 | 0.279 |
| 8 | 0.923 | 0.853 | 0.789 | 0.731 | 0.677 | 0.627 | 0.582 | 0.540 | 0.502 | 0.467 | 0.434 | 0.404 | 0.376 | 0.351 | 0.327 | 0.305 | 0.285 | 0.266 | 0.249 | 0.233 |
| 9 | 0.914 | 0.837 | 0.766 | 0.703 | 0.645 | 0.592 | 0.544 | 0.500 | 0.460 | 0.424 | 0.391 | 0.361 | 0.333 | 0.308 | 0.294 | 0.283 | 0.243 | 0.225 | 0.209 | 0.194 |
| 10 | 0.905 | 0.820 | 0.744 | 0.676 | 0.614 | 0.558 | 0.508 | 0.463 | 0.422 | 0.386 | 0.352 | 0.322 | 0.295 | 0.270 | 0.247 | 0.227 | 0.206 | 0.191 | 0.176 | 0.162 |
| 11 | 0.896 | 0.804 | 0.722 | 0.650 | 0.585 | 0.527 | 0.475 | 0.429 | 0.388 | 0.350 | 0.317 | 0.287 | 0.261 | 0.237 | 0.215 | 0.195 | 0.178 | 0.162 | 0.148 | 0.136 |
| 12 | 0.887 | 0.788 | 0.701 | 0.625 | 0.557 | 0.497 | 0.444 | 0.397 | 0.356 | 0.319 | 0.286 | 0.257 | 0.231 | 0.208 | 0.187 | 0.168 | 0.152 | 0.137 | 0.124 | 0.112 |
| 13 | 0.879 | 0.773 | 0.681 | 0.601 | 0.530 | 0.469 | 0.415 | 0.368 | 0.326 | 0.290 | 0.258 | 0.229 | 0.204 | 0.182 | 0.163 | 0.145 | 0.130 | 0.116 | 0.104 | 0.093 |
| 14 | 0.870 | 0.758 | 0.661 | 0.577 | 0.506 | 0.442 | 0.388 | 0.340 | 0.299 | 0.263 | 0.232 | 0.205 | 0.181 | 0.160 | 0.141 | 0.125 | 0.111 | 0.099 | 0.088 | 0.078 |
| 15 | 0.861 | 0.743 | 0.642 | 0.555 | 0.481 | 0.417 | 0.362 | 0.315 | 0.275 | 0.239 | 0.209 | 0.183 | 0.160 | 0.140 | 0.123 | 0.108 | 0.095 | 0.084 | 0.074 | 0.065 |
| 16 | 0.853 | 0.728 | 0.623 | 0.534 | 0.458 | 0.394 | 0.339 | 0.292 | 0.252 | 0.218 | 0.188 | 0.163 | 0.141 | 0.123 | 0.107 | 0.093 | 0.081 | 0.071 | 0.062 | 0.054 |
| 17 | 0.844 | 0.714 | 0.605 | 0.513 | 0.436 | 0.371 | 0.317 | 0.270 | 0.231 | 0.198 | 0.170 | 0.146 | 0.125 | 0.108 | 0.093 | 0.080 | 0.069 | 0.060 | 0.052 | 0.045 |
| 18 | 0.836 | 0.700 | 0.587 | 0.494 | 0.416 | 0.350 | 0.296 | 0.250 | 0.212 | 0.180 | 0.153 | 0.130 | 0.111 | 0.095 | 0.081 | 0.069 | 0.059 | 0.051 | 0.044 | 0.038 |
| 19 | 0.828 | 0.686 | 0.570 | 0.475 | 0.396 | 0.331 | 0.277 | 0.232 | 0.194 | 0.164 | 0.138 | 0.116 | 0.098 | 0.083 | 0.070 | 0.060 | 0.051 | 0.043 | 0.037 | 0.031 |
| 20 | 0.820 | 0.673 | 0.554 | 0.456 | 0.377 | 0.312 | 0.258 | 0.215 | 0.178 | 0.149 | 0.124 | 0.104 | 0.087 | 0.073 | 0.061 | 0.051 | 0.043 | 0.037 | 0.031 | 0.026 |
| 21 | 0.811 | 0.660 | 0.538 | 0.439 | 0.359 | 0.294 | 0.242 | 0.199 | 0.164 | 0.135 | 0.112 | 0.093 | 0.077 | 0.064 | 0.053 | 0.044 | 0.037 | 0.031 | 0.026 | 0.022 |
| 22 | 0.803 | 0.647 | 0.522 | 0.422 | 0.342 | 0.278 | 0.226 | 0.184 | 0.150 | 0.123 | 0.101 | 0.083 | 0.068 | 0.056 | 0.046 | 0.038 | 0.032 | 0.026 | 0.022 | 0.018 |
| 23 | 0.795 | 0.634 | 0.507 | 0.406 | 0.326 | 0.262 | 0.211 | 0.170 | 0.138 | 0.112 | 0.091 | 0.074 | 0.060 | 0.049 | 0.040 | 0.033 | 0.027 | 0.022 | 0.018 | 0.015 |
| 24 | 0.788 | 0.622 | 0.492 | 0.390 | 0.310 | 0.247 | 0.197 | 0.158 | 0.126 | 0.102 | 0.082 | 0.066 | 0.053 | 0.043 | 0.035 | 0.028 | 0.023 | 0.019 | 0.015 | 0.013 |
| 25 | 0.780 | 0.610 | 0.478 | 0.375 | 0.296 | 0.233 | 0.184 | 0.146 | 0.116 | 0.092 | 0.074 | 0.059 | 0.047 | 0.038 | 0.030 | 0.024 | 0.020 | 0.016 | 0.013 | 0.010 |
| 26 | 0.772 | 0.598 | 0.464 | 0.361 | 0.281 | 0.220 | 0.172 | 0.135 | 0.106 | 0.084 | 0.066 | 0.053 | 0.042 | 0.033 | 0.026 | 0.021 | 0.017 | 0.014 | 0.011 | 0.009 |
| 27 | 0.764 | 0.586 | 0.450 | 0.347 | 0.268 | 0.207 | 0.161 | 0.125 | 0.098 | 0.076 | 0.060 | 0.047 | 0.037 | 0.029 | 0.023 | 0.018 | 0.014 | 0.011 | 0.009 | 0.007 |
| 28 | 0.757 | 0.574 | 0.437 | 0.333 | 0.255 | 0.196 | 0.150 | 0.116 | 0.090 | 0.069 | 0.054 | 0.042 | 0.033 | 0.026 | 0.020 | 0.016 | 0.012 | 0.010 | 0.008 | 0.006 |
| 29 | 0.749 | 0.583 | 0.424 | 0.321 | 0.243 | 0.185 | 0.141 | 0.107 | 0.082 | 0.063 | 0.048 | 0.037 | 0.029 | 0.022 | 0.017 | 0.014 | 0.011 | 0.008 | 0.006 | 0.005 |
| 30 | 0.742 | 0.552 | 0.412 | 0.308 | 0.231 | 0.174 | 0.131 | 0.099 | 0.075 | 0.057 | 0.044 | 0.033 | 0.026 | 0.020 | 0.015 | 0.012 | 0.009 | 0.007 | 0.005 | 0.004 |
| 31 | 0.735 | 0.541 | 0.400 | 0.296 | 0.220 | 0.164 | 0.123 | 0.092 | 0.069 | 0.052 | 0.039 | 0.030 | 0.023 | 0.017 | 0.013 | 0.010 | 0.008 | 0.006 | 0.005 | 0.004 |
| 32 | 0.727 | 0.531 | 0.388 | 0.285 | 0.210 | 0.155 | 0.115 | 0.085 | 0.063 | 0.047 | 0.035 | 0.027 | 0.020 | 0.015 | 0.011 | 0.009 | 0.007 | 0.005 | 0.004 | 0.003 |
| 33 | 0.720 | 0.520 | 0.377 | 0.274 | 0.200 | 0.146 | 0.107 | 0.079 | 0.058 | 0.043 | 0.032 | 0.024 | 0.018 | 0.013 | 0.010 | 0.007 | 0.006 | 0.004 | 0.003 | 0.002 |
| 34 | 0.713 | 0.510 | 0.366 | 0.264 | 0.190 | 0.138 | 0.100 | 0.073 | 0.053 | 0.039 | 0.029 | 0.021 | 0.016 | 0.012 | 0.009 | 0.006 | 0.005 | 0.004 | 0.003 | 0.002 |
| 35 | 0.706 | 0.500 | 0.355 | 0.253 | 0.181 | 0.130 | 0.094 | 0.068 | 0.049 | 0.036 | 0.026 | 0.019 | 0.014 | 0.010 | 0.008 | 0.006 | 0.004 | 0.003 | 0.002 | 0.002 |
| 36 | 0.699 | 0.490 | 0.345 | 0.244 | 0.173 | 0.123 | 0.088 | 0.063 | 0.045 | 0.032 | 0.023 | 0.017 | 0.012 | 0.009 | 0.007 | 0.005 | 0.004 | 0.003 | 0.002 | 0.001 |
| 37 | 0.692 | 0.481 | 0.335 | 0.234 | 0.164 | 0.116 | 0.082 | 0.058 | 0.041 | 0.029 | 0.021 | 0.015 | 0.011 | 0.008 | 0.006 | 0.004 | 0.003 | 0.002 | 0.002 | 0.001 |
| 38 | 0.685 | 0.471 | 0.325 | 0.225 | 0.157 | 0.109 | 0.076 | 0.054 | 0.038 | 0.027 | 0.019 | 0.013 | 0.010 | 0.007 | 0.005 | 0.004 | 0.003 | 0.002 | 0.001 | 0.001 |
| 39 | 0.678 | 0.462 | 0.316 | 0.217 | 0.149 | 0.103 | 0.071 | 0.050 | 0.035 | 0.024 | 0.017 | 0.012 | 0.009 | 0.006 | 0.004 | 0.003 | 0.002 | 0.002 | 0.001 | 0.001 |
| 40 | 0.672 | 0.453 | 0.307 | 0.206 | 0.142 | 0.097 | 0.067 | 0.046 | 0.032 | 0.022 | 0.015 | 0.011 | 0.006 | 0.005 | 0.004 | 0.003 | 0.002 | 0.001 | 0.001 | 0.001 |

## Present Value of an Annuity Table

| | 1% | 2% | 3% | 4% | 5% | 6% | 7% | 8% | 9% | 10% | 11% | 12% | 13% | 14% | 15% | 16% | 17% | 18% | 19% | 20% |
|---|---|---|---|---|---|---|---|---|---|---|---|---|---|---|---|---|---|---|---|---|
| 1 | 0.990 | 0.980 | 0.971 | 0.962 | 0.952 | 0.943 | 0.935 | 0.926 | 0.917 | 0.909 | 0.901 | 0.893 | 0.885 | 0.877 | 0.870 | 0.862 | 0.855 | 0.847 | 0.840 | 0.833 |
| 2 | 1.970 | 1.942 | 1.913 | 1.886 | 1.859 | 1.833 | 1.808 | 1.783 | 1.759 | 1.736 | 1.713 | 1.690 | 1.668 | 1.647 | 1.626 | 1.605 | 1.585 | 1.566 | 1.547 | 1.528 |
| 3 | 2.941 | 2.884 | 2.829 | 2.775 | 2.723 | 2.673 | 2.624 | 2.577 | 2.531 | 2.487 | 2.444 | 2.402 | 2.361 | 2.322 | 2.283 | 2.246 | 2.210 | 2.174 | 2.140 | 2.106 |
| 4 | 3.902 | 3.808 | 3.717 | 3.630 | 3.546 | 3.465 | 3.387 | 3.312 | 3.240 | 3.170 | 3.102 | 3.037 | 2.974 | 2.914 | 2.855 | 2.798 | 2.743 | 2.690 | 2.639 | 2.589 |
| 5 | 4.853 | 4.713 | 4.580 | 4.452 | 4.329 | 4.212 | 4.100 | 3.993 | 3.890 | 3.791 | 3.696 | 3.605 | 3.517 | 3.433 | 3.352 | 3.274 | 3.199 | 3.127 | 3.058 | 2.991 |
| 6 | 5.795 | 5.601 | 5.417 | 5.242 | 5.076 | 4.917 | 4.767 | 4.623 | 4.486 | 4.355 | 4.231 | 4.111 | 3.998 | 3.889 | 3.784 | 3.685 | 3.589 | 3.498 | 3.410 | 3.326 |
| 7 | 6.728 | 6.472 | 6.230 | 6.002 | 5.786 | 5.582 | 5.389 | 5.206 | 5.033 | 4.868 | 4.712 | 4.564 | 4.423 | 4.288 | 4.160 | 4.039 | 3.922 | 3.812 | 3.706 | 3.605 |
| 8 | 7.652 | 7.325 | 7.020 | 6.733 | 6.463 | 6.210 | 5.971 | 5.747 | 5.535 | 5.335 | 5.146 | 4.968 | 4.799 | 4.639 | 4.487 | 4.344 | 4.207 | 4.078 | 3.954 | 3.837 |
| 9 | 8.566 | 8.162 | 7.786 | 7.435 | 7.108 | 6.802 | 6.515 | 6.247 | 5.995 | 5.759 | 5.537 | 5.328 | 5.132 | 4.946 | 4.772 | 4.607 | 4.451 | 4.303 | 4.163 | 4.031 |
| 10 | 9.471 | 8.983 | 8.530 | 8.111 | 7.722 | 7.360 | 7.024 | 6.710 | 6.418 | 6.145 | 5.889 | 5.650 | 5.426 | 5.216 | 5.019 | 4.833 | 4.659 | 4.494 | 4.339 | 4.192 |
| 11 | 10.368 | 9.787 | 9.253 | 8.760 | 8.306 | 7.887 | 7.499 | 7.139 | 6.805 | 6.495 | 6.207 | 5.938 | 5.687 | 5.453 | 5.234 | 5.029 | 4.836 | 4.656 | 4.486 | 4.327 |
| 12 | 11.255 | 10.575 | 9.954 | 9.385 | 8.863 | 8.384 | 7.943 | 7.536 | 7.161 | 6.814 | 6.492 | 6.194 | 5.918 | 5.660 | 5.421 | 5.197 | 4.988 | 4.793 | 4.611 | 4.439 |
| 13 | 12.134 | 11.348 | 10.635 | 9.986 | 9.394 | 8.853 | 8.358 | 7.904 | 7.487 | 7.103 | 6.750 | 6.424 | 6.122 | 5.842 | 5.583 | 5.342 | 5.118 | 4.910 | 4.715 | 4.533 |
| 14 | 13.004 | 12.106 | 11.296 | 10.563 | 9.899 | 9.295 | 8.745 | 8.244 | 7.786 | 7.367 | 6.982 | 6.628 | 6.302 | 6.002 | 5.724 | 5.468 | 5.229 | 5.008 | 4.802 | 4.611 |
| 15 | 13.865 | 12.849 | 11.938 | 11.118 | 10.380 | 9.712 | 9.108 | 8.559 | 8.061 | 7.606 | 7.191 | 6.811 | 6.462 | 6.142 | 5.847 | 5.575 | 5.324 | 5.092 | 4.876 | 4.675 |
| 16 | 14.718 | 13.578 | 12.561 | 11.652 | 10.838 | 10.106 | 9.447 | 8.851 | 8.313 | 7.824 | 7.379 | 6.974 | 6.604 | 6.265 | 5.954 | 5.668 | 5.405 | 5.162 | 4.938 | 4.730 |
| 17 | 15.562 | 14.292 | 13.166 | 12.166 | 11.274 | 10.477 | 9.763 | 9.122 | 8.544 | 8.022 | 7.549 | 7.120 | 6.729 | 6.373 | 6.047 | 5.749 | 5.475 | 5.222 | 4.990 | 4.775 |
| 18 | 16.398 | 14.992 | 13.754 | 12.659 | 11.690 | 10.828 | 10.059 | 9.372 | 8.756 | 8.201 | 7.702 | 7.250 | 6.840 | 6.467 | 6.128 | 5.818 | 5.534 | 5.273 | 5.033 | 4.812 |
| 19 | 17.226 | 15.678 | 14.324 | 13.134 | 12.085 | 11.158 | 10.336 | 9.604 | 8.950 | 8.365 | 7.839 | 7.366 | 6.938 | 6.550 | 6.198 | 5.877 | 5.584 | 5.316 | 5.070 | 4.843 |
| 20 | 18.046 | 16.351 | 14.877 | 13.590 | 12.462 | 11.470 | 10.594 | 9.818 | 9.129 | 8.514 | 8.075 | 7.469 | 7.025 | 6.623 | 6.259 | 5.929 | 5.628 | 5.353 | 5.101 | 4.870 |
| 21 | 18.857 | 17.011 | 15.415 | 14.029 | 12.821 | 11.764 | 10.836 | 10.017 | 9.292 | 8.649 | 8.176 | 7.562 | 7.102 | 6.687 | 6.312 | 5.973 | 5.665 | 5.384 | 5.127 | 4.891 |
| 22 | 19.660 | 17.658 | 15.937 | 14.451 | 13.163 | 12.042 | 11.061 | 10.201 | 9.442 | 8.772 | 8.266 | 7.645 | 7.170 | 6.743 | 6.359 | 6.011 | 5.696 | 5.410 | 5.149 | 4.909 |
| 23 | 20.456 | 18.292 | 16.444 | 14.857 | 13.489 | 12.303 | 11.272 | 10.371 | 9.580 | 8.883 | 8.348 | 7.718 | 7.230 | 6.792 | 6.399 | 6.044 | 5.723 | 5.432 | 5.167 | 4.925 |
| 24 | 21.243 | 18.914 | 16.936 | 15.247 | 13.799 | 12.550 | 11.469 | 10.529 | 9.707 | 8.985 | 8.422 | 7.784 | 7.283 | 6.835 | 6.434 | 6.073 | 5.746 | 5.451 | 5.182 | 4.937 |
| 25 | 22.023 | 19.523 | 17.413 | 15.622 | 14.094 | 12.783 | 11.654 | 10.675 | 9.823 | 9.077 | 8.488 | 7.843 | 7.330 | 6.873 | 6.464 | 6.097 | 5.766 | 5.467 | 5.195 | 4.948 |
| 26 | 22.795 | 20.121 | 17.877 | 15.983 | 14.375 | 13.003 | 11.826 | 10.810 | 9.929 | 9.161 | 8.548 | 7.896 | 7.372 | 6.906 | 6.491 | 6.118 | 5.783 | 5.480 | 5.206 | 4.956 |
| 27 | 23.560 | 20.707 | 18.327 | 16.330 | 14.643 | 13.211 | 11.987 | 10.935 | 10.027 | 9.237 | 8.548 | 7.943 | 7.409 | 6.935 | 6.514 | 6.136 | 5.796 | 5.492 | 5.215 | 4.964 |
| 28 | 24.316 | 21.281 | 18.764 | 16.663 | 14.898 | 13.406 | 12.137 | 11.051 | 10.116 | 9.307 | 8.602 | 7.984 | 7.441 | 6.961 | 6.534 | 6.152 | 5.807 | 5.502 | 5.223 | 4.970 |
| 29 | 25.066 | 21.844 | 19.188 | 16.984 | 15.141 | 13.591 | 12.278 | 11.158 | 10.198 | 9.370 | 8.650 | 8.022 | 7.470 | 6.983 | 6.551 | 6.166 | 5.820 | 5.510 | 5.229 | 4.975 |
| 30 | 25.808 | 22.396 | 19.600 | 17.292 | 15.372 | 13.765 | 12.409 | 11.258 | 10.274 | 9.427 | 8.694 | 8.055 | 7.496 | 7.003 | 6.566 | 6.177 | 5.829 | 5.517 | 5.235 | 4.979 |
| 31 | 26.542 | 22.938 | 20.000 | 17.588 | 15.593 | 13.929 | 12.532 | 11.350 | 10.343 | 9.479 | 8.733 | 8.085 | 7.518 | 7.020 | 6.579 | 6.187 | 5.837 | 5.523 | 5.239 | 4.982 |
| 32 | 27.270 | 23.468 | 20.389 | 17.874 | 15.803 | 14.084 | 12.647 | 11.435 | 10.406 | 9.526 | 8.769 | 8.112 | 7.538 | 7.035 | 6.591 | 6.196 | 5.844 | 5.528 | 5.243 | 4.985 |
| 33 | 27.990 | 23.989 | 20.766 | 18.148 | 16.003 | 14.230 | 12.754 | 11.514 | 10.464 | 9.569 | 8.801 | 8.135 | 7.556 | 7.048 | 6.600 | 6.203 | 5.849 | 5.532 | 5.246 | 4.988 |
| 34 | 28.703 | 24.499 | 21.132 | 18.411 | 16.193 | 14.368 | 12.854 | 11.587 | 10.518 | 9.609 | 8.829 | 8.157 | 7.572 | 7.060 | 6.609 | 6.210 | 5.854 | 5.536 | 5.249 | 4.990 |
| 35 | 29.409 | 24.999 | 21.487 | 18.665 | 16.374 | 14.498 | 12.948 | 11.655 | 10.567 | 9.644 | 8.855 | 8.176 | 7.586 | 7.070 | 6.617 | 6.215 | 5.858 | 5.539 | 5.251 | 4.992 |
| 36 | 30.108 | 25.489 | 21.832 | 18.908 | 16.547 | 14.621 | 13.035 | 11.717 | 10.612 | 9.677 | 8.879 | 8.192 | 7.598 | 7.079 | 6.623 | 6.220 | 5.862 | 5.541 | 5.253 | 4.993 |
| 37 | 30.800 | 25.969 | 22.167 | 19.143 | 16.711 | 14.737 | 13.117 | 11.775 | 10.653 | 9.706 | 8.900 | 8.208 | 7.609 | 7.087 | 6.629 | 6.224 | 5.865 | 5.543 | 5.255 | 4.994 |
| 38 | 31.485 | 26.441 | 22.492 | 19.368 | 16.868 | 14.846 | 13.193 | 11.829 | 10.691 | 9.733 | 8.919 | 8.221 | 7.618 | 7.094 | 6.634 | 6.228 | 5.867 | 5.545 | 5.256 | 4.995 |
| 39 | 32.163 | 26.903 | 22.808 | 19.584 | 17.017 | 14.949 | 13.265 | 11.879 | 10.726 | 9.757 | 8.936 | 8.233 | 7.627 | 7.100 | 6.638 | 6.231 | 5.869 | 5.547 | 5.257 | 4.996 |
| 40 | 32.835 | 27.355 | 23.115 | 19.793 | 17.159 | 15.046 | 13.332 | 11.925 | 10.757 | 9.779 | 8.951 | 8.244 | 7.634 | 7.105 | 6.642 | 6.233 | 5.871 | 5.548 | 5.258 | 4.997 |

**Future Value of an Annuity Table**

| | 1% | 2% | 3% | 4% | 5% | 6% | 7% | 8% | 9% | 10% | 11% | 12% | 13% | 14% | 15% | 16% | 17% | 18% | 19% | 20% |
|---|---|---|---|---|---|---|---|---|---|---|---|---|---|---|---|---|---|---|---|---|
| 1 | 1.000 | 1.000 | 1.000 | 1.000 | 1.000 | 1.000 | 1.000 | 1.000 | 1.000 | 1.000 | 1.000 | 1.000 | 1.000 | 1.000 | 1.000 | 1.000 | 1.000 | 1.000 | 1.000 | 1.000 |
| 2 | 2.010 | 2.020 | 2.030 | 2.040 | 2.050 | 2.060 | 2.070 | 2.080 | 2.090 | 2.100 | 2.110 | 2.120 | 2.130 | 2.140 | 2.150 | 2.160 | 2.170 | 2.180 | 2.190 | 2.200 |
| 3 | 3.030 | 3.060 | 3.091 | 3.122 | 3.153 | 3.184 | 3.215 | 3.246 | 3.278 | 3.310 | 3.342 | 3.374 | 3.407 | 3.440 | 3.473 | 3.506 | 3.539 | 3.572 | 3.606 | 3.640 |
| 4 | 4.060 | 4.122 | 4.184 | 4.246 | 4.310 | 4.375 | 4.440 | 4.506 | 4.573 | 4.641 | 4.710 | 4.779 | 4.850 | 4.921 | 4.993 | 5.066 | 5.141 | 5.215 | 5.291 | 5.368 |
| 5 | 5.101 | 5.204 | 5.309 | 5.416 | 5.526 | 5.637 | 5.751 | 5.867 | 5.985 | 6.105 | 6.228 | 6.353 | 6.480 | 6.610 | 6.742 | 6.877 | 7.014 | 7.154 | 7.297 | 7.442 |
| 6 | 6.152 | 6.308 | 6.468 | 6.633 | 6.802 | 6.975 | 7.153 | 7.336 | 7.523 | 7.716 | 7.913 | 8.115 | 8.323 | 8.536 | 8.754 | 8.977 | 9.207 | 9.442 | 9.683 | 9.930 |
| 7 | 7.214 | 7.434 | 7.662 | 7.898 | 8.142 | 8.394 | 8.654 | 8.923 | 9.200 | 9.487 | 9.783 | 10.089 | 10.405 | 10.730 | 11.067 | 11.414 | 11.772 | 12.142 | 12.523 | 12.916 |
| 8 | 8.286 | 8.583 | 8.892 | 9.214 | 9.549 | 9.897 | 10.260 | 10.637 | 11.028 | 11.436 | 11.859 | 12.300 | 12.757 | 13.233 | 13.727 | 14.420 | 14.773 | 15.327 | 15.902 | 16.499 |
| 9 | 9.369 | 9.755 | 10.159 | 10.583 | 11.207 | 11.491 | 11.978 | 12.488 | 13.021 | 13.579 | 14.164 | 14.776 | 15.416 | 16.085 | 16.786 | 17.519 | 18.285 | 19.086 | 19.923 | 20.799 |
| 10 | 10.462 | 10.950 | 11.464 | 12.006 | 12.578 | 13.181 | 13.816 | 14.487 | 15.193 | 15.937 | 16.722 | 17.549 | 18.420 | 19.337 | 20.304 | 21.321 | 22.393 | 23.521 | 24.709 | 25.959 |
| 11 | 11.567 | 12.169 | 12.808 | 13.486 | 14.207 | 14.972 | 15.784 | 16.645 | 17.560 | 18.531 | 19.561 | 20.655 | 21.814 | 23.045 | 24.349 | 25.733 | 27.200 | 28.755 | 30.404 | 32.150 |
| 12 | 12.683 | 13.412 | 14.192 | 15.026 | 15.917 | 16.870 | 17.888 | 18.977 | 20.141 | 21.384 | 22.713 | 24.133 | 25.650 | 27.271 | 29.002 | 30.850 | 32.824 | 34.931 | 37.180 | 39.581 |
| 13 | 13.809 | 14.680 | 15.618 | 16.627 | 17.713 | 18.882 | 20.141 | 21.495 | 22.953 | 24.523 | 26.212 | 28.029 | 29.985 | 32.089 | 34.352 | 36.786 | 39.404 | 42.219 | 45.244 | 48.497 |
| 14 | 14.947 | 15.974 | 17.086 | 18.292 | 19.599 | 21.015 | 22.550 | 24.215 | 26.019 | 27.975 | 30.095 | 32.393 | 34.883 | 37.581 | 40.505 | 43.672 | 47.103 | 50.818 | 54.841 | 59.196 |
| 15 | 16.097 | 17.293 | 18.599 | 20.024 | 21.579 | 23.276 | 25.129 | 27.152 | 29.361 | 31.772 | 34.405 | 37.280 | 40.417 | 43.842 | 47.580 | 51.660 | 56.110 | 60.965 | 66.261 | 72.035 |
| 16 | 17.258 | 18.639 | 20.157 | 21.825 | 23.657 | 25.673 | 27.888 | 30.324 | 33.003 | 35.950 | 39.190 | 42.753 | 46.672 | 50.980 | 55.717 | 60.925 | 66.649 | 72.939 | 79.850 | 87.442 |
| 17 | 18.430 | 20.012 | 21.762 | 23.698 | 25.840 | 28.213 | 30.840 | 33.750 | 36.974 | 40.545 | 44.501 | 48.884 | 53.739 | 59.118 | 65.075 | 71.673 | 78.979 | 87.068 | 96.022 | 105.931 |
| 18 | 19.615 | 21.412 | 23.414 | 25.645 | 28.132 | 30.906 | 33.999 | 37.450 | 41.301 | 45.599 | 50.396 | 55.750 | 61.725 | 68.394 | 75.836 | 84.141 | 93.406 | 103.740 | 115.266 | 128.117 |
| 19 | 20.811 | 22.841 | 25.117 | 27.671 | 30.539 | 33.760 | 37.379 | 41.446 | 46.018 | 51.159 | 56.939 | 63.440 | 70.749 | 78.969 | 88.212 | 98.603 | 110.285 | 123.414 | 138.166 | 154.740 |
| 20 | 22.019 | 24.297 | 26.870 | 29.778 | 33.066 | 36.786 | 40.995 | 45.762 | 51.160 | 57.275 | 64.203 | 72.052 | 80.947 | 91.025 | 102.444 | 115.380 | 130.033 | 146.628 | 165.418 | 186.688 |
| 21 | 23.239 | 25.783 | 28.676 | 31.969 | 35.719 | 39.993 | 44.865 | 50.423 | 56.765 | 64.002 | 72.265 | 81.699 | 92.470 | 104.768 | 118.810 | 134.841 | 153.139 | 174.021 | 197.847 | 225.026 |
| 22 | 24.472 | 27.299 | 30.537 | 34.248 | 38.505 | 43.392 | 49.006 | 55.457 | 62.873 | 71.403 | 81.214 | 92.503 | 105.491 | 120.436 | 137.632 | 157.415 | 180.172 | 206.345 | 236.438 | 271.031 |
| 23 | 25.716 | 28.845 | 32.453 | 36.618 | 41.430 | 46.996 | 53.436 | 60.893 | 69.532 | 79.543 | 91.148 | 104.603 | 120.205 | 138.297 | 159.276 | 183.601 | 211.801 | 244.487 | 282.362 | 326.237 |
| 24 | 26.973 | 30.422 | 34.426 | 39.083 | 44.502 | 50.816 | 58.177 | 66.765 | 76.790 | 88.497 | 102.174 | 118.155 | 136.831 | 158.659 | 184.168 | 213.978 | 248.808 | 289.494 | 337.010 | 392.484 |
| 25 | 28.243 | 32.030 | 36.459 | 41.646 | 47.727 | 54.865 | 63.249 | 73.106 | 84.701 | 98.347 | 114.413 | 133.334 | 155.620 | 181.871 | 212.793 | 249.214 | 292.105 | 342.063 | 402.042 | 471.981 |
| 26 | 29.526 | 33.671 | 38.553 | 44.312 | 51.113 | 59.156 | 68.676 | 79.954 | 93.324 | 109.182 | 127.999 | 150.334 | 176.850 | 208.333 | 245.712 | 290.088 | 342.763 | 405.272 | 479.431 | 567.377 |
| 27 | 30.821 | 35.344 | 40.710 | 47.084 | 54.669 | 63.706 | 74.484 | 87.351 | 102.723 | 121.100 | 143.079 | 169.374 | 200.841 | 238.499 | 283.569 | 337.502 | 402.032 | 479.221 | 571.522 | 681.853 |
| 28 | 32.129 | 37.051 | 42.931 | 49.968 | 58.403 | 68.528 | 80.698 | 95.339 | 112.968 | 134.210 | 159.817 | 190.699 | 227.950 | 272.889 | 327.104 | 392.503 | 471.378 | 566.481 | 681.112 | 819.223 |
| 29 | 33.450 | 38.792 | 45.219 | 52.966 | 62.323 | 73.640 | 87.347 | 103.966 | 124.135 | 148.631 | 178.397 | 214.583 | 258.583 | 312.094 | 377.170 | 456.303 | 552.512 | 669.447 | 811.523 | 984.068 |
| 30 | 34.785 | 40.568 | 47.575 | 56.085 | 66.439 | 79.058 | 94.461 | 113.283 | 136.308 | 164.494 | 199.021 | 241.333 | 293.199 | 356.787 | 434.745 | 530.312 | 647.439 | 790.948 | 966.712 | 1181.882 |
| 31 | 36.133 | 42.379 | 50.003 | 59.328 | 70.761 | 84.802 | 102.073 | 123.346 | 149.575 | 181.943 | 221.913 | 271.293 | 332.315 | 407.737 | 500.957 | 616.162 | 758.504 | 934.319 | 1151.387 | 1419.258 |
| 32 | 37.494 | 44.227 | 52.503 | 62.701 | 75.299 | 90.890 | 110.218 | 134.214 | 164.037 | 201.138 | 247.324 | 304.848 | 376.516 | 465.820 | 577.100 | 715.747 | 888.449 | 1103.496 | 1371.15 | 1704.109 |
| 33 | 38.869 | 46.112 | 55.078 | 66.210 | 80.064 | 97.343 | 118.933 | 145.951 | 179.800 | 222.252 | 275.529 | 342.429 | 426.463 | 532.035 | 664.666 | 831.267 | 1040.486 | 1303.125 | 1632.670 | 2045.931 |
| 34 | 40.258 | 48.034 | 57.730 | 69.858 | 85.067 | 104.184 | 128.259 | 158.627 | 196.982 | 245.477 | 306.837 | 384.521 | 482.903 | 607.520 | 765.365 | 965.270 | 1218.368 | 1538.688 | 1943.877 | 2456.118 |
| 35 | 41.660 | 49.994 | 60.462 | 73.652 | 90.320 | 111.435 | 138.237 | 172.317 | 215.711 | 271.024 | 341.590 | 431.663 | 546.681 | 693.573 | 881.170 | 1120.713 | 1426.491 | 1816.652 | 2314.214 | 2948.341 |
| 36 | 43.077 | 51.994 | 63.276 | 77.598 | 95.836 | 119.121 | 148.913 | 187.102 | 236.125 | 299.127 | 380.164 | 484.463 | 618.749 | 791.673 | 1014.346 | 1301.027 | 1669.994 | 2144.649 | 2754.914 | 3539.009 |
| 37 | 44.508 | 54.034 | 66.174 | 81.702 | 101.628 | 127.268 | 160.337 | 203.070 | 258.376 | 330.039 | 422.982 | 543.599 | 700.187 | 903.507 | 1167.498 | 1510.191 | 1954.894 | 2531.686 | 3279.348 | 4247.811 |
| 38 | 45.953 | 56.115 | 69.159 | 85.970 | 107.710 | 135.904 | 172.561 | 220.316 | 282.630 | 364.043 | 470.511 | 609.831 | 792.211 | 1030.998 | 1343.622 | 1752.822 | 2288.225 | 2988.389 | 3903.424 | 5098.373 |
| 39 | 47.412 | 58.237 | 72.234 | 90.409 | 114.095 | 145.058 | 185.640 | 238.941 | 309.066 | 401.448 | 523.267 | 684.010 | 896.198 | 1176.338 | 1546.165 | 2034.273 | 2678.224 | 3527.299 | 4646.075 | 6119.048 |
| 40 | 48.886 | 60.402 | 75.401 | 95.026 | 120.800 | 154.762 | 199.635 | 259.057 | 337.882 | 442.593 | 581.826 | 767.091 | 1013.704 | 1342.025 | 1779.090 | 2360.757 | 3134.522 | 4163.213 | 5529.829 | 7343.858 |

**Future Value Tabl[e]**

| | 1% | 2% | 3% | 4% | 5% | 6% | 7% | 8% | 9% | 10% | 11% | 12% | 13% | 14% | 15% | 16% | 17% | 18% | 19% | 20% |
|---|---|---|---|---|---|---|---|---|---|---|---|---|---|---|---|---|---|---|---|---|
| 1 | 1.010 | 1.020 | 1.030 | 1.040 | 1.050 | 1.060 | 1.070 | 1.080 | 1.090 | 1.100 | 1.110 | 1.120 | 1.130 | 1.140 | 1.150 | 1.160 | 1.170 | 1.180 | 1.190 | 1.200 |
| 2 | 1.020 | 1.040 | 1.061 | 1.082 | 1.103 | 1.124 | 1.145 | 1.166 | 1.188 | 1.210 | 1.232 | 1.254 | 1.277 | 1.300 | 1.323 | 1.346 | 1.369 | 1.392 | 1.416 | 1.440 |
| 3 | 1.030 | 1.061 | 1.093 | 1.125 | 1.158 | 1.191 | 1.225 | 1.260 | 1.295 | 1.331 | 1.368 | 1.405 | 1.443 | 1.482 | 1.521 | 1.561 | 1.602 | 1.643 | 1.685 | 1.728 |
| 4 | 1.041 | 1.082 | 1.126 | 1.170 | 1.216 | 1.262 | 1.311 | 1.360 | 1.412 | 1.464 | 1.518 | 1.574 | 1.630 | 1.689 | 1.749 | 1.811 | 1.874 | 1.939 | 2.005 | 2.074 |
| 5 | 1.051 | 1.104 | 1.159 | 1.217 | 1.276 | 1.338 | 1.403 | 1.469 | 1.539 | 1.611 | 1.685 | 1.762 | 1.842 | 1.925 | 2.011 | 2.100 | 2.192 | 2.288 | 2.386 | 2.488 |
| 6 | 1.062 | 1.126 | 1.194 | 1.265 | 1.340 | 1.419 | 1.501 | 1.587 | 1.677 | 1.772 | 1.870 | 1.974 | 2.082 | 2.195 | 2.313 | 2.436 | 2.565 | 2.700 | 2.840 | 2.986 |
| 7 | 1.072 | 1.149 | 1.230 | 1.316 | 1.407 | 1.504 | 1.606 | 1.714 | 1.828 | 1.949 | 2.076 | 2.211 | 2.353 | 2.502 | 2.660 | 2.826 | 3.001 | 3.185 | 3.379 | 3.583 |
| 8 | 1.083 | 1.172 | 1.267 | 1.369 | 1.477 | 1.594 | 1.718 | 1.851 | 1.993 | 2.144 | 2.305 | 2.476 | 2.658 | 2.853 | 3.059 | 3.278 | 3.511 | 3.759 | 4.021 | 4.300 |
| 9 | 1.094 | 1.195 | 1.305 | 1.423 | 1.551 | 1.689 | 1.838 | 1.999 | 2.172 | 2.358 | 2.558 | 2.773 | 3.004 | 3.252 | 3.518 | 3.803 | 4.108 | 4.435 | 4.785 | 5.160 |
| 10 | 1.105 | 1.218 | 1.344 | 1.480 | 1.629 | 1.791 | 1.967 | 2.159 | 2.367 | 2.594 | 2.839 | 3.106 | 3.395 | 3.707 | 4.046 | 4.411 | 4.807 | 5.234 | 5.695 | 6.192 |
| 11 | 1.116 | 1.243 | 1.384 | 1.539 | 1.710 | 1.898 | 2.105 | 2.332 | 2.580 | 2.853 | 3.152 | 3.479 | 3.836 | 4.226 | 4.652 | 5.117 | 5.624 | 6.176 | 6.777 | 7.430 |
| 12 | 1.127 | 1.268 | 1.426 | 1.601 | 1.796 | 2.012 | 2.252 | 2.518 | 2.813 | 3.138 | 3.498 | 3.896 | 4.335 | 4.818 | 5.350 | 5.936 | 6.580 | 7.288 | 8.064 | 8.916 |
| 13 | 1.138 | 1.294 | 1.469 | 1.665 | 1.886 | 2.133 | 2.410 | 2.720 | 3.066 | 3.452 | 3.883 | 4.363 | 4.898 | 5.492 | 6.153 | 6.886 | 7.699 | 8.599 | 9.596 | 10.669 |
| 14 | 1.149 | 1.319 | 1.513 | 1.732 | 1.980 | 2.261 | 2.579 | 2.937 | 3.342 | 3.797 | 4.310 | 4.887 | 5.535 | 6.261 | 7.076 | 7.988 | 9.007 | 10.147 | 11.420 | 12.839 |
| 15 | 1.161 | 1.346 | 1.558 | 1.801 | 2.079 | 2.397 | 2.759 | 3.172 | 3.642 | 4.177 | 4.785 | 5.474 | 6.254 | 7.138 | 8.137 | 9.266 | 10.539 | 11.974 | 13.590 | 15.407 |
| 16 | 1.173 | 1.373 | 1.605 | 1.873 | 2.183 | 2.540 | 2.952 | 3.426 | 3.970 | 4.595 | 5.311 | 6.130 | 7.067 | 8.137 | 9.358 | 10.748 | 12.330 | 14.129 | 16.172 | 18.488 |
| 17 | 1.184 | 1.400 | 1.653 | 1.948 | 2.292 | 2.693 | 3.159 | 3.700 | 4.328 | 5.054 | 5.895 | 6.866 | 7.986 | 9.276 | 10.761 | 12.468 | 14.426 | 16.672 | 19.244 | 22.186 |
| 18 | 1.196 | 1.428 | 1.702 | 2.026 | 2.407 | 2.854 | 3.380 | 3.996 | 4.717 | 5.560 | 6.544 | 7.690 | 9.024 | 10.575 | 12.375 | 14.463 | 16.879 | 19.673 | 22.901 | 26.623 |
| 19 | 1.208 | 1.457 | 1.754 | 2.107 | 2.527 | 3.026 | 3.617 | 4.316 | 5.142 | 6.116 | 7.263 | 8.613 | 10.197 | 12.056 | 14.232 | 16.777 | 19.748 | 23.214 | 27.252 | 31.948 |
| 20 | 1.220 | 1.486 | 1.806 | 2.191 | 2.653 | 3.207 | 3.870 | 4.661 | 5.604 | 6.727 | 8.062 | 9.646 | 11.523 | 13.743 | 16.367 | 19.461 | 23.106 | 27.393 | 32.429 | 38.338 |
| 21 | 1.232 | 1.516 | 1.860 | 2.279 | 2.786 | 3.400 | 4.141 | 5.034 | 6.109 | 7.400 | 8.949 | 10.804 | 13.021 | 15.668 | 18.822 | 22.574 | 27.034 | 32.324 | 38.591 | 46.005 |
| 22 | 1.245 | 1.546 | 1.916 | 2.370 | 2.925 | 3.604 | 4.430 | 5.437 | 6.659 | 8.140 | 9.934 | 12.100 | 14.714 | 17.861 | 21.645 | 26.186 | 31.629 | 38.142 | 45.923 | 55.206 |
| 23 | 1.257 | 1.577 | 1.974 | 2.465 | 3.072 | 3.820 | 4.741 | 5.871 | 7.258 | 8.954 | 11.026 | 13.552 | 16.627 | 20.362 | 24.891 | 30.376 | 37.006 | 45.008 | 54.649 | 66.247 |
| 24 | 1.270 | 1.608 | 2.033 | 2.563 | 3.225 | 4.049 | 5.072 | 6.341 | 7.911 | 9.850 | 12.239 | 15.179 | 18.788 | 23.212 | 28.625 | 35.236 | 43.297 | 53.109 | 65.032 | 79.497 |
| 25 | 1.282 | 1.641 | 2.094 | 2.666 | 3.386 | 4.292 | 5.427 | 6.848 | 8.623 | 10.835 | 13.585 | 17.000 | 21.231 | 26.462 | 32.919 | 40.874 | 50.658 | 62.669 | 77.388 | 95.396 |
| 26 | 1.295 | 1.673 | 2.157 | 2.772 | 3.556 | 4.549 | 5.807 | 7.396 | 9.399 | 11.918 | 15.080 | 19.040 | 23.991 | 30.167 | 37.857 | 47.414 | 59.270 | 73.949 | 92.092 | 114.475 |
| 27 | 1.308 | 1.707 | 2.221 | 2.883 | 3.733 | 4.822 | 6.214 | 7.988 | 10.245 | 13.110 | 16.739 | 21.325 | 27.109 | 34.390 | 43.535 | 55.000 | 69.345 | 87.260 | 109.589 | 137.371 |
| 28 | 1.321 | 1.741 | 2.288 | 2.999 | 3.920 | 5.112 | 6.649 | 8.627 | 11.167 | 14.421 | 18.580 | 23.884 | 30.633 | 39.204 | 50.066 | 63.800 | 81.134 | 102.967 | 130.411 | 164.845 |
| 29 | 1.335 | 1.776 | 2.357 | 3.119 | 4.116 | 5.418 | 7.114 | 9.317 | 12.172 | 15.863 | 20.624 | 26.750 | 34.616 | 44.693 | 57.575 | 74.009 | 94.927 | 121.501 | 155.189 | 197.814 |
| 30 | 1.348 | 1.811 | 2.427 | 3.243 | 4.322 | 5.743 | 7.612 | 10.063 | 13.268 | 17.449 | 22.892 | 29.960 | 39.116 | 50.950 | 66.212 | 85.850 | 111.065 | 143.371 | 184.675 | 237.376 |
| 31 | 1.361 | 1.848 | 2.500 | 3.373 | 4.538 | 6.088 | 8.145 | 10.868 | 14.462 | 19.194 | 25.410 | 33.555 | 44.201 | 58.083 | 76.144 | 99.586 | 129.946 | 169.177 | 219.764 | 284.852 |
| 32 | 1.375 | 1.885 | 2.575 | 3.508 | 4.765 | 6.453 | 8.715 | 11.737 | 15.763 | 21.114 | 28.206 | 37.582 | 49.947 | 66.215 | 87.565 | 115.520 | 152.036 | 199.629 | 261.519 | 341.822 |
| 33 | 1.389 | 1.922 | 2.652 | 3.648 | 5.003 | 6.841 | 9.325 | 12.676 | 17.182 | 23.225 | 31.308 | 42.092 | 56.440 | 75.485 | 100.700 | 134.003 | 177.883 | 235.563 | 311.207 | 410.186 |
| 34 | 1.403 | 1.961 | 2.732 | 3.794 | 5.253 | 7.251 | 9.978 | 13.690 | 18.728 | 25.548 | 34.752 | 47.143 | 63.777 | 86.053 | 115.805 | 155.443 | 208.123 | 277.964 | 370.337 | 492.224 |
| 35 | 1.417 | 2.000 | 2.814 | 3.946 | 5.516 | 7.686 | 10.677 | 14.785 | 20.414 | 28.102 | 38.575 | 52.800 | 72.069 | 98.100 | 133.176 | 180.314 | 243.503 | 327.997 | 440.701 | 590.668 |
| 36 | 1.431 | 2.040 | 2.898 | 4.104 | 5.792 | 8.147 | 11.424 | 15.968 | 22.251 | 30.913 | 42.818 | 59.136 | 81.437 | 111.834 | 153.152 | 209.164 | 284.899 | 387.037 | 524.434 | 708.802 |
| 37 | 1.445 | 2.081 | 2.985 | 4.268 | 6.081 | 8.636 | 12.224 | 17.246 | 24.254 | 34.004 | 47.528 | 66.232 | 92.024 | 127.491 | 176.125 | 242.631 | 333.332 | 456.703 | 624.076 | 850.562 |
| 38 | 1.460 | 2.122 | 3.075 | 4.439 | 6.385 | 9.154 | 13.079 | 18.625 | 26.437 | 37.404 | 52.756 | 74.180 | 103.987 | 145.340 | 202.543 | 281.452 | 389.998 | 538.910 | 742.651 | 1020.675 |
| 39 | 1.474 | 2.165 | 3.167 | 4.616 | 6.705 | 9.704 | 13.995 | 20.115 | 28.816 | 41.145 | 58.559 | 83.081 | 117.506 | 165.687 | 232.925 | 326.484 | 456.298 | 635.914 | 883.754 | 1224.810 |
| 40 | 1.489 | 2.208 | 3.262 | 4.801 | 7.040 | 10.286 | 14.947 | 21.725 | 31.409 | 45.259 | 65.001 | 93.051 | 132.782 | 188.884 | 267.864 | 378.721 | 533.869 | 750.378 | 1051.668 | 1469.772 |

# Glossary

**Accounting**   analysis and evaluation of past events and results, showing how we arrived at the current financial position; also the entire recording and reporting responsibility within a business.

**Accounting System**   the bookkeeping portion of financial management.

**Accounts Payable, also known as Trade Payables**   amounts owed to others for goods or services previously purchased on credit.

**Accounts Receivable**   amounts due to the organization of goods or services or as the result of a contractual agreement.

**Accrual**   a record of a transaction, attributable to a period that is ended, for which the actual completion of the transaction occurs later, such as, accrued payroll, accrued revenues, accrued expenses, accrued taxes.

**Accrual Accounting**   the accounting system that records transactions as they occur, without regard for whether they have been completed. See *Cash Accounting*.

**Accruals**   accounting transactions that estimate revenues and expenses not yet recorded so that the period's financial reports reflect that period's results properly; amounts that will be owed to others based on the calendar date of the statement but not yet due as of the date of the statement, such as payroll or taxes.

**Activity Ratios**   company financial ratios that assess the effectiveness of the company's utilization of assets.

**Balance Sheet**   the financial statement that describes the financial condition of a business at a point in time.

**Bookkeeping**   the accurate and timely recording of transactions, providing the reader with clear financial information; also the function that performs the tasks associated with that recording.

**Book Value**   comprised of the common stock, additional paid-in capital and retained earnings, equal to the net worth of the company. Book value per share is this total divided by the number of shares outstanding.

**Bottom Line**   a term generally relating to the net profit of a business. "Adding to the bottom line" or "dropping to the bottom line" refer to actions that directly affect the profitability of the business.

**Capacity**   in credit management, the ability of the borrower to utilize the amount of credit requested effectively.

**Capital**   in credit management, the investment of the owners in the company, provides some security to the lenders.

**Capitalize**   record as an asset on the Balance Sheet.

**Capital Rationing**   in capital budgeting, the recognition that funds available are not adequate to fund all available acceptable projects; the necessity to rank projects to determine those that are most beneficial to the company.

**Cash**   liquid resources to be spent on goods and services or additional assets for the organization.

**Cash Accounting**   the accounting system that records transactions only when they have had a cash component. Therefore, sales and expenses are only recorded when they have actually been paid for.

**Cash Budget**   the conversion of the operating budget (developed to reflect its accounting treatment) to reflect the timing of cash outflows and inflows.

**Cash Flow**   in credit management, the ability of the business to generate the funds to service the debt.

**Cash Management**   concentrated attention on the attraction, management, and disbursement of cash.

**Character**   in credit management, the integrity and reputation of the borrower.

**Chart of Accounts**   a listing of the accounts included in the Accounting System that enables the accountant to record transactions accurately and effectively.

**Collateral**   in credit management, assets that provide security for the loan.

**Common Stock** represents the actual ownership of the company, based on the number of shares held as a percentage of the total number of shares outstanding; investment in the company in return for an ownership position, with the right to participate in the election of directors, in certain distributions, and in certain company decisions.

**Communications** in credit management, the relationship and transfer of information from the company to the lender.

**Company Stakeholders** people and organizations that have an interest in the company.

**Comparative Analysis** the comparison of a company's financial results for a period to the same company's results from a prior period or to industry statistics or a competitive company's financial results for the same period. This last is also known as competitive analysis.

**Competence** in credit management, of management to manage the company effectively.

**Competition** in credit management, in the lending marketplace, the competitive environment of the lender.

**Competitive Analysis** See *Comparative Analysis*.

**Concentration Account** a centralized account into which balances from small accounts are swept.

**Conditions** in credit management, the economic circumstances of the market in general and of the company.

**Consolidation** drawing together the financial results of all parts of the company and eliminating any transactions that are strictly internal to the company as a whole.

**Convertible Preferred Stock** enables the shareholder to convert the preferred stock into common stock at a defined rate, sometimes offering the shareholder a guaranteed return until the company succeeds in raising its stock price to a level offering the shareholder a significant profit.

**Corporation** a business having a legal identity separate from its owners, who may or may not be actively involved in the business, operated as an entity with its own life, structure, and essence.

**Cost of Capital** the return required to satisfy the provider of a particular type of capital.

**Cost of Equity Capital** the expected or required rate of return on equity.

**Cost of Sales**   those costs and expenses expended to generate revenues, including expenses specifically incurred in the production or acquisition of goods to be sold.

**Credibility**   in credit management, a measure of reliability, particularly related to information related to the borrower.

**Credit**   an entry that decreases an asset or increases a liability on the Balance Sheet or decreases an expense or increases revenue on the Income Statement.

**Current Assets**   those assets expected to be converted into cash or used within one year; those assets that individually are expected to be turned into cash within a year, including cash, marketable securities, accounts receivable, inventories, and prepaid expenses.

**Current Liabilities**   the sum of all obligations expected to be converted to cash or paid within one year.

**Debit**   an entry that increases an asset or decreases a liability on the Balance Sheet or increases an expense or decreases revenue on the Income Statement.

**Debt Ratios**   company financial ratios that assess the management of borrowed funds.

**Default Risk**   the risk that you will not get your money, your principal, back on time or, perhaps, at all.

**Depreciation**   a cost allowance that permits a company to recover the dollars of investment in an asset over its useful life.

**Derivative**   an investment security whose value is derived from other assets, for example, a future contract derives its value from the product on which it is based.

**Dividends**   amounts paid out to shareholders, a distribution of after-tax earnings.

**Elimination**   the removal from consolidated results of the effects of any transactions that are strictly within the company as a whole.

**Equity**   a synonym for net worth, also used to describe what an investor gets when investing in the stock of a company.

**Finance**   managing money on behalf of owners and creditors.

**Financial Analysis**   interpretation of financial results and positions to guide the future actions of the company.

**Financial Management**   the management of a plan of action guiding the attraction, spending, or investing of money on behalf of owners and creditors.

**Fixed Assets**   those assets and resources owned by the organization expected to last more than one year, including such assets as land, buildings, furniture and fixtures, machinery and equipment, leasehold improvements, vehicles, and similar physical assets.

**Future Value**   the value, in terms of some future time, of an amount to be paid today, determined based on a specific interest rate.

**Generally Accepted Accounting Principles (GAAP)**   guidelines established to help assure that financial statements are prepared and presented consistently and can, therefore, be understood and used by informed readers without requiring special knowledge.

**Gross Profit**   the difference between Sales and Cost of Sales.

**Income Statement**   also known as the Profit and Loss Statement, summarizes all of the financial activity that took place during the captioned statement period.

**Inflation Risk**   the risk that when you do get your money back it will have lost some buying power.

**Initial Public Offering (IPO)**   the first time the stock of a company is sold to the public, a complex and exhilarating time for the management.

**Intangible Assets**   valuable nonphysical assets owned by the organization, such as trademarks and patents.

**Interdependence**   in capital budgeting, the recognition that choosing one project automatically requires choosing another, that both projects must be done or the one chosen will be unsuccessful, eliminating the possibility that a manager can circumvent investment authority limitations.

**Interest**   expenses incurred in support of debt undertaken by the organization to finance its activities or the acquisition of assets and resources.

**Internal Rate of Return**   determines that rate of return that exactly equates the present value of the future cash flows with the value of the investment.

**Intracompany Profit**   profit recorded in one part of a company from transactions conducted with another part of the same company.

**Inventory**   if the organization sells product, stocks of product to be sold.

**Inverted Yield Curve**   when short-term rates are higher than long-term rates.

**Journal**   a book of transactions, all of the same type, recording business activity as it occurs. The monthly journals are summarized, now generally automatically by the computerized accounting system, to produce the financial records and statements at the end of the accounting period.

**Just-in-Time (JIT)**   method of managing inventory that, through the use of sound sales forecasts, enables management to minimize stocks held while meeting customer requirements.

**Liquidity Ratios**   company financial ratios that assess the company's ability to meet maturing obligations.

**Liquidity Risk**   the risk incurred if you have to liquidate the loan before it matures. It is a measure of the potential penalty that would be imposed by the market.

**Long-Term Assets**   sometimes known as fixed assets, are assets with a useful life in excess of one year, will include property assets as well as long-term investments and intangibles such as patents, trademarks, and goodwill.

**Long-Term Debt**   usually bank debt, reflects money borrowed for longer than one year.

**Material, Materiality**   an assessment that an activity will or will not significantly affect the accuracy or usefulness of the final results. Those that will are material; those that will not are not material.

**Maturity Risk**   the recognition that if you have loaned your money to someone else you cannot use it yourself, even if a better opportunity arises, maturity premium may also be considered an opportunity premium.

**Mutually Exclusive**   in capital budgeting, the recognition that among capital project alternatives may be some that, if chosen, automatically eliminate others from consideration; that is, choosing one project excludes one or more others.

**Net Present Value (NPV)**   the sum of the present values of all cash outflows and inflows associated with a capital project discounted by the weighted average cost of capital or some other interest rate; a positive NPV denotes an acceptable project from a financial return perspective.

**Net Worth**   the difference between total assets and total liabilities, reflecting the book value of what the owners own after all bills and obligations have been accounted for.

**Normal Yield Curve**  when long-term rates are higher than short-term rates.

**Notes Payable**  short-term funds borrowed, generally from banks, either as a one-time loan or as a revolving line of credit; amounts borrowed by the organization and due within one year.

**Open Book Management**  an approach to financial management where a company provides detailed financial information to all employees and helps them understand how their actions and efforts affect company results.

**Operating Expenses**  expenses incurred to support the general activities of the company, excluding investments in capitalized assets.

**Partnership**  a business owned and operated by two or more people who work together and share in the ownership, operation, and responsibility for the business.

**Payback Period**  the time elapsed from the start of the project until the investment dollars have been recovered by the project's cash inflows.

**Planning**  building on past financial information to direct the future; planning encompasses all levels of budgeting, strategic, and financial planning.

**Preemptive Right**  a provision in the stockholders' agreement that gives a stockholder the right to purchase more shares in a company to preserve an ownership position if the company offers to sell shares to the public.

**Preferred Stock**  investment in the company which generally does not represent ownership, but which gains the investor a right to preferences in distribution of dividends and in certain other situations.

**Prepaid Expenses**  expenditures made in anticipation of future services or obligations, often interest, advertising, or insurance.

**Present Value**  the value, in today's terms, of money to be received or paid in the future, determined based on a specified interest rate.

**Private Placement**  the issuance of debt or equity to a single investor directly by the company.

**Profit**  the amount of money earned by a business after all expenses of the period have been accounted for.

**Profit and Loss Statement**  See *Income Statement*.

**Profitability Ratios**  company financial ratios that assess operating performance.

**Proprietorship**   a business owned and actively operated by one person.

**Repurchase Certificates (Repos)**   overnight or very short-term interest-bearing loans from companies with temporary excess funds to banks and other financial institutions, usually secured by government securities, and enabling the companies to earn some income while permitting the banks to meet reserve obligations or other commitments.

**Retained Earnings**   the cumulative earnings of the company less any dividends distributed to preferred and common stock holders.

**Reversing Journal Entry**   an accounting entry, made in one period and reversed in the next, that helps to assure the accuracy and completeness of the accounting records for each period.

**Revolving Loan**   a loan, generally from a bank, the terms for which permit the borrower to borrow funds, repay them, and later borrow the amounts again.

**Sales**   revenues received or to be received from the sale of the products or services offered by the business.

**Standard Industrial Classification (SIC)**   a classification system used by the United States Department of Commerce to categorize companies by the type of business they do.

**Standard Journal Entry**   an accounting entry, repeated in multiple accounting periods, that reflects the periodic portion of an annual expense. Used to record depreciation, absorption of prepaid expenses, or other evenly spread transactions.

**Strategic objectives**   what we want to accomplish.

**Strategy**   the basic business approach a company follows.

**Subordinated Debt**   amounts owed by a company but which may not be paid until senior obligations have been satisfied.

**Sweeping**   bank initiated transfers of company funds from numerous small accounts into a centralized concentration account, where, due to the larger consolidated balances, the company can earn a higher return or otherwise manage the cash assets better.

**Tactics**   the explicitly identified action steps that will be employed to succeed.

**Taxes**   amounts required by the governmental authorities holding jurisdiction over the company, applied to profits earned by the company.

**Term Loan**   a loan, generally from a bank, the terms for which specify that the funds, when repaid, may not be borrowed again and the whole loan must be repaid by a certain date.

**Total Assets**   the sum of all assets owned by the organization.

**Total Liabilities**   the sum of all amounts owed to creditors by the organization.

**Total Liabilities and Equity**   a total equal to the total assets that confirms that all obligations of the organization have been identified.

**Trading Ratio**   another name for Sales to Net Worth, measures business risk when a company's sales are growing faster than the equity to support them.

**Treasury Bill**   a short-term security issued by the U.S. Treasury, the least risky security, a Treasury Note is medium term, a Treasury Bond is long-term.

**Trend Analysis**   a comparison of a company's financial statistics to similarly computed statistics from a prior period to determine the direction of company financial trends. Usually, trend analysis requires at least three years of data to be useful.

**Trial Balance**   a listing of all of the accounts in the chart of accounts with their respective balances presented in a single sequential statement. The net total of all of these balances when added together will equal zero, that is, the debit balances will equal the credit balances but with opposite signs.

**Weighted Average Cost of Capital (WACC)**   that rate or return that will exactly and adequately compensate all providers of capital to a business, the minimum required rate of return for a capital investment.

# The Final Exam

### Finance and Accounting
### for Nonfinancial Managers

**Course Code 96019**

CREDIT: *On successful completion of this final exam, you will receive 2 CEUs.*

INSTRUCTIONS: *Record your answers on the scannable answer form enclosed with this course. Please follow the directions on the form carefully. Be sure to keep a copy of the answer form for your records. No photocopies will be graded. When completed, mail your answer form to:*

**American Management Association**
## Educational Services
**P.O. Box 359**
**Natick, MA 01760**

1. Generally Accepted Accounting Principles (GAAP) are intended to:
   (a) define precisely acceptable accounting treatments.
   (b) assure that financial statements are exactly correct.
   (c) assure that financial information is useful in making decisions.
   (d) permit managers to predict the future.

2. The Balance Sheet balances by:
   (a) equating assets with liabilities and equity.
   (b) equating revenues with expenses.
   (c) assuring that cash flows are properly recorded.
   (d) measuring managers' ability to balance their responsibilities.

3. The Income Statement is also known as the:
   (a) Statement of Cash Flows.
   (b) Statement of Stockholders' Equity.
   (c) Profit and Loss Statement.
   (d) Assets and Liabilities Statement.

Do you have questions? Comments? Need clarification?
Call Educational Services at 1-800-225-3215, ext. 600,
or email at ed_svcs@amanet.org.

**225**

4. Debits are:
    (a) always good for a company.
    (b) always assets.
    (c) never the same from month to month.
    (d) equal to credits in journal entries.

5. The wealth of a shareholder is found in the:
    (a) revenues of the company.
    (b) equity section of the Balance Sheet.
    (c) assets section of the Balance Sheet.
    (d) net cash flow of the company.

6. The concept of materiality is important because it:
    (a) assures that financial statements are precisely correct.
    (b) permits accountants to focus on the major transactions.
    (c) makes sure all of a period's transactions are included before the books
        are closed.
    (d) assures that the credits equal the debits.

7. Activity ratios, also known as Utilization Ratios, tell an analyst:
    (a) how well the company manages its assets.
    (b) how well the company manages its debt.
    (c) whether the company can pay a dividend this year.
    (d) when the books will be closed.

8. Trend analysis evaluates a company's financial performance in comparison to the:
    (a) company's largest competitors performance.
    (b) company's previous years' performance.
    (c) company's annual budget.
    (d) appropriate international standard of performance.

9. Low asset turnover is an indication of:
    (a) the fact that the company does a good job of acquiring assets.
    (b) potential financial risk.
    (c) too few assets on the company's books.
    (d) sales reaching too high a level for one year.

10. Ratio analysis helps the manager:
    (a) justify his or her actions to management.
    (b) fill out the monthly report all managers are required to write.
    (c) identify critical areas for management attention.
    (d) identify precisely who did not do their job this month.

11. Financial ratios:
    (a) are limited to the ratios developed by professional analysts.
    (b) may not be used by operating managers.
    (c) contain only standard information.
    (d) help to highlight critical characteristics of the business.

12. The purpose of business is to maximize:
    (a) sales.
    (b) profitability.
    (c) profits.
    (d) owner's wealth.

13. Times Interest Earned is a valuable ratio to a vendor because it tells the vendor:
    (a) if the company makes enough operating profit to cover its interest expenses by enough to assure payment to the vendor.
    (b) when to expect payment.
    (c) how much interest the delinquent customer will actually pay.
    (d) how often the company pays its interest bills each month.

14. Bad Debt Expense is:
    (a) accounted for as a debit to Accounts Receivable.
    (b) accounted for as a credit to cash.
    (c) a measure of the quality of current sales.
    (d) accounted for as a credit on the asset side of the Balance Sheet.

15. Sales to Net Worth, also known as the Trading Ratio:
    (a) tells an analyst the rate of return.
    (b) may be an early warning of financial risk.
    (c) cannot be measured as there is no relationship between them.
    (d) tells us if there is too much equity.

16. We can decrease the cash conversion cycle by:
    (a) paying our bills sooner and taking any available discounts.
    (b) allowing our customers to schedule their payments to us.
    (c) buying inventory closer to actual production or shipment dates.
    (d) holding cash receipts until we have a substantial deposit, saving our accounting clerk's time.

17. Inventory carrying costs are:
    (a) approximately 20 percent of the average value of inventory.
    (b) approximately 30 percent of the average value of inventory.
    (c) approximately 40 percent of the average value of inventory.
    (d) impossible to estimate.

18. Companies take physical inventory counts because:
    (a) the balances are significant and need to be verified.
    (b) companies need to be sure they can fulfill all their orders.
    (c) companies pay incentives based on how large the inventory is.
    (d) the computerized systems cannot be relied on.

19. Which of the following is not included in inventory carrying costs?
    (a) Security
    (b) Space costs
    (c) Material costs
    (d) Insurance

20. The write off of inventory requires:
    (a) the immediate sale of all written off stock.
    (b) the disposal of all written off stock.
    (c) the careful storage of all written off stock.
    (d) no recognition in the financial statements.

21. Maturity risk recognizes that:
    (a) the longer you hold your money, the more you accumulate.
    (b) if you have loaned your money to someone else, you cannot use it yourself, even if a better opportunity arises.
    (c) the longer we hold an investment, the harder it is to remember why we made it.
    (d) the older your business is, the easier it is to get a loan.

22. The only type of investment we can make without any default risk is a:
    (a) savings account in a big bank.
    (b) loan to General Electric.
    (c) loan to a member of your immediate family.
    (d) purchase of a U.S. Treasury security.

23. If someone offers an extraordinarily high rate of return, it must mean that:
    (a) there is an extraordinarily high risk associated with the opportunity.
    (b) they have carefully chosen you to be an investor.
    (c) they think you should be given this special opportunity.
    (d) they clearly understand the type of investment you are interested in.

24. The determination of the value of an investment depends on knowing three of the following four variables:
    (a) the present value (PV), future value (FV), interest rate (I) and term, (N, for number of periods).
    (b) the present value (PV), prime rate (P), inflation rate (IR) and term, (N, for number of periods).
    (c) the present value (PV), future value (FV), inflation rate (IR), and time of the year (T).
    (d) the past investment (PI), the future investment (FI), inflation rated (IR), and the term (Y, number if years).

25. The earnings of a corporation belong to the:
    (a) corporation.
    (b) shareholders.
    (c) government.
    (d) Internal Revenue Service.

26. The value of an investment today is the:
    (a) present value of future cash flows discounted at the rate of return required by the investor and determined by applying a risk assessment to the investment.
    (b) future value of present cash flows discounted at the rate of return required by the investor and determined by applying a risk assessment to the investment.
    (c) amount required to make the investor feel rich discounted at the rate of return required by the investor and determined by applying a risk assessment to the investment.
    (d) sum of price, the taxes, and interest you have to pay on it discounted at the rate of return required by the investor and determined by applying a risk assessment to the investment.

27. Free cash flow is:
    (a) the money you get without special management action.
    (b) the amount that can be withdrawn from a business.
    (c) money left over after buying raw materials.
    (d) the difference between sales and cost of sales.

28. Profitable capital projects need to provide a return sufficient to pay for projects that do not offer a return of their own because:
    (a) investors require a return on their investments regardless of where the company invests the money.
    (b) it's the rule of project equality.
    (c) otherwise the companies cannot make these investments.
    (d) all investments for a particular company are equally risky.

29. Changes in working capital:
    (a) affect the cost of a capital investment.
    (b) are specifically excluded from the cost of an investment.
    (c) have no impact on the cost of the investment.
    (d) are included on the Balance Sheet as part of the fixed asset value.

30. The person recommending a new capital investment:
    (a) will be conservative.
    (b) will include all investment costs and operating expenses associated with the investment in his or her recommendation.
    (c) is likely to be optimistic.
    (d) will intentionally overestimate costs in order to be safe.

31. The payback period is:
    (a) the present value of future cash flows.
    (b) how long it takes to earn back the cost of the investment.
    (c) reflects the expected useful life of the asset.
    (d) provides management with a comprehensive analysis of the financial benefits of a project.

32. A positive Net Present Value signifies that a capital project:
    (a) does not earn an adequate return.
    (b) earns exactly the required rate of return.
    (c) earns an acceptable rate of return.
    (d) is the best possible investment.

33. An advantage of the Internal Rate of Return basis for evaluating capital projects is its:
    (a) ease of computation.
    (b) the fact that it enables a manager to rank projects of different sizes.
    (c) the fact that it does not require carefully calculated cash flows.
    (d) the fact that it produces a precisely correct result.

34. Sound business management requires one to match:
    (a) long-term assets with short-term financing.
    (b) long-term assets with long-term financing.
    (c) short-term assets with long-term financing.
    (d) short-term sales with long-term financing.

35. The decision to finance capital investments with equity:
    (a) reduces the riskiness of the business.
    (b) increases the return to the shareholder more than financing with them with debt.
    (c) assures that the company gets the best deal on the assets.
    (d) increases leverage.

36. Depreciation, being a noncash expense:
    (a) increases income and reduces cash flow.
    (b) increases income and increases cash flow.
    (c) reduces income and increases cash flow.
    (d) reduces income and reduces cash flow.

37. Goodwill is the excess of:
    (a) the price paid over the book value in an acquisition.
    (b) book value over purchase price in an acquisition.
    (c) book value over market value in an acquisition.
    (d) the price paid over the market value in an acquisition.

38. Capitalizing assets:
    (a) brings expenses into the current period, sacrificing profits.
    (b) eliminates expenses altogether.
    (c) transfers the cost of the asset to the bank or financing source.
    (d) moves expenses to future periods and brings profits forward.

39. In accrual accounting:
    (a) activity is accounted for in the period it which it occurs, even if the transaction is not complete.
    (b) only cash transactions are valid.
    (c) only transactions completed during the period are included.
    (d) anticipated transactions are recorded as if they had happened.

40. Accruals are intended to:
    (a) confuse anyone seeking to examine the company's financial records.
    (b) adjust incorrect journal entries made in prior periods.
    (c) assure that all months contain the same amount of accounting information.
    (d) enable a company to account for all transactions belonging to a particular period in that period.

41. The best time to borrow money is when you:
    (a) can justify it precisely.
    (b) don't need it.
    (c) are desperate.
    (d) have befriended a banker.

42. Choosing the banker within the bank is important because you want someone:
    (a) whom you have met with before.
    (b) who can represent you well to the loan committee.
    (c) who is readily available to you.
    (d) who has memorized all the bank's loan rules.

43. Proprietorships are characterized by:
    (a) limited liability for the owner, unlimited life of the entity, and double taxation.
    (b) unlimited liability for the owner, limited life of the entity, and single taxation.
    (c) limited liability for the owner, limited life for the entity, and single taxation.
    (d) unlimited liability for the owner, unlimited life for the entity, and single taxation.

44. A corporation, holding the preferred stock of another corporation, is allowed to deduct:
    (a) 50 percent of the dividend received before computing federal income taxes.
    (b) 60 percent of the dividend received before computing federal income taxes.
    (c) 70 percent of the dividend received before computing federal income taxes.
    (d) 80 percent of the dividend received before computing federal income taxes.

45. The Strategic Plan for a company should be:
    (a) written once every five years, covering the next five years.
    (b) updated annually, covering the next five years.
    (c) written whenever the bank requests it.
    (d) written when management determines it is appropriate.

46. The explicitly identified action steps that will be employed by a business to succeed are called:
    (a) the business plan.
    (b) tactics.
    (c) strategic objectives.
    (d) operative plans.

47. Steps to accomplish a strategic objective of achieving a reputation for highest quality in a particular market might include:
    (a) lowest cost.
    (b) dominant market share.
    (c) improved reliability.
    (d) widest distribution.

48. Intracompany profits:
    (a) must be eliminated as part of the company financial consolidation.
    (b) must be combined as part of the company financial consolidation.
    (c) only exist in companies where there is no consolidation.
    (d) have no impact on the computation of company-wide profitability.

**49.** The effort of the individual affects the financial performance of the:
   (a) group, department, division, subsidiary, and whole corporation.
   (b) only the group level.
   (c) only the group and department levels.
   (d) the group, department, and division levels, but not the subsidiary, and certainly not the corporation.

**50.** The focus of division management is on:
   (a) everything the parent company is measured on.
   (b) profits and working capital management.
   (c) capital asset management.
   (d) controlling cash.

# Index

Accounting, 5–6
  closing procedures, 32–33
  cycle of, 30–33
  definition of, 4, 5, 215
  for equity, 180
  financial statements
    preparation, 34–39
  fixed asset, 140–141
  information usage, 23–24
  introduction to, 21–41
  journal entries to record
    transactions, 30–32
  as language of business, 2
  overview of, 21–22
  purpose of, 22–24
  terminology of, basic, 24–29
Accounting system, 22–23
  definition of, 215
  functions of, 23
Accounts payable, 147–148, 215
Accounts receivable
  average collection period and,
    89
  definition of, 215
  inventory versus, 89
  managing, 87, 88–89
  reserve and, 88–89
Accounts receivable to working
  capital, 74
Accrual accounting, 34–35,
  150–151, 215
Accruals, 34–35, 150–151
  definition of, 215
  expenses, 151
  payroll, 151
Acid test ratio. See Quick ratio
Activity ratios, 52–54
  average collection period, 52
  definition of, 215
  fixed asset turnover, 53

  inventory turnover, 52–53
  total asset turnover, 53–54
Additional paid-in capital, 178
Altman, Edward I., 79
American Institute of Certified
  Public Accountants (AICPA)
  on purpose of accounting,
    22
Analysis of financial information,
  44
Annual budget, 193–194
Annuity tables, 211–212
Asset classification consideration,
  136
Asset turnover, 136
Auditor's opinion, 34
Average collection period, 52, 77,
  89

Bad debt expense, 88
Balance Sheet, 8–10
  annotated example of, 9
  bad debts and, 88
  balancing the, 27
  definition of, 8, 215
  deposits on, 93
  division of a company and,
    203
  examining your company's
    balance sheet, 8,10
  examples of, 10, 25, 72
  long-term debt on, 151
  preparing, 35–36
  reserves and, 88–89
  sections of, 136
  timing of, 8
  trial balance and, 38
Banking relationships, 158–164
  cost of bank funds, 159–162
  defining debt, 159

  loan interest rates dictated by
    bank structure, 159
  loan losses, 163
  operating expenses, 162
  profit criteria, 163–164
Banks
  debt pricing, 165–166
  lending officer choosing, 152
  loan pricing example, 166–168
Beta, 105, 106
Bookkeeping, 4–5, 216
Book value, 46, 179, 216
Bottom line, 1, 216
Budgets and actuals, relationship
  between, 206
Business
  liabilities of, 146–147
  outline of plan for,
    190–191
  plan, 188–189, 190–191
  planning, 186–188
  purpose of, 45–46
  structures, 14–16

Capacity
  credit and, 154
  definition of, 216
Capital
  budgeting, 122, 196
  credit and, 154–155
  definition of, 117, 216
Capital asset pricing model, 105,
  106, 116
Capital investment decision
  making, 115–133
  applying cost of capital,
    125–126
  calculating cost of capital,
    116–122
  capital budgeting, 122

cash flow of project
  determining, 127
classes of, 123
components of, 122
evaluating projects and,
  128–130
investment cost determining,
  126–127
overview of, 115–116
project types, 122–128
rate of return requirement for
  project types, 124
reasons for, 137
terminal cash flow
  determining, 127–128
weighted average cost of
  capital, 117–118
Capitalize definition, 216
Capital rationing definition, 216
CAPM. *See* Capital asset pricing
  model
Cash definition, 216
Cash accounting definition, 216
Cash budget, 196–197, 216
Cash conversion cycle, 90, 91
Cash disbursement journal,
  31–32
Cash flow
  credit and, 155
  definition of, 216
  determining for project, 127
  determining terminal, 127–128
Cash Flow Statement. *See*
  Statement of Cash Flows
Cash management, 6–7, 84–86
  definition of, 4, 6, 216
  holding cash reasons, 85–86
  large cash balances, 84
  liquid form of cash, 85
  multiple company locations
    and, 86
  opportunities and, 85
  overdraft check protection, 85
  purpose for holding cash, 85
  techniques for, 86
Cash receipts journal, 31
Cash surrender value of life
  insurance, 141–142
Character
  assessment considerations for,
    153
  credit and, 153–154
  definition of, 216
Chart of accounts, 27–29
  analyzing financial statements
    and, 66–67
  definition of, 216
  numbering system of, 28
  sample, 29
Closing procedures, 32–33
Collateral

credit and, 155–156
  definition of, 216
Common stock, 46, 87, 177–178
  balance sheet and value of, 178
  definition of, 217
  dividend on, 116
  initial public offering of, 178
  paying for investment through
    issuance of, 138
  weighted average cost of
    capital model and, 117
Communications
  credit and, 158
  definition of, 217
Company stakeholders
  definition of, 217
  who are, 23
Comparative analysis, 47–49, 50
  definition of, 217
  source data for, 48
Competence
  credit and, 57–158
  definition of, 217
Competition
  credit and, 156–157
  definition of, 217
Competitive analysis. *See*
  Comparative analysis
Concentration account, 86, 217
Conditions
  credit and, 156
  definition of, 217
Consolidation, 202, 217
Convertible preferred stock, 177,
  217
Corporate strategies defined, 192
Corporation, 15–16
  definition of, 217
  financial statements and, 16
  structure of, 175–176
Cost of capital
  applying, 125–126
  calculating, 116–122
  definition of, 217
Cost of equity capital, 102, 217
Cost of sales
  definition of, 218
  sales versus, 30, 31
Credibility
  credit and, 157
  definition of, 218
Credit
  Balance Sheet and, 26
  definition of, 218
  origin of, 25
  process for, 152–158
  references, 157
Credit, elements of
  capacity, 154
  capital, 154–155
  cash flow, 155

character, 153–154
  collateral, 155–156
  communications, 158
  competence, 157–158
  competition, 156–157
  conditions, 156
  credibility, 157
Current assets
  definition of, 136, 218
  prepaid expenses as, 93
Current liabilities definition,
  136, 218
Current ratio, 51, 73

*D*ays' sales outstanding (DSO).
  *See* Average collection
  period
Debit
  Balance Sheet and, 26
  definition of, 218
  origin of, 25
Debit ratios definition, 218
Debt, defining, 159
Debt management ratios, 55–56
Debt to assets, 74–75
Debt to equity, 75
Default risk, 75, 102, 218
Departmental performance
  relation to big picture,
    201–207
  company, 202
  department, 204–205
  division, 203–204
  finance from broad to specific,
    202–206
  group, 205
  individuals, 205–206
  overview, 201–202
  recap of, 206
  relationship between budgets
    and actuals, 206
  subsidiary, 203
Departments, 204–205
Depreciation, 138–140
  definition of, 138, 218
  method examples of, 139–140
Derivative, 87, 218
Dividends definition, 218
Division, 203–204
Dun & Bradstreet, 48, 157

*E*ffect ratios, 72–76
  accounts receivable to working
    capital, 74
  current ratio, 73
  debt to assets, 74–75
  debt to equity, 75
  inventory to working capital,
    74
  net working capital, 74
  quick ratio, 73–74

short-term debt to equity, 75
short-term debt to total
  liabilities, 75–76
Efficiency ratio, 69
Elements of finance, 4–7
  accounting, 4, 5–6
  bookkeeping, 4,5
  cash management, 4, 6–7
  planning, 4, 6
Elimination, 203, 218
Enterprise resource planning,
  89
Equity
  on Balance Sheet, 27
  definition of, 218
  increasing, 27
  investments, 110
  net worth and, 8
  purchasing, 102, 103
Equity in business, 173–182
  accounting for equity, 180
  business structure and,
    174–179
  investment marketplace,
    179–180
  overview of, 173–174
  recap of, 181
ERP. *See* Enterprise resource
  planning

*F*inance
  basic financial statements of,
    7–13
  business structure and impact
    of financial statements,
    14–16
  definition of, 3, 218
  elements of, 4–7
  introduction to, 1–19
  overview of, 1–3
  vocabulary of, 3–4
Financial Accounting Standards
  Board (FASB) and use of
  reserves, 88
Financial analysis, 5
  comparative analysis, 47–49
  definition of, 219
  objectives of, 47
  using ratios, 43–63. *See also*
    Ratios and financial analysis
  who performs, 46, 47
Financial management
  definition of, 3, 219
  essence of, 25
Financial manager and who is,
  2–3
Financial planning, 183–199
  business type of plan, 188–189,
    190–191
  capital budgets, 196
  cash budgets, 196–197

continuous process of business
  planning, 186–188
essence of, 184–186
exercise for, 185
key players roles, 187
operative plan or annual
  budget, 193–194
overview of, 183–184
process overview, 187
projecting financial future,
  194–197
recap of, 198
requirements estimating,
  194–195
sequence for, 187–188
strategic type of plan, 189,
  191–192
strategy versus tactics,
  192–193
types of plans, 188–194
Financial statements, 25–27. *See
  also* individual statements
Balance Sheet, 8–10
basic, 7–13
common size example, 71
equations for basis of first two,
  7–8
impact on structure of business
  by, 14–16
Income Statement, 10–12
preparing, 34–39
reasons for, 7
revising, 38
Statement of Cash Flows,
  12–13
structure of business impact
  on, 14–16
Fixed asset turnover, 53,
  78–79
Fixed assets
  accounting, 140–141
  acquisition of, 141
  definition of, 219
  depreciation, 138–140
  investment in, 137–142
Future value, 107, 108
  of an annuity table, 212
  definition of, 219
  table, 213

*G*AAP. *See* Generally accepted
  accounting principles
General journal, 32
Generally accepted accounting
  principles, 5, 33
  definition of, 33, 219
  materiality and, 34
Gross profit definition, 30,
  219
Gross profit margin, 54,68
Group, 205

*H*istoric analysis. *See* Trend
  analysis

*I*ncome Statement, 10–12, 67–68
  annotated example of, 11
  bad debts and, 88
  bank versus company sample,
    164
  definition of, 219
  department of a company and,
    204
  division of a company and,
    203–204
  examining your company's
    Income Statement, 12
  example of, 26, 67
  inventory physical counts and,
    92
  preparing, 36–38
  reserves and, 89
  shareholder and, 27
  trial balance and, 38
Individuals, 205–206
Inflation risk, 102, 103, 219
Initial Public Offering, 178, 179,
  219
Intangible assets definition, 219
Interdependence definition, 219
Interest definition, 219
Interest rates, 108
  capital asset pricing model
    and, 105
  determination of, 101
  estimating, 104–106
  loan and, 159
  risk and return relating and,
    105
Internal rate of return, 129
  definition of, 219
  problem with, 129
Internal Revenue Service
  depreciation rules of, 139
  use of reserves and, 88
Intracompany profit, 203, 219
Inventory definition, 220
Inventory management, 89–92
  accounts receivable versus, 89
  carrying costs, 91
  enterprise resource planning,
    89
  just-in-time type of, 91
  manufacturing cash cycle
    example, 90
  materials requirements
    planning, 89
  physical counts of inventory,
    92
  services firms and, 92
  stages, 89
Inventory to working capital, 74

Inventory turnover, 52–53, 78
Inverted yield curve, 103, 220
Investment analysts, 48
Investment cost determination, 126–127
Investment marketplace, 179–180
Investments
  assessing, 109–110
  valuing, 110–112
IPO. *See* Initial Public Offering
IRR. *See* Internal rate of return
IRS. *See* Internal Revenue Service

JIT. *See* Just-in-time
Journal
  definition of, 220
  types of, 31–32
Journal entries to record transactions, 30–32
Just-in-time, 91, 220

Leverage, effects of, 147
Liabilities management, 145–171
  accounts payable, 147–148
  accruals, 150–151
  banking relationships, 158–164
  of business, 146–147
  "C's" of credit, 152–158
  comparison to traditional business cost structure, 164–168
  leverage, 146–147
  long-term debt, 151–152
  notes payable, 148
  overview of, 145–146
  recap of, 169
  short-term or current types of, 147–151
  taxes payable, 150
  traditional business cost structure comparison, 164–168
Limited liability companies, 16
Limited liability partnerships (LLPs), 16, 175
Limited partnerships (LPS), 175
Liquidity ratios, 50–51
  current ratio, 51
  definition, 220
  net working capital, 51
  quick ratio, 51
Liquidity risk, 102, 103–104, 220
Loans
  interest rates dictated by bank structure, 159
  losses, 163
Long-term assets

cash surrender value of life insurance as, 141–142
classification consideration, 136
definition of, 220
financing for, 141
fixed asset investment, 137–142
goodwill as, 141
managing, 135–144
overview, 135–136
patents and trademarks as, 142
Long-term debt, 151–152, 220

Management of cash. *See* Cash management
Managers and what is expected of them, 1
Managing liabilities. *See* Liabilities management
Managing operating performance. *See* Operating performance management
Managing short-term assets. *See* Short-term assets management
Manufacturing cash cycle example, 90
Marketable securities, 86, 87
Material/Materiality, 33, 34, 220
Materials requirement planning, 89
Maturity risk, 102, 103, 220
MRP. *See* Materials requirement planning
Mutually exclusive definition, 220

Net present value, 122, 128–129
  computing, 129
  definition of, 220
Net profit margin, 54, 69
Net working capital, 51, 74
Net worth, 8, 220
Nondiversifiable risk, 103
Normal yield curve definition, 221
Notes payable, 148, 221
NPV. *See* Net present value
NWC. *See* Net working capital

Open book management, 205–206, 221
Operating expenses, 67, 221
Operating performance management, 65–82
  crossover indicators and causal ratios, 76–80
  effect ratios, 72–76

key financial statements, 67–80
making your information useful, 66,67
overview, 65–66
ratios that tell company's story, 68–72
Operating profit margin, 54, 69
Operative plan, 193–194
Overdraft protection for checks, 85

Pacioli, Luca, 25
Partnership, 14–15
  definition of, 221
  structure of, 175
Patents and trademarks, 142
Payback period, 128, 221
Payroll journal, 32
Percent change, 70–72
Personal finance versus business finance terminology, 4
Planning, 4, 6, 221
Preemptive right, 178, 221
Preferred stock, 176–177
  convertible type of, 177
  definition of, 221
  dividend rate, 121
  weighted average cost of capital model and, 117
Prepaid expenses, 992–93
  on Balance Sheet, 93
  definition of, 221
Present value, 107, 108
  of an annuity table, 211
  definition of, 221
  table, 210
Private placement, 179, 221
Profit, 11, 31, 221
Profit and Loss Statement. *See* Income Statement
Profitability ratios, 54–55, 221
Proprietorship, 14
  definition of, 222
  forming, 175
  structure of, 175
Purchases journal, 31

Quartile data, 48, 49
Quick ratio, 51, 73–74

Rate of return
  assessing, 122
  for project types, 124
  recalculating, 124
Ratios and financial analysis, 43–63
  activity ratios, 52–54
  alternative interpretations of ratios, 58

analyzing ratios, 51
average collection period, 52
comparative analysis, 47–49
creating ratios, 57–58
current ratio, 51
debt management ratios,
    55–56
efficiency ratio, 69
fixed asset turnover, 53
groupings of, 50
interpreting ratios, 56–57
inventory turnover, 52–53
liquidity ratios, 50–51
net working capital, 51
nontraditional versus
    traditional ratio analysis, 44
overview, 43–44
power of ratios, 46,47–49, 50
presentation of, 50
profitability ratios, 54–55
purpose of business, 45–46
quartile data and, 48, 49
quick ratio, 51
ratios that tell company's story,
    68–72
total asset turnover, 53–54
traditional ratio analysis, 49,
    50–60
trend analysis, 49, 59
Relating risk and return,
    valuation, and time value of
    money, 97–114
    interest rates estimating,
        104–106
    overview, 97–98
    risk, 98–102
    time value of money, 106–107
    types of risk, 102–104
    valuation, 107–112
Repos. *See* Repurchase
    Certificates
Repurchase Certificates, 86, 222
Reserves, 88–89
Retained earnings, 31, 179
    definition of, 222
    trial balance and, 38
Return on assets, 54–55, 76
Return on equity, 55, 76
Return on sales. *See* Net profit
    margin
Reversing journal entry, 32, 222
Revolving line of credit, 85
Revolving loan, 85, 222
Risk, 98–102
    aversion, 100–101
    characteristics of different
        types of, 101
    default risk, 102–103
    defining, 99–100

inflation risk, 103
interest rates determination,
    101
liquidity risk, 103–104
maturity risk, 103
nondiversifiable risk, 103
orientation, 154
possibility of loss, 101
types of, 102–104
uncertainty of result as, 100
ROA. *See* Return on assets
Robert Morris Associates, 48
ROE. *See* Return on equity

"*S*" corporations, 16
Sales definition, 222
Sales journal, 31
Sales to net worth, 79–80. *See
    also* Trading ratio
Securities and Exchange
    Commission (SEC) and use
    of reserves, 88
Selling, general, and
    administrative (SG&A)
    expenses, 162
Shareholders
    and Balance Sheet, 27
    and Income Statement, 26
Short-term assets management,
    83–95
    accounts receivable, 87, 88–89
    inventory, 89–92
    marketable securities, 86, 87
    management of cash, 84–86
    overview of, 83–84
    prepaid expenses, 92–93
    short-term investment choices
        list, 87
Short-term debt to equity, 75
Short-term debt to total
    liabilities, 75–76
Short-term or current liabilities,
    147–151
SIC. *See* Standard Industrial
    Classification
Small Business Administration
    (SBA) and loans, 154
Standard Industrial
    Classification, 49
    definition of, 222
    Dun & Bradstreet and, 48
Standard journal entry, 32, 222
Statement of Cash Flows, 12–13
    alternative view of, 13
    example of, 13
Statement of Retained Earnings,
    11
Statement of Stockholders'
    Equity, 11

Stocks, 46, 179, 180. *See also*
    Common stock; Preferred
    stock
    book value versus price of
        stock, 46
    common stock, 46
    markets, 179–180
    redemption or sale of, 110
Strategic objectives, 192, 222
Strategic plan, 189, 191–192
Strategy
    defining, 191–192
    definition of, 222
    tactics versus, 192–193
Structure of business and equity,
    174–179
Subordinated debt definition,
    222
Subsidiary, 203
Sweeping, 86, 222

*T*actics
    definition of, 222
    strategy versus, 192–193
Tax effect, 117
Taxes definition, 222
Taxes payable, 150
Term loan, 85, 223
Terminology, basic, 24–29
    chart of accounts, 27–29
    financial statements, 25–27
Terminology of business finance
    versus personal finance, 4
Time value of money,
    106–107
    tables for, 209–213
Times interest earned, 70
Total asset turnover, 53–54,
    79
Total assets definition, 223
Total liabilities definition, 223
Total liabilities and equity
    definition, 223
Trade associations, 48
Trade payables. *See* Accounts
    payable
Trading ratio, 79–80. *See also*
    Sales to net worth
    definition of, 223
    example of, 80
Treasury bill, 104, 223
Trend analysis, 49, 50
    definition of, 223
    exercise for preparing, 59
Trial balance, 38–39, 223
Trusts, 16

*U*ncertainty of result as risk,
    100

$V$aluation, 107–112
  assessing investments, 109–110
  computations for, 108
  illustrative example for,
    108–109
  investment valuing, 110–112
Vocabulary of finance, 3–4

$W$ACC. *See* Weighted average
  cost of capital
Wealth maximization, 46
Weighted average cost of capital
  computing, 118
  definition of, 223
  model, 117–118

Working capital assets. *See*
  Short-term assets
  management

$Z$-formula, 136
Z-score, 79